Eyeball-to-eyeball with the Vietcong . . .

I did a quick 360-degree pedal turn looking for my wingman, my rotor downwash pummeling the Vietcong below with leaves and dirt. The wingman was nowhere in sight.

The same VC began shouting again and once more pointed his AK-47 at the gunner's side of my Loach. This time he released the safety catch on the AK.

The VC's finger was tightening on the trigger of his AK-47, and I was still waiting for permission to fire. I kicked right pedal, immediately placing the rear of the helicopter toward the enemy, a split second before the weapon erupted in a stream of bullets. The familiar sound of bullets penetrating the thin skin of the helicopter pushed me into further action. All three AKs were firing now, the helicopter's engine taking the brunt of the punishment. The Loach began to lose power as I dropped over the cliff, gliding toward the river several hundred feet below . . .

CHARLES HOLLEY

POCKET BOOKS

New York   London   Toronto   Sydney   Tokyo   Singapore

An *Original* Publication of POCKET BOOKS

POCKET BOOKS, a division of Simon & Schuster Inc.
1230 Avenue of the Americas, New York, NY 10020

ISBN: 0-671-76055-6

First Pocket Books printing June 1992

10 9 8 7 6 5 4 3 2 1

POCKET and colophon are registered trademarks of
Simon & Schuster Inc.

Cover art by Gaylord Welker

Printed in the U.S.A.

for MONICA JAN,
THE WIND BENEATH MY WINGS.

High Flight
By
John Gillespie McGee, Jr.

Oh, I have slipped the surly bonds of earth
   And danced the skies on laughter-silvered
   Wings.
   Sunward I've climbed, and joined the tumbling mirth
Of sun split clouds—and done a hundred
   Things
You have not dreamed of—wheeled and
   Soared and swung
   High in the sunlit silence. Hov'ring there,
I've chased the shouting wind along, and flung
   My eager craft through footless halls of air.
   Up, up the long, delirious burning blue
   I've topped the windswept heights with
   Easy grace
   Where never lark, or even eagle flew.
And, while with silent, lifting mind I've trod
   The high untrespassed sanctity of space,
   Put out my hand, and touched the face of God.

Low Flight
Dedicated to all Helicopter Pilots
(Author Unknown)

Oh, I have slipped the surly bonds of earth
  And hovered out of ground effects on semi-rigid blades;
Earthward I've auto'ed and met the rising brush of
  Non-paved terrain;
  And done a thousand things you would never care to
Skidded and dropped and flared
  Low in the heat soaked roar.
Confined there, I've chased the earthbound traffic
  And lost the race to insignificant
  Headwinds;
Forward and up a little in ground effect
  I've topped the General's bridge with drooping turns
  Where never Skyhawk or even Phantom flew.
Shaking and pulling collective, I've lumbered
  The low untrespassed halls of victor airways,
  Put out my hand and touched a tree.

Contents

■ ■ ■ ■ ■ ■ ■ ■ ■ ■ ■ ■ ■ ■ ■ ■

CONTENTS

Author's Note

This book represents a personal narrative of events and people from an important period in my life, and the life of our nation. Each of the events described herein is based on fact; however, to maintain the "flow" of the narrative it was not always possible, nor was it necessary to the story, to correctly ascribe events to characters. The names of the characters are fictitious (my own excepted), although in general they represent real people and the Vietnam geography is mostly accurate (see map: "Republic of Vietnam, II Corps").

I have attempted to write the book from the perspective of what I was then: a Warrant Officer Aviator. The reader should be forewarned that this breed—as a whole—deliberately projects certain attitudes, particularly in its view toward authority. The reader should not incorrectly interpret comments or events to represent cynicism. While the warrant officer aviator will typically curse the ancestry of the "idiot who thought up this stupid mission" all the way to the flight line, this projected attitude represents a facade, belied by their combat aviation exploits.

I have tried to capture the essence of the Army Aviator, particularly in Vietnam: bold, courageous, reckless, insubordinate, naive, foolhardy, and often just plain foolish. We enjoyed a collective reputation that was well-deserved. On several occasions since Vietnam I have had a grunt, on discovering that I was a helicopter pilot in Vietnam, insist on paying my bar tab. "But I was a scout pilot," I would protest. And invariably he would respond by saying, "It don't matter. You guys are all alike anyway. And I owe you."

The following article, published in 1968, eloquently describes this essence to which I refer:

YOUNG PILOTS IN VIETNAM:
'YOU JUST CAN'T KEEP THEM DOWN'

SAIGON—He's young, perhaps 21 or 22. He wears the gold and brown bars of a junior warrant officer. Chances are he sports a moustache.

He's just a few years out of high school, yet your life depends on his steady hands and agile mind every time you board his slick or call on his guns when you're pinned down.

The young Army aviator in Vietnam is a phenomenon. He will risk his life to save yours when nothing else could, but he will just as calmly gun down two dozen enemy soldiers in an open field.

"These kids are young," said Maj. Gen. Robert R. Williams, CG of the 1st Avn Bde. "But they're not the hotshot pilots of World War II. They're young—but they're responsible, professional. And their spirits are high."

Williams cited a conversation he had with a young pilot just after the pilot had brought his disabled gunship down without damage.

"He kept looking at his watch," Williams said, "and pretty soon he said, 'Sir, I've got to go. I'm taking off in 15 minutes.' "

One pilot in the Mekong Delta was shot down three times in one day. Each time he got another chopper and went back out looking for Charlie.

Once when three CIDG soldiers were cut down by an enemy machine-gun near Rach Gia, two LOH pilots flew right into the gun to find out if any still lived. Once was alive, and the pilots volunteered to try to rescue him, though he was lying 20 feet from the still active enemy gun.

"The stories of the heroics of our young pilots are legion here," Williams said. "But to really get a good idea of their value you have to talk to the ground commanders."

Williams recommended Col. Ira A. (Rice Paddy Daddy) Hunt, CO of the 1st Bde, 9th Inf. Div., as a ground commander who makes effective use of his air support.

"The performance of our air cav element has been phenomenal," Hunt told Army Times. "I simply can't brag enough on the job they've done."

"The thing that gets me most about these young men is their spirit," Williams said. "You just can't keep them down."

He described a bedside awards ceremony at a Vietnam hospital. Gen. Dwight Beach, CINCUSARPAC, was presenting the Distinguished Service Cross to a young Army aviator as an interim award for the Medal of Honor.

The flyer had lost an arm above the elbow.

"Gen. Beach asked him how he felt," Williams said. "There were tears in [the pilot's] eyes when he answered, 'Sir, I'm sorry I lost the aircraft.'"

Army Times, October 23, 1968

Another aspect of the Army Aviator was demonstrated by Chief Warrant Officer Hugh Thompson during the My Lai massacre. After several unsuccessful attempts—via radio—to halt advancing American troops who were firing on Vietnamese civilians that had taken shelter in a bunker, Mr. Thompson landed his Loach between the Americans and the Vietnamese and ordered his door gunner to shoot at the Americans if they continued firing. He then left the helicopter and led the civilians to safety. In later years, when asked about the order to shoot at his own countrymen, Mr. Thompson replied, "Thank God they stopped shooting."

In the days of the great Texas cattle drives, the cowboys had a saying: "He'll do to ride the river with." This was the highest compliment that could be paid to another cowboy, implying ultimate trust and confidence. In a similar vein, Army Aviators use the phrase: "He can fly my wing anytime." I would like to acknowledge the particular contributions to this book of three of my fellow aviators and "wingmen," each of whom provided both critique and input to some of the material: Robert R. "Bobby" Taylor ("Good . . . good. But the details are all wrong."), Robert A "Bob" Gardner ("Taylor's details are all wrong."), and Ottis L. "Lynn" Morgan ("Some of it I liked . . . some I didn't."). Such unbridled enthusiasm provided me with great encouragement for finishing the project.

My wife, Monica, provided numerous technical contributions to the style and content, including several improved anecdotes. Her assistance provided the catalyst that moved the book from an idea to reality.

A special thanks goes to John Irsfeld and John F. "Rick" Stetter whose excellent editorial comments produced a much-improved manuscript.

I would also like to acknowledge the contributions of all those daring young (and old) men (and women now) who comprise Army Aviation. It is not possible to name each of those aviators who in some manner influenced this book. However, one in particular deserves mention: Captain Michael Wright, one of the finest commanding officers I ever knew. May he rest in peace.

Prologue

On July 20, 1968, Delta Troop 2/1st Cavalry Regiment (Air) boarded an Air Force C-141 cargo plane at Austin, Texas; its destination: Camp Enari, home of the Fourth Infantry Division, located near Pleiku in II Corps, the Republic of Vietnam. There was still hope for American efforts in Vietnam. The Cavalry was coming to the rescue.

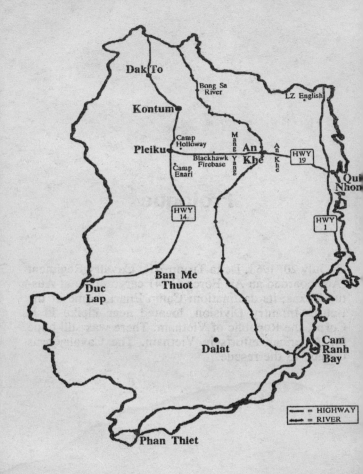

THE REPUBLIC OF VIETNAM, II CORPS.

PART
ONE

∎ ∎ ∎ ∎ ∎ ∎ ∎ ∎ ∎ ∎ ∎ ∎

The
Path
to
Vietnam

1

■ ■ ■ ■ ■ ■ ■ ■ ■ ■ ■ ■ ■ ■

Greetings

IT WAS COLD IN THE GARAGE, A FOUR-BAY SHEET-METAL building near the center of town. Five blocks west a highway department sign marked the city boundary. Fritch, Texas, Pop. 1836. The perpetual West Texas wind howled its fury in a never-ending onslaught against all obstacles in its path. Above the garage's door a weather-beaten wooden sign proclaimed the establishment: Johnson's Gulf Service and Garage. The original sign, made of Plexiglas with flashing orange and blue lights, had not lasted long in the Panhandle, and the wooden sign, more impervious to natural hazards, had been constructed to take its place. The sign was artfully—if unskillfully—done in a multicolored scheme that displayed the three different colors available, in half-pint quantities, from Howard's Lumber Yard and Café.

Inside the garage I got into the Ford and cranked the engine, which sprang instantly to life—a reward for my endless hours of mechanical tinkering. The high-performance camshaft caused the engine to idle roughly, shaking the entire car. The deep, mellow roar of the twin glass-pack mufflers provided an unbridled announcement of the power beneath the throttle. Herschel Winters opened the door, and I backed the Ford out. Herschel and I had been close friends for a couple of years. He ungracefully stuffed

5

his 220 pounds of All-Regional football center into the front seat, the button-and-tuck upholstery suffering abnormal wear and tear, and we headed to Howard's for lunch.

"What are we going to do about it?"

The query came from Herschel as he stuffed down his second cheeseburger, with double fries.

"What's 'it'?"

"Don't play dumb," he said, finishing off the last of his meal and looking around for more. " 'It' is the big letter . . . our appointment for induction physicals tomorrow."

"Oh, that 'it,' " I replied as he reached for one of my french fries. I stabbed his hand with my fork, drawing blood.

"Damn," he shouted, jerking his hand away.

"Never, ever take someone else's food without an invitation."

"Sorry. Lost my head," he said, sucking the blood from his wound. "Can I have a potato?"

"No."

"But I'm still hungry."

"Then order some more food. Just because you wolf down your meal doesn't entitle you to mine."

Herschel shouted at the waitress to bring him another order of fries. "So, what are we going to do?"

"We're going to go over to Amarillo tomorrow and take our physical exams."

"You know we'll be drafted."

"Sure, they're drafting everyone these days." The physicals were just a formal prelude to the draft notice, our student exemptions having been revoked after we'd flunked out of college for three consecutive semesters.

"It'll cost us two years."

"You got anything better to be doing?"

"Naw. Not really. It'll be good experience, I guess. We should just look on it as a paid vacation."

"Strange idea of a vacation."

"I'm trying to think positive. You know what the army will do with us?" he asked rhetorically.

"Sure. Most draftees get assigned to the infantry. In six months we'll be slogging around rice paddies and dodging bullets."

"Yeah, well, I don't want to do that."

"I don't think we'll have a lot to say about it."

"We could. But it'll cost us another year."

"How's that?"

"I've been talking to a recruiter. If you get drafted, it's a two-year hitch and if you enlist, it's three years, but you get to choose your job assignment. Provided you pass all the qualifying tests, of course."

"That's got possibilities. It might be worth an extra year not to get stuck in the infantry."

"That's what I figure. And I know what I want to do."

I was impressed. I wished I knew what I wanted to do vocationally. No profession intrigued me. "What's that?" I asked.

"Helicopter pilot."

"Helicopter pilot! Where on earth did you come up with that?"

"The recruiter."

"But don't you have to have a college degree to be a pilot?"

"Nope. The army has this program, Warrant Officer Flight Training, and you only have to have a high school diploma to qualify."

"What's a warrant officer?"

"Beats me. But the pay is good, and you get saluted. And you draw sergeant's wages and flight pay while you're in training."

"But why helicopters?"

" 'Cause that's the program. The army uses a lot of helicopters. Anyway, it's a helluva lot better than the infantry."

"I don't know. Those things seem pretty dangerous to me."

"You think getting shot at in the infantry isn't dangerous?"

"You get shot at in helicopters, too, and you make a better target. It's also a lot further to the ground when you get hit."

"I don't care. It sounds like fun. I'll bet the girls really go for helicopter pilots. You even get to wear these really neat sunglasses. It's what I want to do. I've decided."

"Fine. You've decided. It doesn't sound particularly attractive to me."

Herschel looked crushed. "They have this enlistment option called the buddy program. You can sign up together, and you do all your training together."

"So?"

"So, I want us to sign up for it and go to flight school together."

"But I don't want to go to flight school."

"Come on. I got a feeling on this. It's going to be the best thing that ever happened to us. Trust me."

Oh, hell, I thought. He obviously had his heart set on this. And I didn't really have any better ideas. "All right."

"You'll do it?"

"I said 'all right.' But I'm holding you accountable for this being a good idea."

"You'll see."

The next morning, Thursday, we took our physical exams, an introduction to the army's never-ending hurry-up-and-wait process. We had chits that provided lunch in a nearby restaurant, after which we took our entrance exams. We passed easily (Choose the correct response: If you were going to nail two wooden boards together, would you use a saw, a hammer, a screwdriver, or a wrench?) and enlisted for Warrant Officer Flight Training. The recruiter spent a considerable amount of time explaining what a lovely place Fort Polk, Louisiana, would be for basic training. According to him, it was a real paradise, second only to Hawaii, but the army didn't offer basic training in Hawaii. He scheduled us to leave the following afternoon, after the results of our physicals came back. We were given vouchers for a hotel, where we spent a nervous night.

Early Friday morning we got the results of our physicals: I had passed with flying colors; Herschel had flunked. The army did not feel that he had completely recovered from a kidney disease he had had two years earlier. He was crestfallen. I began to suspect that this was another fine mess he'd gotten me into.

That afternoon Herschel bade me farewell as I departed on my first airplane ride. It was three years before I saw him again. He had graduated from college; I had graduated from Vietnam. Herschel hadn't changed much. I had.

I was terrified throughout that first flight and was convinced that becoming a pilot wasn't the smartest decision I'd ever made, particularly when the Boeing 707 shuddered through rough turbulence to land at the El Paso Airport. I thought it was a strange way to get to Louisiana. It was even stranger to discover that my enlistment papers showed that I had volunteered for the infantry. Three posts and more than a year later I finally arrived at flight school. The intervening year, which included a hitch in the infantry and a three-week stretch of KP (kitchen police), had made me a more enthusiastic candidate—and one that was determined to succeed. However, the training program on which I was about to embark seemed to have been designed by a Charles Darwin enthusiast. Determination was only one attribute required for survival.

9

2

■ ■ ■ ■ ■ ■ ■ ■ ■ ■ ■ ■ ■ ■ ■

Above the Best

I ARRIVED AT FORT WOLTERS, TEXAS, THE ARMY'S PRIMARY
Helicopter School, on an icy winter day. The long and wind-
ing road to flight school had taken more than a year, but I
had doggedly pursued my objective. That it had taken Ulys-
ses twenty years to return to Penelope was no longer a
mystery to me; he, also, was at the mercy of bureaucracies.
Nevertheless, I had made it. Finally. It was time to reap
the reward of my perseverance. I triumphantly drove
through the main gate, passing between two helicopters
mounted on display pedestals and a sign proclaiming the
Army Aviation motto: Above the Best. It was February 5,
1967. It was also extremely cold, with freezing rain driven
by a strong wind. The weather outside was frightful. But I
was too excited to be mentally sidetracked by such mortal
complaints. I was about to join the ranks of Charles Lind-
bergh, Amelia Earhart, and Wiley Post. There was only
one thing standing between me and my aviation destiny:
nine months of survival against one of the deadliest terrors
ever to stalk the earth, the tac officer. I soon ceased to
worry about either the weather or other matters involving
creature comforts.

The tac officer's principal responsibility was to ensure
that no individual with human frailties ever pinned the sil-

ver wings of the army aviator on his chest. He did this by using a variety of ingenious and dastardly tactics—passed down to him from previous generations of evildoers—designed to turn brave young lads into whimpering jelly. And woe unto the foolish candidate who whimpered. Warrant officers were to be forged from sterner stuff. I never whimpered. I complained . . . once. I had been unfairly assigned some demerits, and when I politely attempted to point out the tac officer's mistake, he doubled the demerits. When I said, "But, sir," he doubled them again. I learned to keep my mouth shut. The tac was my temporary god, and there was no appeal from his judgment. And my god was an evil god.

For warrant officer candidates, known as WOCs, the first four weeks were called preflight. There was no flying. It was a period devoted to being completely at the mercy of a merciless tac officer. If you survived preflight, you moved up to the Hill, as the permanent barracks were called, and began primary flight training. If you survived those four months, you went on to advanced flight training at Fort Rucker, Alabama. But the army's principal training strategy was to separate the wheat from the chaff before the chaff ever set foot in a helicopter. Preflight was twenty-eight very long, very demanding days of pure hell.

Everything in flight school was organized as a time-based series of rites of passage, which occurred formally about once a month. As you moved successfully past these hurdles you got more privileges and less harassment. In fact, you were sanctioned and encouraged to harass candidates who were behind you. Preflight candidates were, of course, the low men on the totem pole. In fact, they were so low they held the totem pole up. Fortunately, they were physically isolated from the Hill, where the "real" candidates were housed, and this provided an obstacle to one source of torment. The tac officers ensured that this gap in harassment was adequately remedied.

When we moved up to the Hill—those of us who had survived preflight—we went as a company organized in platoons. Our training was scheduled by platoon, and we became a close-knit unit at that level. We were housed by alphabetical order, with three men per room. My roommates were Randal Hoft and Bill Holder. There were three "Holleys" in the platoon: Sam Holley, Bill Holly, and myself. Due to the alphabetical split in room assignments, the other two were next door. This twist of fate was to cause my first serious encounter with an irate tac officer.

I had pretty much avoided being an individual target up to that time. We had learned early that one way of coping with the tac officers was to stick together one hundred percent: united we stand, divided we fall. Tac officers were like lions foraging on a herd of wildebeests. They couldn't attack the herd because of its collective strength, so they went for the stragglers. A fundamental tactic for WOC survival was to avoid becoming a straggler.

Despite that general strategy, tac officers also loved to harass the entire group whenever the chance presented itself; the most opportune time occurred daily, at lunch. We were required to march to the mess hall in formation; we returned individually. The mess hall ritual was highly synchronized: fall out of the barracks at 11:35, report attendance, march to the mess hall, stand in line, eat, return to barracks, and fall out of the barracks at 12:15 for either afternoon classes or flying. If everything happened exactly on schedule, there was just enough time allocated to gulp down some food. And that's exactly what the tac officers counted on.

As soon as we fell out of the barracks to get into formation they would descend and heckle us for fifteen or twenty minutes, just enough time to make us spend a hungry afternoon (that is, of course, if we were scheduled for classroom instruction. They would never send us to the flight line hungry). There was only one way to avoid this: to be faster than the tac officers. We had to fall out of the barracks, get into formation, report attendance (we couldn't leave until everyone was accounted for), and depart the area before the tac officers had time to catch us. This was no easy trick. It required clockwork precision from forty candidates. But we got the system down pat.

"Where's Sam Holley?"

Sam was platoon leader for the week. All of the student command positions were rotated on a weekly basis. We were lined up in the hallway, waiting for the lunchtime dash, but we were missing our leader.

"Here I am," Sam shouted as he rushed out of his room and moved to the main doorway. He quickly perused the assemblage, organized in order by squads, and asked, "Is everyone accounted for?"

His query was greeted by silence, signaling assent.

"Doormen?"

"Ready," the two candidates assigned the task of handling the doors for the quick escape responded in unison.

"Okay. On three. One . . . two . . . three."

The double doors were flung open, and the platoon spilled forth in a single surge, racing for the street. With luck we would have a five-second head start on the tacs. As I scrambled for my position in the third-squad lineup I saw the door across the street swinging open. The tacs had been waiting for us. We didn't get the five-second head start.

"Fall in," Sam Holley bellowed. We had already fallen in, but everything had to go by the book.

"Report," he barked.

The squad leaders quickly reported.

"Right face."

Just before we turned I glimpsed a tac officer streaking toward us. Approaching the rear of the platoon, he yelled at Sam, "Candidate, hold that mob."

To my surprise, Sam hollered, "Forward, march." We took one step, and then he commanded, "Double time, march," putting us into an immediate run.

The tac raced after us, screeching at Sam to halt the platoon. Instead Sam picked up the pace and began a singalong cadence, drowning out the pursuing tac officer. After about three blocks the tac bent over in the middle of the street, gasping for breath. Sam had pulled it off! He was the hero of the moment. My admiration for his deed, however, was to be short-lived.

Like the other candidates, I ate quickly and returned to the barracks. The few precious minutes between lunch and the next formation were our own; five or ten minutes of relaxation was a valuable commodity in a nonstop schedule. As I entered the main door and headed toward my room I passed several other candidates who were lounging about the hallway. They averted their faces as I passed by. Strange, I thought, maybe I've suddenly developed the plague.

I pushed open the door to my room and stepped inside. I immediately froze. Two tac officers were standing on the far side of the room: the one we had outrun to the mess hall, Mr. Williams, and the senior tac, Mr. Brady. They looked like two cats who were about to pounce on an unsuspecting mouse. It occurred to me that something was amiss. Perhaps I had entered the wrong room by mistake. I took a step backward to check the room number, which was painted above the door in the hall. No such luck. It was my room.

"Candidate, get in here and post," Williams boomed.

I quickly crossed the room and posted in front of Mr. Williams.

"Sir, Candidate Holley, sir."

Mr. Brady moved behind me and closed the door. Uh-oh, I thought as he rejoined Williams.

I still had no idea of what transgression I had committed. My mind raced through the possibilities: grades okay, demerits okay, no pink slips. Perhaps I had just been randomly chosen as a sacrificial lamb. Maybe the rumor was true: Tac officers had a quota of busted WOCs to maintain, like police officers with traffic tickets. One thing I knew for sure: the senior tac officer did not attend trivial ass-chewings.

Williams began verbally lambasting me, ranting about my disrespect; how I didn't deserve to be a warrant officer; how he was a hero in Vietnam while I had still been a punk on some street corner; etc., etc. This went on nonstop for about ten minutes. Finally the light bulb clicked on. I understood what was happening: He didn't realize there were three "Holleys" in the platoon. He was really after Sam, whose room was next door. This put me in a quandary. I didn't want to sic him on Sam, but if I didn't set him straight, he was going to be even more upset. I decided the safest thing to do was to point out his mistake.

"Sir," I interjected in his tirade.

"Don't you interrupt me, Candidate! You're at attention. You speak only when you're asked to speak."

And the onslaught continued, sparked with new life. After another five minutes I tried again. Same result.

Finally Mr. Williams ran out of steam. "Well, you sorry excuse for a human being, do you have anything to say for yourself before we kick your butt back to the infantry?"

"Sir, Candidate Holley, yessir. You've got the wrong Candidate Holley. The one you want is in Room 8."

It took a moment to sink in. Then his mouth dropped open—literally. He'd just wasted the best ass-chewing he'd ever given. With difficulty I kept a straight face. The senior tac officer turned away from Williams, discreetly covering his snicker.

With a confused expression Williams looked first at me, then at Mr. Brady. Then at me, then at Brady. He struggled for words. Finally, in a barely audible voice, he asked Mr. Brady, "What do I do now?"

He was so deflated, so pathetic, I almost pitied him. Almost, but not quite. You could never allow yourself to forget, even for a moment, that the tac officer was by nature the sworn enemy of candidates. He would recover to strike again.

Brady looked compassionately at him and said, "You say 'excuse me,' and we leave."

That was my first high-profile encounter with a tac officer. It was hardly my last. But usually such incidents involved minor offenses. On one occasion, however, I received what might be considered cruel and unusual punishment for a virtually nonexistent infraction of the rules.

I had been summoned to Mr. Brady's office. I was to report during the "counseling period" after dinner. I knew the reason for the summons: The class grades from the meteorology exam had come back, and nearly half the class had flunked, myself included. It seemed to me that meteorology could be made into a simpler subject: good clouds and bad clouds. Mr. Brady was calling all of the flunk-ees in for a "fear of God" lecture prior to the makeup exam. I knew why I had failed, but I couldn't tell Mr. Brady. I had become engrossed in *The Agony and the Ecstasy* and had read it instead of studying the meteorology text. That, of course, would never suffice as an excuse.

I arrived outside Mr. Brady's office, still sifting through my brain for plausible explanations. His door was open, but another candidate was posted in front of his desk, getting his lecture on the importance of meteorology. I followed the standing rules of candidate behavior for such a situation: parade rest, against the wall, outside the door. Mr. Brady continued to admonish the other candidate.

About five minutes later Mr. Carter—tac officer for the first platoon—came wandering down the hallway and spotted me outside the door. "Candidate, why are you eavesdropping?" he roared.

"Sir, Candidate Holley, sir. Begging the tac officer's pardon, but I am not eavesdropping. I am in the correct parade rest position, waiting to report to the senior tac officer."

"Candidate, that door is open. You are standing outside the door. Can you hear what is being said inside?"

"Sir, Candidate Holley, yes, sir."

"Then by dingies, that's eavesdropping!"

"Sir, Candidate Holley, sir. I am simply following the specified procedure: assuming the parade rest position in the hallway and waiting until the senior tac officer is free."

"Are you arguing with me, Candidate?"

"Sir, Candidate Holley, no, sir."

"Very well, Candidate. You've been caught red-handed committing a most serious offense. You have also admitted your guilt. I should probably bounce you right out of flight school, but I'm a generous and kindhearted fellow. You've got until 0800 hours tomorrow morning to have a twenty-five-page military format letter on my desk explaining why you were eavesdropping and why you'll never do it again. Do you understand the assignment?"

"Sir, Candidate Holley, yes, sir."

"Do you have any questions?"

"Sir, Candidate Holley, no, sir."

"Very well, 0800 hours. Have a good night."

And with that he moved on down the hall, stalking other unsuspecting victims. I waited for Mr. Brady's invitation to enter his office—obviously, continuing to "eavesdrop"—

received my lecture, and returned to my room. I began working on Mr. Carter's letter. After a half page I ran out of reasons and explanations that could apply to "eavesdropping." I convinced myself that the assignment was too Mickey Mouse to take seriously. I'll bet he doesn't even remember the letter by tomorrow, I thought. It was one of the few bets I won.

Although the clashes with Mr. Williams and Mr. Carter were spurious, I dreaded the day a tac officer would discover, and hold me accountable for, two real offenses that I had committed: destruction of government property and violating the altitude ceiling during a solo flight. The destruction of government property had been an accident, but try explaining that to a tac. He would just say, "Sure, sure," while he continued to supervise the packing of my luggage.

I am not a naturally tidy individual. I would like to be, but something always goes wrong. Break starch on a new pair of fatigues and the shirt is torn or a button is missing or the zipper is broken. Put on pair of spit-shined boots only to discover they belong to my roommate; I forgot to polish mine. Highlight my name tag in black ink and five minutes later the "permanent" ink has run, making the name tag illegible. Such situations have plagued me throughout life but were particularly problematic in flight school, because sloppiness was not tolerated. Consequently I was forced to masquerade as a neat and tidy person. This might have been my greatest challenge in attaining my aviator wings.

It was because of the masquerade that I destroyed government property. I was always lousy at shining shoes. Regardless of their starting condition, by the time I finished polishing a pair of shoes or boots they looked like refugees from Goodwill. But I was determined to do better. I was talented. I was persevering. I knew I could succeed. All I needed was a little instruction from an expert, Candidate Harvey Miller. Harvey's combat boots always shone like a mirror. Literally. You could shave by the reflection from his boots.

I paid Harvey ten dollars for boot shining lessons, including the secret to his success. There were two key ingredients to his formula. First, after you spit-shined using black paste wax, you put a glaze on the shine with clear paste wax. Not too difficult. That one I could handle. It was the second ingredient that proved to be my undoing: you melted the wax before putting it on the boots, allowing it to saturate the pores of the leather.

On my first attempt at implementing Harvey's formula I assembled all the necessary components and placed them on my nightstand, a rather ugly piece of furniture with a gray vinyl top. It was, of course, highly functional, having adequately served the army's needs for quite some time. On the top of the stand I lined up two freshly opened cans of boot wax—one black and one clear, large sizes—Zippo lighter, cotton balls, water, and black liquid dye for the soles. Prepared with all the necessities, I flicked the Zippo and stuck it against the can of black wax.

A small flame began rising from the polish, gradually spreading to encompass the entire surface. I had only to judge the desired melting point and extinguish the blaze. My friendly little fire soon became an inferno. I decided the desired melting point had been achieved, the fusion of the can with the vinyl tabletop providing a good thermometer. At this point it also occurred to me that Harvey's instructions had not included how to put out the fire. For most people over the age of three that would probably have been an unnecessary set of instructions.

I began to panic. The flames were leaping higher, and the can was progressively burying itself deeper and deeper into the vinyl covering of the nightstand. In desperation, I took a deep breath and blew fiercely at the flaming can of wax. This did not put out the fire. It did, however, cause a goodly portion of the flaming liquid to leave the confines of the can and spread across the tabletop. I had quite successfully escalated the problem. President Johnson and I had much in common.

I took another deep breath and tried smaller puffs. Little tiny ones. Puff . . . puff . . . puff. The fire seemed to like that. It leapt higher. But I was determined. "I'll huff and I'll puff until I burn these barracks down," I shouted at the fire.

Fortunately, my roommate chose that particular time to

return, immediately sized up the situation, grabbed a towel from my bunk, and placed it over the flaming nightstand. The fire died out.

"Aha!" I exclaimed. "Oxygen deprivation. That's what I was going to try next."

The tabletop was not a pretty sight—black shoe polish embedded in melted vinyl. If I turned the table in for a new one, the damage would have to be explained. The truth did not seem like a plausible explanation for an elimination board. I could vividly picture the board saying, "And what would you do if your helicopter was on fire, Candidate? Blow on it?" "No, sir," I would respond. "I'd throw a towel over it."

Confession may be good for the soul, but in this case I would wait to get caught before I confessed. In the interim I decided to try camouflage. I cleaned the table up as best I could and then coated it heavily with beeswax. About five coats. It shone like a new dime. This caused the damage to appear to have occurred at a much earlier date. Like Tuesday instead of Wednesday. Then I arranged the table furnishings as best I could to cover the more damaged areas. When I was finished it didn't look too bad—if you didn't move anything, and if you didn't look too closely. For the rest of my time at Fort Wolters I feared that a tac officer would inadvertently move something on the table while inspecting for dust. They never did. They came close, but they never did. And I knew I had been blessed with a strong heart.

The other episode that kept me terrified during my tenure at Fort Wolters involved violating altitude restrictions while flying solo. I also have trouble with rules, particularly arbitrary ones. Candidates were restricted to a maximum altitude of 3,000 feet AGL (above ground level) while solo. I didn't understand this. Regulations allow aircraft to be flown between 10,000 and 14,500 feet for thirty minutes before oxygen masks are required, with masks always required above 14,500 feet. So why could we only go to 3,000 feet? This was a mystery in need of resolution, particularly since helicopters had been flown at altitudes in excess of 30,000 feet.

At my first opportunity I challenged the 3,000 feet rule.

It took me almost an hour of climbing at max power in my Mattel Messerschmidt, but finally I passed through 13,000 feet, somewhere over Mineral Wells, Texas. Shortly thereafter the engine quit abruptly. I lowered the collective, entering autorotation, and floated earthward.

As I watched the altimeter needle reverse itself ever so slowly, I contemplated my unusual predicament. I was so high that I had my choice of virtually any helicopter staging field in the vicinity of Fort Wolters as a forced landing area. It occurred to me that it would look a little fishy to have an engine failure in a helicopter and be able to glide to an improved airfield for an emergency landing. Too suspicious. I decided some farmer's field would be more appropriate.

Five minutes later I had lost sufficient altitude to make the situation plausible. I had also identified a nice, large— I estimated it at about forty acres—flat field as a landing area. I made my Mayday call, giving my location, and then concentrated on performing my first solo autorotation, my attempts at restarting the engine having been in vain. I lined up perfectly for the center of the forty acres. I wasn't taking any chances. I concentrated on airspeed, altitude, and ground closure rate, just as I'd been taught. I also watched in horror as the helicopter floated on past the forty-acre field. What a klutz, I thought, a 13,000-foot approach and you overshoot a forty-acre field.

Fortunately, things worked out for the best. The tiny, tree-bounded clearing that I was forced to settle for as an alternate landing area not only eliminated potential suspicion regarding the episode—no one in his right mind would have deliberately chosen it as a landing area—but also allowed me to demonstrate my dexterity as a helicopter pilot. Actually, I just closed my eyes and hoped for the best. But that's not the way the story came out, and truth is often a matter of interpretation. I was satisfied with their interpretation. However, I spent several terrifying weeks waiting for the results of the maintenance analysis of the helicopter. I had no doubt that the engine had failed from oxygen starvation. Fortunately, the analysis revealed a broken carburetor. I had dodged another bullet in the quest for my silver wings.

*   *   *

For a human, flying is a complicated psychomotor task. It is, however, a relatively simple task for a chimpanzee. I know this to be true because our flight instructors continually claimed that they could teach a champanzee to fly a helicopter. They usually implied that would also be an easier feat than teaching a WOC to fly. In the words of my first instructor pilot: "I was looking at the stacks of meat in the butcher's counter, and I noticed three types of brains: cow brains for a dollar a pound, chimpanzee brains for five dollars a pound, and WOC brains for ten dollars a pound. So I asked the butcher: 'Why are WOC brains so expensive?' And he says: 'Because it takes so many WOCs to make a pound of brains.' "

There were two major flying-type rites of passage at Fort Wolters: hovering by the fifth hour of instruction and soloing by the seventeenth. Otherwise, you were out. Hovering was the most difficult task, soloing the most frightening. To hover properly, you must maintain the aircraft stationary, three feet off the ground. This requires the continuous and simultaneous manipulation of four very sensitive controls: throttle (power), collective pitch (vertical control), cyclic pitch (horizontal control), and anti-torque pedals (yaw control). If one control position were altered, all others had to be correspondingly altered: manual homeostasis. And it was constantly necessary to alter a control position. A helicopter is inherently unstable. It doesn't fly; it beats the air into submission.

The instructors used two successive approximation techniques to teach hovering. First, they only allowed you to manipulate one control at a time—while they handled the other three controls—gradually increasing the number of controls you were allocated until you were handling all of them by yourself. Second, they started you out with a football-size field to try to hover in, gradually reducing the size of the field.

The frightening thing about soloing was having to do an autorotation if the engine failed. The instructor pilots continually drilled us on performing an autorotation—constantly cutting the throttle when we least expected it—until the mechanics of the maneuver were reflexive actions. And of course, we also practiced touchdown autorotations at the staging field. But performing a practice autorotation with an instructor sitting next to you is a far cry from doing a solo autorotation. There's no security blanket.

In fact, the army recognized this distinction. Previously they had required students to perform three solo autorotations, the final requirement for graduation from primary training at Fort Wolters and progression to advanced training at Fort Rucker. But that had all changed with Candidate Roy Schneider, who had been two classes ahead of me. I, along with most other WOCs, would be eternally grateful to him for causing the solo autorotation requirement to be canceled, although the episode cost him his candidacy.

Candidate Schneider had completed all requirements for graduation, with the exception of performing three solo autorotations. He brought his OH-23 around the traffic pattern at the staging field and turned final for his first autorotation. It was a beautiful day for flying, and the day was a momentous occasion in his life. Three more landings and he was off to Fork Rucker. Despite the OH-23's poor autorotative capability, he was confident. Timing was critical, but he knew he could handle it.

He held his altitude and centered the helicopter over the runway. As he passed over the near end of the runway Candidate Schneider closed the throttle and lowered the collective, entering autorotation. Almost one down . . . two to go. The helicopter began gliding toward the earth, which, in an OH-23, means it began falling like a rock. He used the cyclic to adjust airspeed as the ground rushed toward him. He was undoubtedly talking out loud to himself, articulating the procedural steps for successfully completing the autorotation: "Hold attitude. Everything nice and easy. At twenty-five feet, flare to reduce airspeed. Level the skids at ten feet. Pull collective to cushion the landing." We all talked out loud when we were solo.

When he estimated the altitude to be twenty-five feet Candidate Schneider pulled the cyclic toward him, executing the flare. The runway was rushing up at an incredibly fast rate. At ten feet he pushed the cyclic forward, leveling the aircraft. The helicopter continued its relatively unimpeded earthward plunge and crashed forcefully into the runway. He was temporarily stunned by the impact, the helicopter disintegrating in the middle of the runway. Candidate Schneider had forgotten the last step in the autorotative maneuver: pull collective.

As the fire trucks and flight instructors arrived at the wreckage he untangled himself from the carnage and climbed out. Spotting his own flight instructor rushing toward him, along with the flight commander, he raised his right hand into the air, elevated two fingers, and said, "Bring me two more helicopters."

Candidate Schneider was eliminated from flight school. Not for wrecking the helicopter, but for having a bad attitude. I thought his attitude was quite appropriate for a future army aviator. In my case, the pre-event anxiety associated with soloing turned out to be unnecessary. The actual event was performed, to my gratitude, without incident, and I received my ritual dunking in the swimming pool at the Mineral Wells Holiday Inn. God was good to me that day. In fact, he was good to me the rest of the time I was at Fort Wolters, including my radio procedure foul-up with Dempsey Tower. The army was death on using proper radio procedures: constant threats regarding FAA regulations, fines, imprisonment, physical disfigurement, and public humiliation. They were particularly adamant about not using profanity over the radio. The last WOC who used profanity and got caught was still hanging by his thumbs in the WOC dungeon. Unfortunately, I committed the unpardonable sin of using profanity over the radio. I also committed the pardonable sin of not getting caught.

It was late afternoon, about 1700 hours. In civilian terminology that's five P.M. In fixed-wing terminology, the little hand was on the five, the big hand was on the twelve, and the sun was shining. I was solo in my Mattel Messerschmidt, heading back to Dempsey Field, through for the day. There were about three hundred other helicopters doing the same thing: ending the day's flying and landing at Dempsey. It was a daily fiasco. Three hundred helicopters, two thirds of them with inexperienced candidates getting solo time, trying to land at one time, dodging one another and jockeying for position in the landing pattern. We WOCs had an apt saying for this particular situation: The dangers of Vietnam are bound to be relatively insignificant compared to the Dempsey traffic pattern at five o'clock in the afternoon.

Like most candidates did when flying solo, I had my hot mike switch turned on. That way you could talk out loud to yourself over the intercom without using the push-to-talk switch. The trick to this procedure was to make sure that your transmit select switch was in the intercom position. Otherwise, everything you said was transmitted over the radio.

On this day, however, Murphy's Law caught up with me. I failed to place the transmit select switch back in the intercom position after making my initial radio call to the tower for landing instructions. As I approached Dempsey's downwind leg at a proper 45° angle for entering the traffic pattern I unintentionally cut another helicopter out of the pattern. Vocally, I criticized my amateurish mistake.

"Boy, did I fuck up," I said aloud, presumably over the intercom.

A few seconds later Dempsey Tower responded, "Fucked Up, this is Dempsey Tower. Over."

Surely he couldn't be talking to me, I thought.

The tower repeated its call, "Fucked Up, I say again, this is Dempsey Tower. Over."

Nobody else was responding. I frantically checked the transmit select switch and discovered, with despair, that it was in the transmit position. Oh, shit, I thought, he *is* talking to me. I decided to respond; otherwise the tower operator would continue repeating his request.

"Dempsey Tower, this is Fucked Up. Over," I transmitted.

"Roger, Fucked Up. Tower requests your position. Over."

"Roger, Tower. Fucked Up is in the Dempsey traffic pattern. Over." That seemed safe. Me and a couple of hundred other helicopters fit that description.

"Roger, Fucked Up. Tower requests your tail number. Over."

"Roger, Tower. I understand you want my tail number. Over."

"Roger, Fucked Up."

"Tower, this is Fucked Up. I'm not that fucked up. Out."

Five torturous months after arriving at Fort Wolters I graduated from primary flight training and headed for Fort Rucker. A major hurdle had been surmounted. At Fort Rucker there was less harassment and more flight training. Most of the Mickey Mouse stuff was behind us. And except for instrument flight training, we got to fly real aircraft: Hueys. During instrument training we flew the Bell OH-13, which was similar to the aircraft we had left behind at Fort Wolters. My primary objective at this point was simply to stay out of trouble. I knew that if I accomplished that, in four short months I'd be pinning silver wings on my chest. I wasn't completely successful at accomplishing my objective.

3

■ ■ ■ ■ ■ ■ ■ ■ ■ ■ ■ ■ ■

Mother Rucker

ON ARRIVING AT FORT RUCKER, AFFECTIONATELY REFERRED to as Mother Rucker by its alumni, I noticed two things. First, the afternoon sunshine that I had been enjoying disappeared, replaced by a half hour of drizzling rain and obscured skies. Such daily downpours, I learned, were standard fare for Alabama in the summertime. Second, everything was aviation-oriented, from the continuous "whomp, whomp" of Hueys passing overhead to virtually every soldier and civilian you encountered. One couldn't help feeling a lot of pride at being a part of this. Of course, you had to graduate before you were a permanent offspring of Mother Rucker. And I was determined to do just that. With the exception of two episodes, the four months passed quickly and uneventfully. The first occurred in an OH-13 during initial instrument training. It resulted in the only pink slip I received during flight school.

"Well, Candidate Holley. What are you going to do if I cut the throttle right now?"

I surveyed the situation before responding to the instructor pilot's question. The dense Alabama forest covered the ground for miles in every direction. There were no forced landing areas, only trees. He couldn't possibly be serious,

26

I thought. Simulated forced landings were strictly controlled in this particular model of helicopter, the OH-13, because the engine had a tendency to quit when it was reduced to flight idle.

The luck of the draw had given me Mr. Cooke for my final check ride in initial instrument training. All of the students lived in terror of Mr. Cooke. In his rather lengthy tenure at Fort Rucker, only three students had passed their final check rides with him. He was referred to as Mr. Pink Slip—not to his face, of course. We had gotten off on the wrong foot right from the beginning of the flight.

"Well, sir, I guess I would just pull the collective up under my armpit and bend over and kiss my butt goodbye."

"You ever had a pink slip, Candidate?"

The guy obviously has no sense of humor, I thought as I responded in a properly compliant tone, "No, sir."

"You just keep working your smart mouth, and that'll change real quick."

"Yes, sir. It's just that the OH-13 is restricted from simulated forced landings when there aren't any landing areas available."

"So it is," Mr. Cooke responded.

The throttle suddenly twisted beneath my hand. The low RPM warning tone began screeching as I quickly lowered the collective and entered autorotation. The man's a certifiable lunatic, I thought. Fortunately, the engine RPM stabilized at flight idle. At least we would be able to make a power recovery. I turned the helicopter into the wind and established a glide angle for minimum rate of descent. The only choice I would have in the landing was which tree to hit.

"Very good, Candidate. You fly better than you talk. Now just hold what you've got and pick out a nice fat tree to land in."

I selected the fattest tree I could find and adjusted my flight path accordingly. We were about two hundred feet above the trees now. Very soon Mr. Cooke would execute a power recovery, since regulations prohibited us from going below two hundred feet. Regulations also prohibited us from performing simulated forced landings in this situation. Lunatics didn't seem to pay much attention to regulations. The trees loomed closer and closer.

"Now put in a little aft cyclic and hold it," Mr. Cooke said.

I complied, and the helicopter slowed. We were about ten feet above the tree that I had selected.

"Pull collective, then add a little forward cyclic."

Again I complied with the instructions. I felt the throttle being twisted open and heard the engine spring back to life as the helicopter began to settle into the branches at the top of the tree. The skids were touching the tree as the helicopter stabilized at a hover.

"Excellent job, Candidate. You show promise. Someday you might make a decent aviator."

This was high praise from the legendary Mr. Cooke. "Thank you, sir."

"Remember, there are lots of trees in Vietnam. If you have to go down in them, do it right. You'll lose the aircraft, but you'll walk away."

"Yes, sir," I responded. "Are you still going to give me a pink slip?"

"Of course," Mr. Cooke replied.

The second Fort Rucker episode occurred during advanced instrument training, also in an OH-13. I was to do a real autorotation for the second time in my brief aviation career. This time, however, I was not alone—although after landing I discovered that the comforting presence of the instrument instructor pilot had been an illusory security blanket.

"Flying can be very boring, can't it, Candidate Holley?"

The question came from my advanced instrument instructor pilot, Captain Anderson, a grizzled veteran who would never make it to the higher ranks of the army. Like Mr. Cooke, he terrorized most of his students, leaving them quaking with pink-slip fear at the end of each flight. Fear as motivation seemed to be a primary army training strategy for future aviators, Machiavelli having consulted on the syllabus.

Unlike my relationship with Mr. Cooke, however, Captain Anderson and I got along great, primarily because I readily took to instrument flying and didn't take his gruff manner seriously. He both understood and appreciated my sense of humor. For example, he would have chuckled at the sly remark that had drawn a pink slip from the humorless Mr. Cooke. On this day we were doing a cross-country instrument flight: two hours outbound, refuel, two hours inbound. We were on the inbound leg, heading back to Fort Rucker with about a half hour to go. I was under the hood, which meant I couldn't see outside the helicopter. I had to rely solely on my instruments.

"Sometimes," I responded noncommittally. You had to be careful with Anderson. He had a way of leading your answers down the primrose path.

"You know, we have a saying in aviation: Flying is hours and hours of boredom, punctuated by moments of stark terror."

"A very clever cliché," I replied. I couldn't see him, but I could feel his eyes boring into me.

"I think you need some stark terror," he said as he closed the throttle.

I didn't see why he thought this would be so frightening. An autorotation under instrument flying rules was a simple procedure. Theoretically, you couldn't see outside of the aircraft; therefore, the autorotation simply represented a controlled crash, with a guess at cushioning the ground impact. And simulated autorotations were terminated two hundred feet above the ground, unless they were done at a staging field. I lowered the collective and stabilized the aircraft in an autorotative descent. Then I made the simulated emergency radio call.

I also observed that the engine RPM had gone to zero. The engine had died when Anderson had abruptly closed the throttle to the flight idle position. The OH-13 was bad about that. As the altimeter needle passed through a thousand feet I peeked under the hood and stole a glance at Anderson. He was staring contentedly outside the aircraft, unaware that we had experienced an actual engine failure.

"Sir, did you want to take the controls?" I asked.

"Why would I want to do that? You're doing just fine."

"Well, I just thought that since we've had a real engine failure, you'd want to finish off the autorotation."

This calmly spoken remark produced an appropriate stark terror reaction. "I have the aircraft," he blurted, grabbing the controls.

"You have the aircraft," I responded.

While Anderson was making a hysterical Mayday call over the emergency frequency I calmly removed my hood and the panels that were blocking my view outside the aircraft. Then I quite properly locked my seat belt and shoulder harness in preparation for Anderson's superb demonstration of his autorotative skills. I had the utmost confidence in my instructor pilot; after all, an autorotative landing was a simple feat compared to walking on water.

My confidence began to wane when he failed to flare the aircraft. We hit the ground at sixty knots. Fortunately, he did remember to pull collective, cushioning our impact. However, we were going so fast that every time we hit a bump we were thrown back up into the air. Then we would wham back into the ground. Up . . . down . . . wham. Up . . . down . . . wham. Finally the helicopter skidded to a halt, facing back the way we had come.

"Nice touch," I said as the dust began to settle.

Anderson didn't respond but immediately scrambled out of the helicopter and began throwing up. Then he moved away from the helicopter and lit a cigarette. Actually, it took him several attempts to get the cigarette lit. His hands were shaking rather badly. I turned off the cockpit switches, tied down the rotor blade, and then joined the chain-smoking Anderson. He offered me a cigarette, but I declined. I didn't smoke.

"You know, Candidate Holley, you are a calm son of a bitch. Don't you ever get excited?"

"Oh, I didn't see much to get excited about, sir. I knew I was in good hands."

"I appreciate your confidence in me, Mr. Holley, particularly since that was my first real autorotation."

"Sir, could I borrow one of those cigarettes?" I asked.

* * *

Captain Anderson and I were quickly picked up by the Fort Rucker dustoff helicopter, whose crew replenished our defunct inventory of cigarettes, and returned to base.

The rest of my time at Fort Rucker was anticlimactic. I somehow managed to stumble through the escape and evasion course without breaking a leg, getting captured, or starving to death (nobody should eat bunny rabbits). I also got to fly a helicopter in John Wayne's movie *The Green Berets,* which was being filmed while we were in tactics training. David Janssen dined with us in the field mess hall, where the main menu item was the chef's special, concocted from mystery ingredients. John Wayne declined lunch, citing a pressing schedule. Janssen rejoined the film crew after a short recovery period.

The guest speaker at our graduation ceremony was General Hamilton Howze, whose "Howze Board Report" had produced radical changes in Army Aviation's organization and employment. He spoke to us at some length about combat helicopter tactics in desert warfare. I found the lecture confusing. While I am not a student of geography, I did not think Vietnam was noted for its desert terrain.

That aside, I endured the ceremony, pinned on the silver wings of an army aviator, saluted my first enlisted man ("One dollar, please"), and marched off to war. At least I thought I was marching off to war. The orders I received might have had me marching off to war, but without great haste.

4

■ ■ ■ ■ ■ ■ ■ ■ ■ ■ ■ ■ ■ ■ ■

Cav Country

MY ORDERS READ: ASSIGNED TO D TROOP, 2/1 CAVALRY (Air), Fort Hood, Texas. Things had changed since the cavalry rode horses, wore yellow ribbons around their necks, and rescued the pioneers from the Indians at the last minute. Progress. The cavalry had traded in horses for tanks, armored personnel carriers, and helicopters. In tribute to tradition, however, they had retained their Stetsons and spurs.

They had also kept an image of independence and a can-do attitude. These characteristics combined to bode ill for both the enemy and the superior headquarters to which a cavalry unit was attached. Superior headquarters did not care for subordinate units that were difficult to discipline. On the other hand, they could not ignore combat results. The cavalry's job was to find the enemy, and it was very good at the job. Occasionally, it was too good. As I had discovered back at Fort Rucker when I compared postgraduation assignments with the other candidates, a tour with the air cavalry was not necessarily considered opportune, particularly for a pilot who cherished longevity. Most of the reactions fell into one of two categories: "God, that's really bad luck" or "Whatever you do, stay out of scouts."

By the time I signed in at Fort Hood headquarters I was

more than a little apprehensive about my future. The duty officer did not ease my anxiety. With an official-looking demeanor he scrutinized my orders, shook his head sadly, and said, "I'm so sorry for you."

"What are you sorry about?"

"Oh . . . nothing . . . just a slip of the tongue. It's really a plush assignment. You're very lucky."

I remained skeptical. Back in Amarillo the recruiter had convinced me that Fort Polk would be like Hawaii. I never made it to Fort Polk, but some of my flight-school buddies had. It was not Hawaii.

"Can you give me directions to my unit?"

"Sure. It's easy enough to find. You just go out to Killeen Base and follow the signs to Gray Army Airfield. The cav's quartered there."

"Where's Killeen Base?"

"Take Highway 190 west out of the main gate. About six miles. You'll see the signs."

"Why's the cavalry way out there?"

"The general doesn't like to have them on the main post. You get my drift?"

"No, I don't. But it doesn't matter. Thanks for the info."

"You're welcome. And good luck. You'll need it."

The next morning I reported to Delta Troop and began my indoctrination into the cavalry and the cavalry way of life. I learned that the combat elements of an air cavalry troop consisted of ten Hueys (Aerolift Platoon), ten gunships (Aeroweapons Platoon), ten Loaches (Aeroscout Platoon), and an infantry platoon (Blue Platoon). Delta Troop was the air unit of a ground cavalry squadron. The other three units of the squadron were ground cavalry troops, and they were already in Vietnam. We would be joining them in about six months. Our primary mission was reconnaissance—finding the enemy, but not becoming decisively engaged, so the big boys could come in and wipe them out. The primary method of operation was to locate the enemy by using the scouts as bait: They hovered around the trees, tracking the enemy until they drew fire; ipso facto, they had located the enemy.

The survival rate for scouts was very low. I breathed a

sigh of relief when I received my platoon assignment: gunships, UH-1Cs. As it would turn out, my relief was temporary.

But the air cavalry was more than the mission and table of organization that could be read in official publications. It embodied a spirit of tradition that extended more than a hundred years into the past. You learned this aspect of the cavalry by listening to cavalry veterans whenever the opportunity presented itself. And one of the best places for this was at the Officers Club Annex, where we spent a lot of off-duty hours.

The stale odor of popcorn, cigarette smoke, and beer greeted me as I passed through the aging doorway of the Annex. While waiting for my eyes to adjust to the darkness, I listened to the familiar sounds of a thousand other crowded barrooms. Gradually vague shadows took form, and voices began to belong to people. The decor consisted mainly of various parts of helicopters and military apparel displayed on the walls and ceiling. Behind the mirrored bar a portrait of an AH-1G helicopter gunship—with its menacing rockets and guns—ominously welcomed the patrons. A caption under the portrait read: "Deadliest Snake in the World."

The loud thud of a dice cup hitting a tabletop drew my attention to a nearby table. As his tablemates laughed at his expense, a pseudo-indignant soldier, trapped in the tangled web of the liar's dice, anted up for another round of drinks. On a platform in the center of the room a go-go dancer unrhythmically struggled with the beat of a Creedence Clearwater tune, which was blaring from a well-worn jukebox. Above the dancer a large red-and-white banner—emblazoned with a cavalry hat, crossed sabers, spurs, and the words "CAV COUNTRY"—hung from the ceiling. In the far corner two soldiers were throwing darts into a board covered with a map of Vietnam; various targets on the map were identified with point values.

Like myself, most of the customers were wearing gray flight suits that identified them as army pilots. There were two cavalry troops stationed at Killeen Base, and the Annex was their favorite watering hole. Recognizing a familiar face at a corner table—Larry Seaman of the Gun Platoon—I joined him and was quickly introduced to the other members of the impromptu party. An Oriental waitress dropped off an empty beer mug, and I helped myself to one of the pitchers on the table.

"Now this ain't no BS," Jim Simpson, a member of the Scout Platoon, drawled from beneath a non-regulation mustache. "Must've been in early spring—maybe February. We were working near the Cambodian border, west of Dak To. 'Course, this was before we were authorized to cross the border, and we had to be real careful about that to keep the Old Man from getting called on the carpet—international incidents, they were called.

"We were working with two Charley Models and two Loaches. I was flying the lead Loach, and Crazy Joe Murdock was my door gunner. You fellers prob'ly remember me talking 'bout Crazy Joe before. Helluva guy, Murdock. Nicest fellow you'd ever want to meet—long as you weren't a commie and he didn't have a machine gun. When Crazy Joe wasn't flying, he was practicing with his M-60. He set up his own firing range, with dummy targets made up to look like Vietcong and NVA troops. He got so good that he could put his initials in one of those targets from two hundred yards away while holding his M-60 in one hand.

"Crazy Joe used to say things like, 'There's only three good things in life: whiskey, women, and shooting VC; not necessarily in that order.' This gave the pilots Joe flew with a great sense of security. I used to fly with him a lot.

"Anyway, we were working near the border, and it had been a real nothing kind of a day—the way they always were before things went to hell in a handbag. Now, you have to realize that us scout pilots didn't carry maps, so I wasn't responsible for us getting on the wrong side of the border. We depended on the gunships for our navigating, usually the lead. He'd tell us scouts to do things like 'turn left' or 'turn right'—things we could understand.

"It was getting on toward late afternoon, and all of a sudden we find ourselves smack dab in the middle of a regimental-size NVA base camp. This place was like a full-fledged army post—flags, barracks, headquarters building, tanks, artillery. Probably even had a PX. Here we were, two Loaches—at a hover, ten feet off the ground—eyeball-to-eyeball with what must have been three or four thousand NVA regulars. It wasn't until later that I learned we were in Cambodia—our illustrious navigator had misread his map.

"Needless to say, in a matter of seconds there were so many fireworks going off that it would have caused Philadelphia's centennial celebration to pale by comparison. Even with Crazy Joe along, I figure the odds aren't tipped in our favor—hell, we only carried 1500 rounds for the M-60. So I pull the collective up under my armpit, intending to perform an immediate retrograde operation.

"By this time my Loach is starting to get punched full of bullet holes; everyone's screaming on all channels of the radio; broken Plexiglas is flying all over the place; one of our smoke grenades has taken a hit and gone off in the cockpit; my warning lights are flashing; the low RPM audio is blaring in my ears; and I'm being personally assaulted by ejecting M-60 shells—I can't tell if I'm being killed by the NVA or Crazy Joe.

"Things are real hectic right then, but I manage to jump my Loach over a tree line and temporarily break line of sight with the NVA. However, I'm losing engine power and cyclic control. I make it a couple of hundred yards, limping along over the trees, and I come to a clearing—must've been about the size of a football field. My old Loach breathes its last gasp just as I slam it down in the middle of that clearing.

"Sometime during the fighting my radio had been shot out, and me and Crazy Joe had no idea what had happened to the other Loach or the gunships. For all we knew, we were the only ones left. So we start gathering up our personal weapons to make a dash for the trees. I had my pistols, a shotgun, a grenade launcher, an M-16, an M-2, and my Bowie knife. Besides his pistol Crazy Joe carried the M-60, an AR-15, and a case of assorted grenades. Scouts tried to be prepared for these kinds of situations.

"About that time NVA soldiers began oozing out of the trees. Within seconds they're three and four deep and still coming. We're completely surrounded! I look at Crazy Joe, and he looks at me. Slowly he clears his M-60 and feeds in a fresh belt of ammunition. Then, in his slow Southern drawl, he says, 'Well, Mr. Simpson, them NVA are in front of us, behind us, and on both sides.' He paused to light a cigarette. 'This is one time they sure as hell won't get away.' "

Laughter erupted from our table. Customers at other tables and at the bar turned to see what was going on. Larry Seaman yelled at the waitress for more beer. Jerry Hornaker, also a veteran scout pilot, commented, "Yep, I never been in a Cav outfit that didn't have a couple of door gunners like your Crazy Joe Murdock."

Curiosity was gnawing at me. The others were apparently satisfied with the story's ending, but to me it seemed that Pauline was still tied to the tracks in front of an onrushing locomotive. "So here the two of you were, surrounded by several hundred NVA soldiers. How did you escape?"

With a puzzled expression Jim looked at me, while apparently searching his memory for the answer. He took a long pull on his beer and then carefully sat the mug on the table. Finally he spoke. "You know, every time I tell that story someone asks that question. And I'll be damned if I can remember for sure. The best I can figure is this: Since there were less than a thousand NVA soldiers in that clearing and they were up against two Cav soldiers, we had a definite combat advantage. We must've just killed them and then walked home."

I learned a lot about the cavalry by listening to experienced soldiers like Jim Simpson. But the time at Fort Hood wasn't simply for drinking beer and telling war stories. We were there for a purpose: to be formed into a close-knit combat organization. We worked long, hard days and longer nights. For six months we trained together as a unit, then we were shipped to Vietnam. Green troops, off to war. We were fearless and naïve. We had a send-off ceremony at Fort Hood, wherein the post chaplain prayed for our safe return. Being air cavalry, few of us took him seriously. Prayer was for mortal men.

PART
TWO

■ ■ ■ ■ ■ ■ ■ ■ ■ ■ ■ ■ ■

Prelude
to
Scouts

5

■ ■ ■ ■ ■ ■ ■ ■ ■ ■ ■ ■ ■ ■

In Country

THE AIR FORCE C-141 STARLIFTER THAT TRANSPORTED THE troop's personnel to the Republic of Vietnam departed Austin, Texas at 0900 hours on 20 July 1968. The passenger manifest included the new CO we'd gotten right before we shipped out, Major Harold Williams. The new major came equipped with his own intricate theories about guerrilla warfare, mostly involving tactical employment of gas. There were unflattering rumors floating around about the new major's background. For example, it was said that on a previous tour in Vietnam as an infantry platoon leader he had burned his mouth on the tail pipe when he was sent out to blow up an enemy truck.

I chose to ignore such rumors, preferring to give a person the benefit of the doubt until I personally observed such opinions to be well-founded—my own version of *tabula rasa*. I would eventually conclude, however, that knowing the major could have prompted Albert Einstein's aphorism regarding the two infinities: "Two things are infinite, the universe and human stupidity." The members of Delta Troop would soon discover that Victor Charlie wasn't the only enemy we were to face.

Our equipment, including helicopters, was sent earlier by ship and was scheduled to arrive a week or so after us. In keeping with normal bureaucratic practices, the "or so" turned out to be more realistic. We had also sent an advance party a month earlier. Its job was to ensure that everything was prepared for the arrival of the main body.

Transport on the C-141 was similar to that on a commercial airliner, with a couple of exceptions: the passengers were seated facing the rear of the aircraft, and they had no windows. During the long flight, interrupted only by a short refueling stop in Alaska, we passed the time by chatting, napping, eating, reading, and playing cards. The more gung-ho members of the outfit studied military maps of Vietnam and planned their strategies for destroying the enemy.

By chance I was seated next to Mr. O'Brian, the ranking warrant officer in the troop, who was en route to his third tour. We didn't know it at the time, of course, but the legendary O'Brian would be leaving us soon, his tour of duty curtailed by the cancer already eating away at him. It would take a while for the medical staff to provide the diagnosis, the disease being symptomatically similar to the effects of eating mess-hall chow. It was to be an ignoble ending for a valiant warrior. Were there a kinder God, O'Brian would have died in a flaming helicopter, riddled with bullets.

I spent as much of the trip as I could picking his brains. While I learned vicariously from his wisdom born of experience, I would soon discover that true learning comes from your own experience. Unfortunately, the learning can be fatal, particularly in a combat zone.

Many hours after our departure the wheels of the C-141 touched down at Pleiku, RVN. After the long flight we were looking forward to our barracks and some real sleep before we went about the task of unpacking and getting set up for war. We could anticipate that a lot of the housekeeping details had been taken care of by our advance party, as evidenced by our awaiting ground transportation. Four army buses waited to drive us to our base, Camp Enari, home of the Fourth Infantry Division. The windows of the buses were covered with poultry wire to prevent grenades from being tossed in. The wired windows were one of the myriad combat-zone precautions to which we would quickly adapt. They served as constant reminders that we were in a hostile environment.

During the slow twelve-mile drive to Camp Enari we warily watched the terrain, alert to the possibility of a VC attack. To our knowledge we did not spot any VC, although there was some debate regarding the political affiliation of a mama-san who was relieving herself behind a bush near the main thoroughfare. Amidst cultural shock we discovered that the Vietnamese were early originators of the concept of porta-potty.

As we approached Camp Enari our thoughts were on bed rest and later, possibly, some food. What we got was a band and a parade. Since we were arriving as a complete unit, the division commander insisted that we receive our fair quota of pomp and circumstance. Tradition! Our new commander, Major Williams, gave a rousing reception speech emphasizing the tactical employment of gas in guerrilla warfare. Three enlisted men keeled over during the forty-five-minute discourse, but they were quickly propped up by their comrades to avoid embarrassing the major.

The "three-hour" ceremony began at 1430 hours and ended at 1530 hours, leaving little time to get settled in before dinner, which was being hosted by Delta Troop, 1/10th Cavalry (Air)—the famous Buffalo Soldiers. They had been given the chore of being our "sister unit" during our in-country transition period. We were guided to our billets by several members of our advance party. During the half-mile hike they made several comments to the effect that the division hadn't known we were coming and had to erect temporary quarters for our housing. We wrote their comments off as combat exhaustion. After all, they'd been in Vietnam for almost a month, and everyone knew that war was hell. The army couldn't possibly fail to let someone know that they were receiving an entire cavalry troop.

When we arrived at the troop area we discovered two important survival facts. First, the advance party was not suffering from combat exhaustion. Second, the army was perfectly capable of not informing someone that they were receiving an entire cavalry troop. Our "billets" amounted to several large tents—in general, one officers' and one enlisted tent per platoon—that had been erected in the middle of a large, muddy field. This was to be our home for the next few weeks. While we were repeatedly assured that this situation was temporary, I kept remembering the adage that there is nothing so permanent in the army as that which has been erected to be temporary.

Spending several weeks in a tent during monsoon season is an experience that one should forego if at all possible. The joys of this existence simply defy description. We did, however, have maid service. It was mandatory, but you had to pay for it; sort of like charitable contributions at payday. The army's Civilian Personnel Office screened Vietnamese—eliminating those actively carrying grenades—and hired them to perform a number of menial tasks, such as cleaning the barracks, doing laundry, cleaning latrines, burning waste, and marking targets for VC mortar attacks. I thought paying hooch maids to sweep mud floors during monsoon season was pointless, but the opinion of a Wobbly One didn't carry much weight with the army.

Living—actually, existing is semantically more correct—in a tent while being continually bombarded with millions of gallons of water can be rather unpleasant, but that's not to say it's all bad. After all, one can usually find a sunny side to any street. For example, mildew is not as undesirable a fungus as many people have been led to believe. It can be quite entertaining, and once you learn the individual personalities of the various fungi you can develop some really meaningful relationships.

Another aspect to the sunny side of the street dealt with nighttime bladder draining. This is a generally irksome problem for which our current living conditions provided a ready solution. If you needed to empty your bladder during the night, it was not necessary to trek through the rain to the latrine. You simply opened a tent flap and did your business; the outside world was in a constant state of flush. Normally, one would expect some criticism of this approach from occupants living downhill, but none ever occurred. Some of the more creative members of the troop even improved on the basic bladder draining procedure. They would hang a two-foot stalk of bamboo next to their bunks. During the night they would relieve themselves into the bamboo stalk and the next morning dump the contents outside the tent. This approach proved to be less sleep-interruptive.

While we awaited the arrival of our helicopters, which were coming by boat, our days were occupied mostly with make-work activities. Things like attending classes on required military subjects, being inoculated against the dreaded tsetse fly, and maintaining imaginary equipment. We also got caught up in imaginary paperwork for the imaginary equipment, but in truth, a helicopter pilot without a helicopter is about as useful as an extra Indian at the Little Big Horn. Our nighttime entertainment consisted mostly of playing darts at the local officers' club to the accompaniment of Wild Turkey or Jack Daniels. We learned quickly that war could be very boring. Finally—after what seemed months but was only two weeks—we got word that our helicopters were on the dock at Qui Nhon. We simply had to go and get them and fly them back to Camp Enari—after reassembling them, of course.

We took off from Qui Nhon Airport as a flight of nine. We departed to the south, over the ocean, and then swung back to the east, crossing the rugged mountains overlooking the city. I was the number five aircraft in the formation. It was good to be back in the saddle again. The right seat of the Charley Model seemed like an old friend. My copilot, Mike Burton, sulked in the left seat. In a two-pilot helicopter, the pilot-in-command was designated aircraft commander and the copilot was referred to as a Peter Pilot, the latter term indicating a less-experienced aviator. One of the advantages—or disadvantages, depending on your perspective—of having very few experienced aviators in the troop was that some of us became instant aircraft commanders, a selection process that was quite possibly random.

Mike Burton was suffering from the eternal pilot's malady, bruised ego. Although he had a month's seniority, based on graduation from flight school, I had been selected as an aircraft commander. In his opinion, this was a serious blow to the concept of seniority; however, we had no union. If the situation had been reversed, I would have felt the same way. All pilots seem to have large and sensitive egos. Two pilots could get into a fistfight because one of them had an ego so large that the other one would notice it.

I tried to compensate for the damage to Mike's ego by letting him do most of the flying. This strategy worked out fairly well, and the flight progressed smoothly until we were about fifteen minutes away from our landing at Camp Enari. Then the master caution light came on. Since the aircraft had been disassembled prior to shipment to Vietnam and then reassembled upon arrival, it was not surprising that something would break or shake loose on the maiden flight. We'd performed a doubly thorough preflight inspection looking for potential gotchas, and the obvious ones had been corrected prior to departure. However, we couldn't possibly find them all, particularly with a maintenance strategy that emphasized Band-Aiding the birds together to get them to Camp Enari and then properly repairing them there.

"What is it?" Mike asked.

"Number one hydraulics . . . tail rotor," I responded as I checked the caution panel and reset the master caution indicator. "Check your pedals."

Mike pushed forcefully on the pedals; left leg, then right leg. "They're stiff as a board."

"Well, at least its not the complete hydraulic system. O'Brian told me about a Charley Model crew that lost its complete hydraulic system. Both pilots put their weight on the collective, trying to force it down. All they succeeded in doing was bending it."

"Didn't they use the emergency accumulator?"

"This was before the emergency accumulator." Beginning with Aircraft 66-491, the army began installing emergency accumulators on the Charley Models. In the event of a complete hydraulics system failure, the accumulator supposedly allowed four movements of the collective, provided they were performed within approximately ten minutes after the accumulator switch was turned on. The operator's manual also contained the proviso that the four collective movements would only be available if the stored energy hadn't been lost because of damaged lines between the accumulator and the hydraulic cylinder. This was product liability language for saying don't depend on the emergency accumulator.

"Jeez. How'd they get down?"

"Pretty much straight . . . after they ran out of fuel," I responded, then I called the lead aircraft to report our situation. "Blackhawk 26, this is Blackhawk 28. Over."

"Yeah, 28, go ahead."

"We've got a number-one hydraulics failure. We'll drop back and land separately so we can make a running landing. Over." Since a helicopter tends to streamline in forward flight, having limited anti-torque control was not a serious problem as long as we maintained our airspeed. The tricky part would come when we landed, which would call for a running landing to keep our airspeed as high as possible. Even this was not particularly serious, since we could still provide some manual control over the anti-torque system. However, it did call for caution.

"Roger, 28. Situation understood. Go easy on the Papa Tango," Blackhawk 26 responded, advising caution with my pilot technique.

"Two-eight, out," I replied, reaching for the flight controls. "I have the aircraft," I said to Mike.

"Roger, you have the aircraft."

I tried the stiff-as-a-board pedals. With maximum force they were clumsily movable. With both of us on the pedals during landing we would be able to crudely manage the input to the flight controls. I lowered the collective a bit and eased back slightly on the cyclic, slowing the helicopter and moving out of the formation. The eight other aircraft gradually distanced themselves from our broken bird. I swung to the east to set up a long final leg for landing at Enari.

The master caution light suddenly illuminated again. This time it wasn't necessary to check the caution panel to diagnose the problem. The collective lever was frozen. According to the operator's manual, which simply stated that additional manual force would be required in this situation, the collective lever wasn't actually frozen. The guy who wrote that was probably the same one who determined that bumblebees couldn't fly. I reset the master caution and alerted Mike, who apparently hadn't observed the latest malfunction, to our deteriorating situation.

"Say, Mike. You know that full hydraulics failure we were discussing?"

"Yeah."

"Well, we've got it . . . we just lost the number-two system."

"Come on. Don't joke about stuff like that."

"Try the controls."

Mike tried his hand at moving the collective. "This is not good."

"No, but it could be worse."

"I hate optimists."

While I continued to hold the helicopter in the wide arc, gradually losing altitude so as to put us into a very long and very shallow final leg for landing, I notified Enari Tower of our emergency situation and intentions.

It was fortunate that I'd eased off on the power just before the failure occurred. This left me with at least a limited ability to control altitude with the throttle and cyclic. I beeped the engine RPM up to redline and then rolled it back manually. I wanted the full range of manual control for the throttle. Timing would be critical for this landing, and I wasn't going to depend entirely on the emergency accumulator working. There wasn't likely to be a second chance, since I couldn't bring in collective power to climb. Either undershooting or overshooting the runway at Enari would produce the same disastrous result. There was also the large hill at the departure end of the runway that had claimed several gunships during night scramble missions.

When our altitude had dropped to five hundred feet, I eased the Charley Model around to the final approach leg. We were about two miles from the runway, the helicopter continuing its gradual descent. As the ground ever so slowly edged toward us Mike began exhibiting symptoms of advanced nervousness. His hands started to shake, and he licked his lips continuously. We passed over the approach end of the runway at sixty knots with twenty-five feet of altitude. So far, so good. I breathed a sigh of relief—one major hurdle behind us—and turned on the emergency accumulator switch. The collective still did not respond.

I manually decreased the engine RPM while maintaining airspeed. The helicopter continued to settle toward the runway.

As the skids of the Charley Model began scraping the runway I eased the nose up slightly and continued reducing the throttle. The helicopter continued skidding down the runway, its weight gradually shifting to the skids. Finally friction did its intended job, and we ground to a halt three fourths of the way down the runway, surrounded by fire trucks. As I shut down the engine Mike opened his door and retched outside the helicopter. I wondered if he really had what it took to be an army aviator. We'd just been given a golden opportunity to demonstrate our superior skills, and instead of being elated, he was throwing up. Who could figure it? I left him to his own devices and headed for Maintenance.

Two days later, fully equipped and operational, we began flying real cavalry missions. Our first assignment was to the north, conducting screening operations for a brigade of the Fourth Infantry Division that was operating near Kontum. Two gunships, two scouts, and a C & C slick—our routine flight configuration for combat—departed at dawn for this, our first official performance at war. We were eager to lose our combat virginity. We would soon discover—not on this mission, which only involved tree-shooting—that remaining a virgin was not particularly undesirable. The realities of war in the air cavalry were presented to us on our fourth mission.

We maintained a loose orbit at 1500 feet, keeping a distance of a couple of hundred meters between us and the lead Charley Model, which was piloted by Gil Lewis. The C & C Huey circled a thousand feet above us. The Lift Platoon leader, Captain Reese Foreman, was at its controls, commanding the operation. Reese had the reputation of being a straight shooter with his subordinates, and he was well respected for his competence. Below us, hovering among the jungle trees, the two Loaches tracked the enemy. They were hot on a fresh trail a few miles southwest of Dak To.

I kept my Charley Model in an easy left bank to maintain a constant angle on the lead Loach. One of the two gunships was always in position to dive immediately and put covering fire in the vicinity of the scouts. Tactics. The quicker we could get munitions on target, the better chance the Loaches had of surviving an attack. I monitored the scouts' progress over the FM radio, which was reserved for their communications. The rest of the flight operated on UHF.

They had just turned north, tracking along a narrow creek bed, when the nose of the lead Loach dipped violently and swung to the right. I quickly rolled the Charley Model into a steep dive, anticipating the radio call.

"Blackhawk 18, receiving fire! Receiving fire! Smoke's out. Bad guys are twenty meters north of the smoke."

We punched off a round of rockets, not waiting for the smoke. From the way the Loach had reacted, we could predict the general vicinity of the enemy soldiers. The rockets spewed forth with a smoking whoosh, streaking toward the jungle floor. The wing Loach had provided a few seconds of covering fire for his lead and then vacated the area, knowing the rockets would be inbound. Identifying the smoke, we adjusted on target, punched off several more pairs of rockets, and then raked the jungle with the wing-mounted miniguns.

I broke off the run with a hard right bank, my copilot pumping the jungle with the 40mm mounted on the nose turret. An enemy bullet shattered the Plexiglas below my feet, exiting through the greenhouse above my copilot's head. Gil Lewis, in the lead Charley, was putting fire on target now, covering my break. I raced outbound, skids clipping the treetops, watching the eight-day clock on the instrument panel. In fifteen seconds I would swing back inbound to cover Gil's break.

"This is Blackhawk 18. We're shot up pretty good," the pilot of the lead Loach radioed over the FM. "I'm heading for the hospital pad at Dak To."

"Eighteen, this is 36," Captain Foreman responded from the C & C ship. "How bad are you hit? Over."

"Arm and leg. Gunner's hit worse. Don't know for sure

about the Loach . . . engine's running hot, and she's hard to handle."

"Roger, 18. Set the aircraft down and ride into Dak To with your wingman. Over."

"Negative, 36. I can make it. Out."

"Blackhawk 18, this is 36. Follow my instructions. That's an order. Over."

Captain Foreman's demand was greeted by silence. He repeated it to no avail. Finally Blackhawk 11, the scout wingman, responded, "Three-six, this is 11. Over."

"Go ahead, 11."

"One-eight won't be responding. He just creamed in at a hundred knots."

"Understood, 11. What's the location?"

"About five klicks northeast of you. Over."

"Roger the five klicks. I'll be sending a medevac to pick up the crew and the Blues to secure the aircraft. Remain on station to guide them in if you're able."

"Wilco. One-one out."

As I turned inbound for my third run I observed an airmobile flight approaching from the direction of Dak To: eight slicks flanked by two gun teams. That would be our ready reaction force. The Cav's task was to find the enemy so these guys could come in and finish the job. An infantry company would be initially inserted. If necessary, depending on how the situation developed, it would be followed by others. In the Dak To area it wasn't unusual for these encounters to escalate into brigade-size operations. It all depended on what the cavalry had stumbled across.

Our on-station relief ships also arrived. They would conduct screening operations while the infantry engaged the enemy. Guns empty, we headed for Dak To to rearm and refuel. Delta Troop had taken its first casualty. Surprisingly, it did not come from the Loach that had been shot down. There was something about the egg shape of the little aircraft that provided phenomenal protection for the crew during a crash. The pilot and gunner were evacuated to Japan with an early ticket home.

The casualty was Captain Foreman in the C & C ship. While orbiting at 2500 feet, which was well out of the effective range of small-arms fire, an AK round passed through the open cargo door of the Huey and between the armor-plated seats of the pilot and copilot. It struck Captain Foreman in the side, entering behind his chicken plate, killing him almost instantly. His death brought a sobering reality to Delta Troop.

During this initial period of transition the Troop was also acquiring pilots with combat experience as part of the infusion program. Those of us who were previously aircraft commanders stayed with the unit as Peter Pilots, while our Peter Pilots went to other units. In late August the troop acquired three of these infused aviators, whose destinies were to become intimately intertwined with my own: John Larkin, Dave Horton, and Eric Masterson. John and Dave flew guns; Eric was a scout. They'd come to us from the Buffalo Soldiers. John and Dave were best friends and had been together a long time, including flight school.

Sometimes there were hidden reasons for these in-country transfers. While the gaining commander was always assured of acquiring an experienced combat aviator, the losing commander often used the program as a method to get rid of his troublemakers. I felt sure that the troublemaker strategy had played no role in the reassignments of John, Dave, and Eric. There was a rumor that Eric's CO had once chided him regarding his lack of military courtesy, and he'd responded by saying, "I can't do a military curtsy, but I can do a helluva good military bow." But it was probably just that, a rumor. These three guys were straitlaced, by-the-book, strictly-business soldiers. Sort of.

During this early period of in-country adaptation we also moved to An Khe, which was roughly halfway between Pleiku and Qui Nhon, and we were placed under the operational control of the 173d Airborne Brigade. We didn't particularly care who controlled us; the important thing was that we were out of our tents and into real billets. Most of the First Cavalry Division, the previous occupants at An Khe, had moved to I Corps, and they'd left a lot of empty buildings behind. After Tent City the sparse barracks seemed like the Holiday Inn, which is exactly what we called our new quarters. We also began trading in our old Charley Models for Cobras, although it would be a couple more months before we'd completely converted over. More importantly, we began receiving real missions that, to say the least, were not boring. Like night scramble missions to support long-range reconnaissance patrols, or LRRPs.

The small two-man hooch was crowded with an impromptu gathering of aviators. All available perching space seemed to have been allocated, yet when a new participant slipped through the doorway somehow a shifting of bodies occurred and a new perch was created. The sun had set several hours earlier, but the jungle heat still persecuted the occupants of the tiny enclosure. The less modest inhabitants were clad only in their underwear, attesting to the informality of the occasion. The electric fan, purchased for $16.95 at the Post Exchange and mounted in an upper corner of the rear wall, did little to suppress the heat. However, its periodic emitting of loud, peculiar noises resembling the mating cries of a male bullfrog did serve to keep the assemblage awake. Overhead the familiar *whomp, whomp* of Huey rotor blades could occasionally be heard as the aircraft departed from the airfield adjacent to Delta Troop. At periodic intervals the radio would let forth with Vietnam's most requested song, the Animals' You've Got to Get Out of This Place, and the gathering would burst into immediate, albeit off-key, accompaniment.

As time in country increased, the frequency of these "parties" also increased. The primary purpose was to consume vast quantities of alcoholic beverages to the accompaniment of progressively embellished war stories. Since we hadn't really been in country that long, such stories should have been in short supply. They weren't. Jerry Harris of the scout platoon was about to entertain us with his thirty-third rendition of "the day I pulled out six LRRPs with my Loach while holding off seventeen VC with my .38" when he was summarily selected to go fetch another bottle of Wild Turkey from the troop's Officers Club. He left grudgingly, his space immediately occupied by a newcomer.

This particular gathering began breaking up around ten o'clock, which was normal. Sometimes they lasted longer. But with two thirds of the pilots either on standby or scheduled for dawn-departure missions, late parties were relatively rare. Our crew rotation schedule usually had us flying one day, on standby the next, and off the third. Frequently you ended up flying more when you were on standby than when you were scheduled to fly. Just as often, you never got that third day off.

As the group straggled from the hooch I hurried to catch up with John Larkin, who was quickly gaining a reputation as our best gunship pilot. I had been assigned as his copilot. Normally he preferred to fly with Dave Horton, but the experienced pilots were currently teamed with the inexperienced pilots. We were on standby that night; John and I in the lead Cobra, Dave Horton and Jerry Thomas in the wing. With luck, no emergencies would occur, and we'd get some rest.

"John," I called as he passed through the door ahead of me. He waited for me outside. "All the equipment's in the ship. I preflighted a couple of hours ago."

"Good. Now take it easy and get some rest. We won't be flying tonight."

"How do you know?"

"Feel it in my bones. When you've been here longer you'll be able to feel it, too. It's sort of like being able to tell the difference between incoming and outgoing mortar rounds. It's a skill you develop."

"You ever wrong?"

John pondered the question. "Let's see . . . no . . . wait . . . yes! Back in fifty-four, once . . . I thought I was wrong, but I turned out to be right. Nope, you can bank on it: We won't be flying tonight. Trust me."

Trust me, I thought. That's what Herschel had said when he talked me into signing up for flight school. That's what my recruiter had said. I was becoming skeptical.

At four o'clock the next morning John was wrong for the second time in his life.

6

■ ■ ■ ■ ■ ■ ■ ■ ■ ■ ■ ■ ■ ■

Seventeen Pounders

IN THE PRE-DAWN DARKNESS I RACED DOWN THE SHORTCUT behind the mess hall, chasing John Larkin, who was some distance ahead of me. The well-trodden dirt path cut a hundred meters off the quarter-mile distance to the flight line. The reduction in distance, however, was at the expense of personal safety. The path was unlighted, and as we were racing in the darkness at full speed, a miscue could have unfortunate consequences. The week before, one of the new pilots had made a wrong turn, fallen down an embankment, and broken his wrist. There was also the problem of unwittingly encountering nocturnal creatures of the jungle.

However, this was a scramble mission, so we kept running blindly. You had to depend on experience and ability, and hope that luck was on your side. We had no control over the nocturnal creatures, but we would not make a misstep on the shortcut route. Part of our training involved practicing this run while wearing a blindfold. Professionals covered all the angles.

Because of the darkness and the twisting path I couldn't see John, but I could occasionally hear his footsteps. As usual, he would win the race to the aircraft. He believed in leading by example. And he'd already lost face with his team by proclaiming they wouldn't be flying tonight. Because of an unfortunate delay by Operations, this would also be the first time he had failed to get his team off the ground within the five-minute deadline for scramble missions. While personally disappointing for him, the real tragedy was that it had occurred when LRRPs had requested support. We had a high regard for LRRPs, the small groups of infantrymen who stalked the jungle nights searching for the enemy. To our minds, LRRPs, scout pilots, and medevac pilots demanded respect and admiration. The soldiers that filled these roles were a special breed. They seemed oblivious to the potentially deadly consequences of their routine tasks. While necessarily compelled to call their actions courageous, we suspected that psychopathic labels might be more appropriate.

Ahead, the lights from the revetment area—where the aircraft were parked—outlined the trees and bushes at the end of the path. With the backlighting from the revetments I could see John clearly, about fifty meters ahead. Suddenly his feet were jerked from beneath him, and he hit the ground heavily, momentarily stunned by the force of the impact. A flare, ignited by the trip wire that had been stretched across the opening to the path, shot into the air. At the apex of its flight the flare burst, flooding the area with incandescent illumination.

I caught up with John as he began struggling to his feet, vehemently expressing his opinion of the hidden trip wire. As I helped him up a voice called out the familiar warning of the army sentinel: "Halt! Who goes there?"

" 'Tis I, fair Juliet," John yelled angrily in the direction of the hidden voice.

"Orchid," cried the voice. We froze. An official request for a password demanded an official response. In the Vietnam circus you never gave anyone an excuse to pull a trigger. We did not know the password. They had never been required on the flight line. The guard was hidden, but the voice appeared to come from behind the nearest revetment. We couldn't be certain, but the voice seemed to belong to SP4 Bullard, an infantryman in the Blue Platoon.

"Bullard. Bullard, is that you?" Larkin asked loudly.

"Orchid," the voice replied.

"Bullard, this is Mr. Larkin."

After a brief pause, the voice responded, "Mr. Larkin? The Cobra pilot?"

"Yes, Bullard. Mr. Larkin, the Cobra pilot. Look, I'm on a scramble mission. I've got to take off."

"Sorry, sir. I can't let you through without the password."

"Bullard, I've been in this unit for two months. We've never required passwords on the flight line before."

"Orders from the major, sir. If you don't know the password, I'm supposed to throw gas and then shoot you."

The flare had burned itself out by now. Faint spirals of gray smoke hung in the air as evidence of its former presence. In the returning darkness we were quietly joined by the pilots of our wing Cobra, Dave Horton and Jerry Thomas.

"What's going on?" Dave asked as they crouched down beside us.

"It seems that the major has tightened security. We're about to be gassed and then shot," Larkin replied. "Any of you guys know the password?"

The question was greeted by silence.

"Orchid," Bullard shouted.

"Try Cardinal," Jerry Thomas said.

"Cardinal," Larkin hollered.

"That ain't it. I'm going to have to throw gas," came the reply.

"I thought you said Cardinal was the password," Larkin screeched at Thomas.

"I didn't say it was the password. I said try it," Thomas rebutted. "It was the password in a book I was reading last week."

"Damn it. This is not a laughing matter. By the time we get to the LRRPs it may be too late." In a louder voice he called to Bullard. "Listen, Bullard. I don't know the password, but I can prove it's me."

"How can you do that, sir?" Bullard replied.

"Look, we sat next to each other in the mess hall last week. Do you remember?"

"Yes, sir, I remember."

"We were talking about the UCLA–Houston basketball game. Right?"

"That's right."

"You claimed that Big E won the game for Houston, and I claimed that Goodrich lost the game for UCLA. Is that right?"

"Yes, sir, that's right."

"Then obviously it's me. How else would I know what we talked about? Let us through to the aircraft."

There was a slight pause while Bullard considered this line of reasoning. Then he responded, "I can't do that, sir. You don't know the password. The VC could have captured you and gotten that information. The major said he'd take my stripes if anyone got through here without the password. I'm going to have to gas you and shoot you."

"I've got an idea," Horton said. Before Larkin could respond, Dave bellowed, "Bullard! Bullard, where are you? This is Mr. Horton. The duty officer sent me with a message for you."

"I'm down in the revetments, Mr. Horton. What's the message?"

"The VC have broken our codes. Effective immediately, the new password is Tricky Dicky."

"For chrissakes, Dave. Nobody's that stupid," Larkin whispered.

"Tricky," Bullard shouted.

"Vulcan logic does not apply to humans," Dave responded to John's criticism.

"Dicky," Larkin yelled as we scrambled to our feet.

"Advance and be recognized."

We raced to the aircraft. While I untied the main rotor blades John quickly climbed into the rear seat of our Cobra. Our scramble procedure was synchronized. Each of us performed a task that complemented the other's, thereby allowing us to be airborne quicker. He flipped the battery switch on, checked the throttle position, and pressed the starter button. I had set up the cockpit for a quick start when I had done the preflight the previous evening. The turbine engine responded with its familiar whine, increasing in pitch as the RPM increased and the needle rose on the EGT gauge. John glanced outside to be sure the rotor blades were turning and then kept his eyes glued to the EGT gauge. This was no time for a hot start.

In the meantime I had climbed into the front seat, put on my flight helmet and chicken plate, and buckled my seat belt and shoulder harness. Then I turned on the radios, position lights, and rotating beacon. Observing that the engine and rotor RPM had stabilized at flight idle, I began increasing the throttle to achieve operating RPM while John buckled in. When the RPM was at one hundred percent John took the controls and brought the helicopter to a hover, checked the go/no-go limits, and began backing out of the three-sided revetment.

Four revetments further down the lights of the second Cobra were also flashing. Switching his radio to VHF, John said, "Hawk 24, this is Hawk 22. Are you ready? Over."

"Roger, 22," Dave replied from the wing Cobra.

While switching to the tower frequency John turned the nose of the Cobra into the wind and initiated his takeoff. Overloaded with fuel and ammunition, the sluggish Cobra struggled through translational lift and then began to increase its altitude and airspeed. "Ramsey Tower, this is Army Copter 17843. Flight of two, departing Pad Delta to the north. Over."

"Army Copter 17843, this is Ramsey Tower. Hold at Pad Delta for departure clearance. Over," the tower operator replied. The unnecessary holding instructions were his way of letting the pilots know that they were not in charge of takeoffs and landings at the airport. That was the duty of the tower operator. It was a mindless power game, given the circumstances. However, all tower operators who played it well eventually found their way into satisfactory career patterns with the Defense Contract Audit Agency.

"Ramsey Tower, Army Copter 17843. Unable to comply with your request. Out," John responded. He turned off the UHF receiver to avoid the ensuing tirade from the tower operator, who would spend the rest of the morning writing up Army Copter 17843 for a flight violation. The report would cycle through channels in quintuplicate and eventually arrive on the major's desk. This would present the major with a problem. Army Copter 17843 was still in support maintenance at Qui Nhon. We were flying 17858.

"Hawk Operations, this is Hawk 22. Over."

"Roger, Hawk 22. Contact Bronco 7 on 36.6. He's in the

vicinity of Point Zulu. Sorry for the delay on the scramble message. Over."

"Roger," John replied, ignoring the apology and switching to the new frequency. He continued our northbound departure and leveled off at three thousand feet, holding the torque near redline and letting the airspeed build. To the east the sky was beginning to brighten. Soon the early-morning rays of the sun would begin streaking across the horizon. We waited impatiently for five minutes as our racing Cobra shortened the distance to the LRRPs.

"Bronco 7, this is Hawk 22. Over."

John's transmission was greeted by silence. Adjusting the squelch on the FM radio, he repeated the call. "Bronco 7, this is Hawk 22. Over."

The whispered response was barely audible above the background noise of automatic rifle fire. "Hawk 22, Bronco 7. Over."

John turned the volume up on the FM receiver. "Bronco 7. What's your location and situation? Over."

"Roger, Hawk. We're about two klicks southwest of Point Zulu. I don't know how many bad guys we're in contact with—a bunch. They've been chasing us for two hours. So far we've been able to move and shoot, but we're getting low on ammo and close to the river. If they pin us against the river, they'll have us. Over."

"Roger, 7. Do you have any casualties? Over."

"No casualties yet. Over," came the whispered response.

By this time the sun had broken over the horizon. In the distance we could make out the hill mass known as Point Zulu. I marveled at the breathtaking beauty of the early-morning jungle, a beauty that belied the reality of the constant struggle for survival. Soon the sun's rays would penetrate the canopy, bringing light to the jungle floor. The LRRPs had survived the past two hours because darkness was their shield. In a few more minutes the shield would be gone.

"Bronco 7, Hawk 22. I should be within range of your location. Can you ID me? Over."

"Negative, Hawk. We're under the canopy, and there's too much noise to hear your helicopter. Over."

"Roger, Bronco. Standby to pop smoke. Out."

"Hawk 24, Hawk 22. Call Operations. Have them send another gun team and a Huey to extract the LRRPs. We'll make our runs from east to west, with a left break. Over."

"Wilco," Hawk 24 responded to John's instructions.

"Bronco, 7, Hawk 22. Pop smoke. Over."

"Roger, Hawk. Smoke's out. The bad guys are fifty meters due north."

"Roger, Bronco. We'll be making our runs from east to west. Out."

We began scanning for the smoke. It would take a few seconds for it to weave through the canopy and rise above the jungle tops. I spotted it first. "Green smoke at ten o'clock . . . about four klicks," I transmitted over the intercom.

"Roger," John replied as he, too, identified the green smoke.

"I've got yellow smoke, south of the green," I continued.

"Roger. And there's purple and red. It's beginning to look like a rainbow down there. Guess Charlie's been listening in," John responded.

"Bronco 7, Hawk 22. What color did you pop? Over."

"Hawk, yellow. I repeat yellow. Over," Bronco 7 replied.

"Roger, 7. I confirm yellow. We're inbound. I'll spot with the first pair of rockets. Over."

"Roger, Hawk. They're breathing down our necks. Out."

John set the rocket control switch to one pair and selected an imaginary target fifty meters north of the yellow smoke. Reducing power, he lowered the nose of the Cobra until the grease-penciled X on his windshield lined up with the target. As he pressed the firing switch he brought the nose of the diving aircraft up and to the left to compensate for range and wind direction. The rockets whooshed as they ignited and left the pods, one from each whside of the Cobra. We watched as the finned rockets stabilized their flight path and spiraled toward the target. Their impact was obscured by the jungle canopy.

Bronco 7 confirmed the location. "Hawk, you're on target. Over."

"Roger, Bronco 7. Out," John responded as he changed the rocket selection switch and then pressed the firing switch. The Cobra shuddered as eight rockets were propelled from the pods. He fired the rockets again, shifting to the wing miniguns as the distance to target closed, and then he put the aircraft into a hard left turn and increased power. The main rotor blades were only inches from the treetops as he powered the heavy ship through the turn. From the front seat I opened up with the 40mm, which was mounted in the nose turret, to cover the break. Without looking we knew that Hawk 24 would be inbound on his rocket run now.

John pulled the power near redline and held his altitude. The trees whipped past, barely missing the skids as the airspeed indicator climbed past 140 knots. He had to get enough distance between us and the target for the second rocket run and also swing back inbound in time to cover Hawk 24's break.

"Bronco 7, Hawk 22. There's a clearing one hundred meters due south of your position. A Huey will be there to pick you up. Move out. Over."

"Roger, Hawk. We're moving, but the bad guys are going to be right on our heels. Over."

"Roger, Bronco. We'll be firing twenty-five meters further to the south. Let us know if we get too close to you. Over."

"Roger, Hawk. Did you ever hear about the fellow who got tangled up with a bobcat? Told his buddy to just shoot in among them, that it didn't much matter which one he hit. You won't get too close. Out."

John held the power near redline and abruptly pulled the cyclic toward him. The Cobra shot skyward. When the airspeed fell to fifty knots he banked hard to the left and brought the nose around to the target. I began firing the 40mm just as Hawk 24 broke off the target. As our Cobra dived inbound John pressed the firing switch three more times. With each press he shifted his aim further south Once more he broke left and skimmed the treetops on the outbound leg. Checking the rocket status, he observed that we were out of ten pounders. The only remaining rockets were seventeen pounders.

"Hawk 22, this is Hawk 28. Over."

"Roger, Hawk 28. Over."

"I'm inbound with two Snakes and a Huey, twenty-five klicks south of Point Zulu. Over."

"Roger, 28. The PZ is a one-ship clearing at 738942. I'll have them pop smoke when you're three klicks out. Over."

"Roger, 22. Coordinates 738942. Out."

"Hawk 22, Bronco 7. We're at the clearing, but we'll never make it out. We're looking at the proverbial whites of their eyes. Over."

"Roger, 7. Hang tight. We'll get you out. Precisely how far away are the bad guys? Over."

"Twenty-five meters and closing. We can't hold them back. Over."

"Roger, 7. Wait one. Out."

"Hawk 24, Hawk 22. What's your rocket status? Over."

"I just shot my last pair. Over," Hawk 24 replied.

"Roger, 24. All I've got left is seventeen pounders. I'll have to use them. Over."

"You can't do that, 22. It's too close. Even if you hit right on top of the bad guys, the burst radius will get the LRRPs. Over."

"I know, but Hawk 28 is still too far away. By the time he gets here it will be too late. I'm going to have to risk it. Out," John responded. "Keep your fingers crossed," he said to me over the intercom.

"Bronco 7, Hawk 22. Has your situation changed? Over."

"Negative, Hawk. They're twenty meters due north and moving in for the kill. Over."

"Roger, Bronco. Pop smoke to mark your location. Over," John replied as he broke off our climb and turned the Cobra inbound for the final run.

"Roger, Hawk. Red smoke's out. Over."

"Roger the red smoke, Bronco. Do you have cover? Over."

"Roger, Hawk. We're dug in behind some dead trees. Over."

"Roger, Bronco. I'm inbound. I want you to count to ten and then get all your men down behind those trees. I'll be firing seventeen pounders on this run. I repeat . . .

seventeen pounders. They make big boom boom. I'm going to put them exactly twenty meters north of your smoke. Do you understand? Over.''

"Roger, Hawk. Count to ten and hit the dirt. The sky will be falling. Out.''

John said a silent prayer as he, too, counted to ten. Then he dropped the nose of the Cobra and placed the X on a position twenty meters north of the red smoke that had begun to trickle above the trees. Precision rocket firing this close to friendlies was risky business, even with ten-pound rockets. He hesitated momentarily, apparently reassessing his decision to use the seventeen pounders, but there were no viable alternatives. He made a final adjustment on the target and pressed the firing switch.

We both mentally crossed our fingers as the rockets sped from the aircraft and arched gracefully toward the target. This time we were able to observe their impact. The rockets erupted, scattering jungle foliage in all directions. I sensed John breathing a sigh of relief. Both rockets had hit exactly on target.

"Medevac! Medevac! This is Bronco 7. We've been shot to hell by the rockets. We need a medevac. Over.''

Shocked, John responded to the frantic request, "Roger, Bronco. The Huey's inbound. Out.''

"Hawk 28, Hawk 22. Do you have the red smoke? Over.''

"Roger 22. Over.''

"The bad guys are twenty meters north of the smoke. We'll hold to the south while you make the extraction. Over,'' John responded.

"Roger, 22. Out.''

In the wing Cobra Dave Horton fell in on our trail as we moved three klicks south and orbited at three thousand feet. From our position we observed the Huey approach the PZ and drop beneath the trees while the other Cobra team pummeled the surrounding jungle. After a brief pause the Huey reappeared above the trees and quickly turned south, toward An Khe.

"Hawk 33, Hawk 22. What's the status of the LRRPs? Over,'' a worried John Larkin asked the Huey pilot.

"They're all ambulatory. Lots of blood, but nothing too

serious. I'll drop them at the hospital helipad. Over," Hawk 33 responded.

"Roger, 33. Out."

We followed the slick to An Khe and orbited while it discharged the LRRPs at the hospital. When the Huey departed we took its place on the helipad. Cutting the throttle to flight idle, John waited the required two minutes for the engine to cool down and then closed the throttle. "Don't bother to tie down the blades," he said. "We'll be right back."

"Roger," I replied as we scrambled out of the helicopter.

We quickly walked down the grassy knoll surrounding the helipad and entered a door marked EMERGENCY. Inside, white-uniformed personnel were bustling to and fro.

"Hi, Larkin." The greeting came from a youthful man in a white jacket. I had never met him, but he obviously knew John. A stethoscope hung carelessly from his right pocket. "What are you guys doing here?"

"Hi, Doc. I'm looking for the LRRPs they just brought in," John replied.

"How come?"

"I shot 'em."

"Oh! I see. Third door on the right. Don't be too long."

"Thanks, Doc," John acknowledged as we moved down the hallway.

Outside the door John paused and took a deep breath. Bracing himself for the worst, he cautiously pushed the door open. The six LRRPs inside the room were in various stages of undress. Nurses were picking bits and pieces of shrapnel from various parts of their bodies while soothing and pampering the wounded warriors.

"I'm looking for Bronco 7," John said.

An unkempt young soldier with a two-day growth of beard responded, "Sergeant Burroughs, sir."

"I'm Hawk 22—Larkin."

The response was not what we expected. "Hawk 22! Mr. Larkin, that was the finest shooting I've ever seen. I've been supported by lots of Cobra pilots, but you've got to be the best. You saved our bacon, sir," exclaimed the enthusiastic sergeant as he extended his hand to John.

Puzzled, John shook the sergeant's hand. "I don't understand, Sergeant. I just shot you guys up . . . and you're grateful?"

"Sir, it wasn't your fault we got hit," the sergeant responded. "You put the rockets right on target. But you see, sir, we'd never seen seventeen pounders go off before. So we stood up to watch. Those suckers pack a helluva wallop!"

On the way back to the troop revetment area John kept muttering over the intercom about LRRPs, scout pilots, medevac pilots, and genetic inbreeding. Dave Horton and Jerry Thomas were waiting for us when we arrived and parked the Cobra. As the four of us walked toward Operations, John explained what had happened with the LRRPs.

"Well," Dave commented, "the only thing I can say is that they were damn lucky we were using Cobras. Our Charley Models would never have had enough punch to get them out." Dave's comment referred to the fact that we were still in the process of turning in our old UH-1C gunships for the newer Cobras. Currently we had five of each, which gave you a fifty-fifty chance of flying either gunship on any given mission.

Dave continued to disparage the Charley Models. "With any luck, I'll never have to fly one of those things again." He intensely disliked the old gunships. It was hard not to, after you'd flown the Cobra.

Unfortunately, he didn't have the luck that he'd hoped for. A week later he was called on to lead a team of Charley Models to cover an extraction for our Blue Platoon, which had stumbled into a major battle to the north. Jerry Murcheson, our first in-country new guy, was his copilot. It became a mission that neither of them would forget.

7

■ ■ ■ ■ ■ ■ ■ ■ ■ ■ ■ ■ ■ ■ ■

Morphine

IT WAS A SUNNY AFTERNOON IN EARLY OCTOBER. THE SUN-shine provided a welcome respite from the typical cold, gloomy weather. Most of the pilots were lounging around the patio outside the troop Officers Club, easing through the digestive process of a mess-hall lunch. Somehow the cavalry had cornered the market in dried-out roast beef and reconstituted potatoes. Fresh vegetables were a lingering memory from the past.

The bar was closed, all flight crews having been placed on half-hour alert. This meant we didn't have to remain dressed for combat, most of us having mastered the technique of quick-change artistry. Blue jeans and sweatshirts comprised the customary lounging attire. The quasi-alert status was prompted by the insertion of the Blues earlier in the day. They were still on the ground chasing Charlie. Until they were back home we'd remain in a ready-action posture.

I was in the process of contemplating the odds of drawing a fifth club to fill the flush I was working on. The game was seven card stud. I had two cards to go to salvage my investment in a sizable pot.

"Raise a quarter," John Larkin said, tossing yet another quarter on the mound of coins in the center of the table.

This produced moans from other members of the quintet, who reluctantly added their fees to the growing pile. Like me, they had an investment to protect. The problem with nickel-dime-quarter stakes was that a quarter never seemed like much to pay to see that next card. Before you realized it, the quarters deceptively added up, and you could end up borrowing money to make it to payday. Dirty Ernie McWhorter was the troop's loan shark, the nickname stemming from his self-reported sexual habits. His interest rates were exorbitant, particularly for scout pilots. He considered them a poor security risk, given their longevity rates.

With the pot straight, Eric Masterson dealt the last face-up card. The final card would go facedown. I got a spade to go with my four clubs and a diamond . . . so far, so bad. John continued obsessively building the pot. It cost me seventy-five cents to see my last card: another spade. I folded during the last round, saving another seventy-five cents.

John, the heavy bettor, was finally called. He produced a pair of threes. John liked threes. That's why he bet on them. It had nothing to do with their quality as a poker hand, thereby producing an unintentional bluff. Fortunately, he was a much better gunship pilot than he was a poker player. Bluffing seldom worked with nickel-dime-quarter stakes. Dave Horton won the hand with a baby straight.

"At least you win the deal," Eric chided John, passing him the cards.

John began meticulously shuffling the cards, convinced that receiving the winning hand was directly related to the quality of the shuffle. With precision borne from placing rockets on target from 2500 feet, John ensured that every other card crisscrossed as he shuffled the deck. This was painstaking work, to be repeated four times. Normally we would use the interlude of John's-turn-to-shuffle to go to the bar and replenish our Wild Turkey-and-waters. That option wasn't available today. So we sipped our canned Cokes and twiddled our thumbs . . . and waited . . . and waited.

John was on the third step of his four-step shuffling process when the messenger from Operations came screeching around the corner of the club, tripped over a chair, and careened into our poker table. As the table toppled over, a mad scramble ensued for the money that was now flying around the patio. Despite the chaos John somehow managed to hang on to the cards and continued with his intricate shuffle, perfection being more important to him than money.

In the midst of the confusion the messenger remembered his original purpose and shouted, "All pilots report to Operations. The Blues are in deep shit!"

The Blue Platoon had picked up the VC trail a little before noon, shortly after leaving the LZ. The Loaches had guided them to the trail, in the rugged terrain northwest of Mang Yang Pass, based on an earlier exchange of gunfire with the concealed enemy. The canopy and undergrowth were so thick that the Loaches couldn't continue to follow their quarry. That's when it became the job of the Blues: to go where the Loaches couldn't.

In theory it made a lot of sense. But in theory the Blues should never have gotten trapped. An infantry company— or battalion, depending on the situation—was always supposed to be on alert status to come to the rescue when the Blue Platoon got into heavy stuff. Twenty-four men with light weapons couldn't afford to become decisively engaged with a superior force. Yet here they were, about to become decisively engaged. The Blues were up against at least a company-size unit. And there was no backup infantry company, someone at Division having diverted it to another AO.

The VC trap had not been a spur-of-the-moment happening. With ingenious premeditation Charlie had quite deliberately suckered them. Shooting at the Loaches had just been part of their greater plan, aimed at enticing the Blues deep into the jungle and getting them isolated. The chase had moved slowly through the undergrowth; the elusive enemy deliberately provided an occasional trail clue, so the Blue Platoon neither got lost nor gave up. For three hours they moved painstakingly through the foliage, chopping their way with machetes, each man stepping cautiously in the footprints of another. They moved like a slow and ponderous snake, crawling along the jungle floor. The Blues methodically stalked the enemy, never receiving a clue that anything was amiss. The lack of booby traps along the trail should have alerted them sooner. Charlie was never in such a hurry that he didn't leave a couple of booby traps behind. But the Blues were apparently too intent on the chase to notice this lapse.

Their first awareness of the entrapment had come, loudly and disastrously, at 1500 hours. The L-shaped ambush had taken out the first squad, and most of the second, with its opening salvo. It had also taken out the LT, who had insisted on leading from the front. That had left Stan McDonald, the platoon sergeant, in charge. He formed the remnants of the platoon into a hasty defensive position, the thick undergrowth acting as both their salvation and their damnation. It impeded the VC's encirclement of their position, but it also provided no potential landing zones for a rescue mission.

Beyond the Blues' hasty perimeter the VC continued their encirclement, obviously confident, not even bothering with their usual harassing sniper fire. The Blues tried to gauge the VC's intentions and their own best defensive strategy, which normally would have been an immediate retrograde operation. However, that was not a currently feasible option. There was no place for a helicopter to land, and that would have been their only way out. While they waited for the inevitable onslaught the Blues worked feverishly, in shifts, to carve a PZ through the jungle canopy.

At 1530 hours the C & C ship had checked in with the Blues, right on schedule. McDonald was about to acknowledge the C & C's radio transmission when incoming mortar rounds began falling thunderously on their position. The VC had completed their encirclement. The C & C pilot promptly called Operations for help.

The Ready Room was bustling with activity when Dave Horton arrived carrying his boots and zipping his flight suit. I motioned to him, and he quickly slid into the chair I'd been saving for him. According to the assignment boards, I'd be flying Dave's wing today. That was the good news. The bad news was that we'd be in Charley Models. While

Captain Masters briefed the frag order, Dave struggled clumsily into his boots, muttering under his breath about the "goddamned Charley Models."

"Gentlemen, here's where the Blue Platoon is pinned down," Masters said as he pointed to the Operations map, which rested on a tripod in the front of the room. "It's nasty terrain, and an even nastier situation. They've already lost a lot of men, including Lieutenant Johnson." He paused for effect, then continued. "If we don't get there in a hurry, they'll lose a lot more. They're under attack right now, and we can expect the PZ to be very hot.

"The Blues are carving out a PZ—they're in triple-canopy stuff—big enough for a Loach. We're going to use the Loaches as slicks. Loaches, it also means you'll have to go in without door gunners. But door gunners probably wouldn't help anyway. Also, you're going to have to be very fast: in and out in a hurry. We'll take seven Loaches; the seventh is a spare. I want you to go in fifteen seconds apart. That means you've got to be very good, and timing is essential. You can't afford to linger in the PZ, because another Loach will be right behind you, and if you haven't cleared the PZ, you'll both be between a rock and a hard spot. You pull out four Blues per Loach. They'll also be tough, but they'll be traveling light. Don't worry about counting the load—you won't have time. The Blues will have received their loading instructions. Also, don't worry about over-torquing your birds. They're expendable; the Blues aren't. Remember, if you have to go down, keep the PZ clear. Otherwise you'll be signing some death warrants.

"Guns. We'll take two heavy teams, one of four Charley Models and the other of four Cobras. Horton leads the Charleys, Larkin the Cobras. John, your Cobras will get there first. You'll have to milk the ammo as best you can. Try to cover at least the first four extractions. Remember, there's no relief on station. They only thing coming behind you is the Charleys, and they don't carry a lot. We've got no reserves. It's up to us."

The entire briefing had lasted thirty seconds, a half minute in which the pilots continued to dress while assimilating the information.

"Each aircraft scrambles individually, with flight join-up

en route. Don't worry about contacting the tower for departure. Operations will get a blanket clearance. Any questions?"

No one spoke. Captain Masters was about to release the men when the major interrupted from the rear of the room.

"Excellent briefing, Captain. However, you left out an important point."

"Sir, there wasn't time for me to cover all aspects of METT-T, nor did I consider it necessary. We really need to be going."

"Never lose sight of the bigger picture, Captain. Sure we could rush right out and maybe save a few Blues. But in the process we could lose aircraft and flight crews, and it takes a lot longer to train a pilot than an infantryman. Consider the cost-effectiveness issue. Thou shalt not rush into a tactical situation.

"Now, what's the most important tactical consideration in this little war?"

A large army-issue clock—white face, black hands—hung above the door in the rear of the Ready Room. Masters watched anxiously as the second hand marched around the dial. It wasn't just ticking off seconds. It was ticking off men's lives. The major's question was purely rhetorical. He availed himself of every opportunity to espouse his treatise on the application of gas as the only sensible approach to the tactical situation in Vietnam.

"I assume you mean gas, sir."

"Exactly! This situation is ideal for gas. It's made to order."

"Sir, we don't really have time to rig a ship for gas. Also, the Blues aren't carrying gas masks."

"What? Why aren't they carrying gas masks?"

"The VC have never used gas, sir. Leaving the masks behind allows the Blues to carry more ammunition."

"Who authorized that? From now on, nobody leaves this compound without a gas mask."

"Captain, you use gas. Next time the Blues won't leave their masks at home."

Time was marching on, and arguing the point would be futile. "Very well, sir. I'll do the job myself. I'll rig a Huey and catch up with the flight," Masters replied. He caught Larkin's eye and gave a slight nod of his head. Just as surreptitiously John acknowledged the hidden communication: Don't wait for the gas.

"Excellent, Captain. If we all keep thinking tactically, we may just win this war." The major was about to continue when Masters took advantage of the pause to yell "Dismissed."

Dave Horton had gotten the jump on me when Masters had suddenly dismissed us. I raced after him. I had already beaten him to the Ready Room for the briefing. With a little luck I would beat him into the air. Thus far it had not been Dave's day. Nor was it going to be.

The Cobras, Loaches, and Charley Models departed as three separate flights: first the Cobras, then the Loaches, then us. The C & C ship took off later, after the crew had gotten the gas rigged. We probably set a record for getting fifteen helicopters off the ground in a coherent manner. Since it was only twenty-five miles to the Blues, the faster speed of the Cobras didn't produce a lot of separation between them and the other two flights. From our trailing vantage point we were close enough to watch the Snakes begin their gun runs and the Loaches spread their formation to begin the extraction.

The incoming mortar fire hadn't lasted long . . . and that was bad news. It hadn't been doing any damage to speak of, the shells unable to effectively penetrate the thick jungle canopy. But as long as it continued, it meant the VC would not be rushing the Blues' position. They would be smoking pot, mentally preparing themselves for their desperate charge into the jaws of death. They usually got high before a battle. It made them fearless. And damned hard to kill. There was no psychological impact when the bullets hit them, and apparently no pain either. They just kept coming, determinedly.

John Larkin called on the radio just as a concerted barrage of AK-47s began rattling the Blues' position. In the other helicopters we were all tuned to the FM frequency, monitoring the battle.

"Blackhawk 46 Alpha, this is Blackhawk 22. Over."

"Hawk 22, this is Alpha. Over."

"Roger, Alpha. We're on station. Pop smoke for the

Loaches. Give me a SITREP and tell me where you want the ordnance. Over.''

"Hawk 22, purple smoke's out. Put your ordnance twenty-five meters from the smoke, in any direction. We're under heavy fire, particularly from the east. Over."

"Roger the purple smoke and the ordnance. We're inbound. Out."

In a matter of seconds rockets began bursting in the jungle near the Blues, and the miniguns began raking the area at 4800 rounds per minute. The Blues still received incoming fire, but it was sporadic. The gunships were thwarting a concentrated attack. Most of the VC's weapons were pointing skyward now, attempting to bag more lucrative prey. There were direct rewards for any VC that downed an American helicopter.

From out trailing flight of Charley Models we continued to observe the action as the lead Loach dropped through the narrow window the Blues had carved through the jungle canopy, their field-expedient PZ. It was a tight squeeze, even for a Loach. The small helicopter began a rapid vertical descent, its rotor blades chopping foliage obstructing its downward path. Finally its skids cushioned its impact against the jungle floor, and four Blues simultaneously scrambled aboard, shedding their gear behind them. Almost instantaneously the Loach began to rise, the heavy coning of its main rotor blades indicating a severe struggle with the overweight condition. Ever so slowly it rose in its fight against the laws of physics, the small turbine engine straining in protest. Finally it cleared the tops of the trees, and the pilot dropped the nose, edging the aircraft forward into translational lift. It was quickly replaced by another Loach, and the process was repeated.

During the extraction the VC's anti-air attack was ferocious. One of the wing Cobras, on its initial gun run, suddenly began leaving a streaming trail of black smoke in its wake. The pilot jettisoned his weapon pods, making the aircraft lighter, and began nursing his rapidly diminishing altitude as he searched for a nonexistent forced landing area. There was nothing but trees for miles in every direction. Inevitably the crippled bird came to earth, the resulting fireball identifying its final resting place. I marked the location on my map. We'd need it for the subsequent and futile search-and-rescue mission. None of the Cobras had thus far escaped undamaged. Despite the thick canopy, the VC had been able to position their machine guns advantageously. As the battle continued to rage, one by one the Loaches depleted the number of stranded Blues. The last lift—with no Blues left on the ground to provide covering fire—would be the trickiest. As the fourth Loach began its departure Larkin again called McDonald on the radio.

"Hawk 46 Alpha, this is Hawk 22. Over."

"Alpha. Over."

"We're switching gun teams. Hawk 24 will be taking over. How's the situation? Over."

"Understood, 22. Situation is improving. We've still got seven on the ground. Two more Loaches and we're home free. Over."

"Understood, Alpha. Good luck. I'll see you at home base."

"Roger, 22."

Larkin switched to the UHF frequency and called Dave Horton. "Hawk 24, Hawk 22. Over."

"Hawk 24. Over."

"You've got the show, Dave. Two to go. We're empty and headed for home."

"Understood, 22. See you back at the ranch. Out." Dave switched to the FM frequency. "Hawk 46 Alpha, Hawk 24. Commo check. Over."

"This is Alpha. I've got you lima charlie. Over."

"Roger, Alpha. Just letting you know I'm covering your backside now. Over."

"Roger, 24. Alpha, out."

As we began making our gun runs in the Charley Models we got occasional glimpses of the ground battle, now in its final stages. McDonald and the two other remaining Blues continued pumping covering fire into the surrounding jungle as the fifth Loach departed the PZ. The sixth Loach quickly took its place, and the three remaining Blues made a run for it. They were completely vulnerable now, with no one to provide direct covering fire on the ground. The only covering fire available was what we could provide from upstairs. The VC were also aware of their vulnerability. In a matter of seconds the ground attack was renewed, and a fresh fusillade of bullets began ripping the PZ. Holes erupted in the side of the Loach as the VC concentrated on destroying the escape vehicle. Inside, the pilot scrunched down low in his seat, striving for as much armor protection as he could muster.

Inbound in the wing Charley Model I helplessly witnessed Stan McDonald's desperate race against steel for the sixth Loach. For a moment I thought he was miraculously going to run the gauntlet and remain unscathed. For a moment . . . then the first bullet hit him. He was only a couple of strides from the Loach. It had been that close . . . but they weren't playing horseshoes. The impact caused him to stagger, but he did not go down. The helicopter began to rise on its skids, the pilot's allotted time on the ground having expired. McDonald struggled forward, stumbling, toward salvation. The second bullet hit him in the leg, and he went down. Still he forced himself forward, crawling determinedly. As the Loach cleared the ground one of his comrades reached out and grabbed his arms, dragging McDonald aboard. The unexpected additional weight caused the helicopter to settle momentarily back to earth, but the pilot wasted no time making corrections and clearing the PZ. They headed for An Khe, the extraction complete.

From the wing position I watched Dave Horton turn his Charley Model inbound for a final rocket run. Dave had apparently milked his rockets, holding some back for a special target: the machine-gun nest that had been raking the gunships on every pass. He had its position pinpointed. And he wasn't going to miss.

From my vantage point on the outbound leg of the gun pattern I watched apprehensively as the gap between Dave's Charley Model and the target got narrower and narrower. Still, Horton held his fire. Quite obviously he was intending to put his remaining rockets right down the VC's throats, come hell or high water. The flashing barrel of the machine gun could be seen clearly now as it spewed its stream of deadly projectiles skyward. Observing the tracer line, I knew that some of the bullets had to be finding their target. Finally Dave punched off his rockets at nearly point-blank range. The machine gun disappeared in a cloud of fire and smoke as Dave put his Charley Model into a hard right bank. Despite having a now-empty ammunition load, the tired old UH-1C gunship lumbered slowly through the air as it struggled to gain airspeed and altitude.

Having been forced into the role of powerless observer as Dave recklessly challenged the VC's machine-gun position, I watched with relief as he broke off the run and headed for An Khe, leaving the enemy position smoldering in his wake. I moved my ship into loose trail formation for what I expected to be a routine flight back to home base. Shortly afterward Dave's helicopter began wandering aimlessly, and he did not respond to my radio calls.

I pulled up beside him, finally getting his attention, and motioned for him to follow me. Which he did. Out of curiosity, I suppose. When we arrived at An Khe Dave made an uncharacteristically hard landing. I left my copilot at the controls and raced to Dave's ship, quickly opening the left door of his bird. Normally the aircraft commander of a Charley Model flew in the right seat, but Dave insisted on flying from the left seat when he had a newby for a copilot because it gave him more control over the weapons.

I discovered that in his present state of euphoria Dave wouldn't have noticed the rough landing. He was feeling no pain . . . and didn't for several hours thereafter. While we waited for an ambulance to arrive, his copilot Jerry Murcheson, whose left arm was shattered badly from a bullet wound, explained what had happened.

Both Jerry and their crew chief had been hit just before Dave punched off his rockets on that final run that had knocked out the machine-gun nest. While their door gunner tended to the crew chief, Dave attempted to tend to Jerry, who was in considerable pain from his shattered arm. Flying the ship with one hand, Dave used his other hand to remove the morphine injector from the pocket of his survival vest. The injector was a foolproof design, allowing any soldier to become an instant medic. You simply removed the plastic tip that covered the needle and then jabbed the injector into a muscle. The correct dosage was injected automatically.

This procedure, of course, was not intended to be undertaken by a pilot who was attempting to fly a helicopter with one hand. As Dave thrust the injector at Jerry's left leg the helicopter chose that inopportune moment to encounter an air pocket that buffeted it roughly. This caused Dave's aim to be slightly off-target. The injector deflected off the copilot's collective stick and buried itself in Dave's hand, giving him a full dose of the morphine.

Jerry Murcheson refused to fly with Dave again. I don't know if it was because of his clumsiness with the morphine injector or his duel-to-the-death gun run. But Jerry was petrified with fear whenever Dave's name was mentioned. Thereafter, they never set foot in the same helicopter.

Stan McDonald got thirty days at a hospital in Japan. When he returned there were many new faces in the Blue Platoon, including a new lieutenant, our token leg officer. More than half the Blues had been lost during the VC ambush. McDonald had his work cut out for him: The replacements were mostly green hands. But he was a good soldier, and he knew his job. Soon he had the Blues functioning together as a unit, like a well-oiled piece of machinery. His efforts would eventually prove futile. The Blues had a date with destiny that training and experience couldn't thwart.

Thanks to Major Williams, I also had a date with destiny.

8

■ ■ ■ ■ ■ ■ ■ ■ ■ ■ ■ ■ ■ ■

Reassignment

I WAS SOUND ASLEEP IN MY BUNK—AT LEAST AS SOUND asleep as one dared become—when the footsteps outside the hooch woke me up. It was still dark. I quickly slipped my hand under the pillow, removing the .38-caliber pistol. It was loaded with illegal bullets that I'd gotten from the Special Forces at Pleiku—guaranteed to stop a charging elephant or an angry husband instantly. One of the VC's favorite tactics was to slip around hooches and toss in a grenade or a satchel charge. The footsteps came closer, stopping outside the door. In the bunk on the other side of the room, Doc Post—the flight surgeon—continued snoring loudly, oblivious to the world. As usual, he'd overconsumed Johnnie Walker Black at the troop's Officers Club the night before. Doc had two obsessions: alcohol and women. He planned to specialize in gynecology when the army was finished with him.

The covered screen door to the hooch began to open slowly, stopping when the slack was removed from the slip latch on the inside of the door. I cocked the .38.

"Mr. Holley," a voice called from outside, accompanied by three light taps on the door. "Mr. Holley."

I uncocked the .38 and returned it to its resting place beneath the pillow. "Yeah," I said, although only the "ah" got vocalized. Sometimes my first word of the day got clipped off. I tried again. "Yeah. Holley here."

"Sir, the major left a message with the duty officer that he wants you in his office at 0630."

"Okay. He say what it's about?"

"No, sir. Just for you to be there."

"Roger. I'll be there."

I gathered up my toilet bag and headed for the officers' shower. I would have preferred to know what the meeting would be about. That way I could have a relatively believable story rehearsed. From experience, I knew the summons meant trouble. The major didn't call warrant officers into his office as a matter of routine.

The shower had warm water for a change. Usually the hot water was depleted by the early birds before I managed to struggle out of bed. Today I was one of the early birds, albeit reluctantly. I would gratefully have traded the hot shower for a couple more hours of sleep. I finished the morning ritual quickly and returned to my hooch. I dressed spic-and-span for the meeting with the major. He put great store by such things.

Fifteen minutes later, having received the first sergeant's go-ahead, I knocked on the major's door and entered his office.

"Mr. Holley reporting, sir."

The major continued with his paperwork, not bothering to look up. "Sit down, Mr. Holley. I'll be with you in a moment," he said, motioning me to a chair in front of his desk.

I took the indicated seat and proceeded to twiddle my thumbs for two or three minutes. Finally the major finished writing and looked up. "Well, now, Mr. Holley. I have a number of items to discuss with you."

Uh-oh, I thought. More than one item to discuss was definitely a bad omen.

"I have some paperwork here where you've applied for a direct commission to second lieutenant."

"Yes, sir."

"I've given the matter some thought, and to tell you the truth, I'm just not sure you're cut out to be a commissioned officer."

"I see," I responded, disappointed. No one likes to hear the truth if it's unflattering. "Any particular reason, sir?"

"Well, yes. There is one reason in particular. You're rather young, and your military education has been somewhat limited. For example, you can't know much about tactics."

"My approach to tactics is fairly straightforward, sir. If it shoots at me, I kill it."

"But what if it's friendly troops shooting at you? That happens, you know."

"If it's shooting at me, it's not friendly."

"Actually, I was thinking of tactics in a broader sense."

Aha, I thought, I didn't just fall off the turnip truck. "I'm very keen on the use of gas in the tactical situation, sir. Particularly in unconventional warfare."

"Perhaps you're more of a tactician than I realized. Tell you what, Mr. Holley. I'm going to hold your application while I scrutinize your performance. I'll let you know my decision in three or four weeks."

"Yes, sir," I responded halfheartedly.

"Now, the other thing I need to discuss. Do you like being in this troop?"

"Yes, sir. I've been with it for more than a year now, including the time at Fort Hood."

"Well, the time we spent at Fort Hood is what's created our problem. Coming over together as a unit means that we all have the same DROS. Except, of course, for the few infusion pilots and new assignees that we've gotten since we've been in country. Basically, Division has ordered me to spread out the DROS dates."

"Yes, sir."

"What this means to you is that you will either have to extend your DROS for sixty days or transfer to another unit."

So far this had really been a day for good news.

"It's entirely up to you, Mr. Holley. You can extend and stay with the troop, or you can go to another troop. Do you want some time to think it over?"

"That won't be necessary. I'll stay with Delta Troop."

"Great!" the major exclaimed. "I always like to see loyalty in my troops.

"This will also weigh favorably on my decision regarding your application for a direct commission. You need to sign this for me."

I scrawled my signature on the proffered form and returned it to the major. He examined it carefully and then placed it in his out basket. "One last thing."

"Yes, sir."

"Starting tomorrow, you'll be in the Scout Platoon."

Flabbergasted, I managed to stammer, "But why, sir?"

"It's all tied into this DROS problem. I've also got to balance the rotations within the platoons. Putting you in scouts will help that."

"But sir, surely there's another way."

"Yes. But not a better way. I've made my decision. If you're still around in six months, we'll talk about putting you back in the Gun Platoon."

"Sir, about that DROS extension," I interjected. Going to another unit suddenly didn't seem like such a bad idea. Particularly if I went before I transitioned to scouts: I would be transferring as a gunship pilot.

"Yes," the major responded frostily. "What about it?"

It occurred to me that I was in a no-win situation. If I transferred to another unit, the major would vindictively kill my application for a commission. On the other hand, if I went into scouts, I would probably be dead before I got the commission. Which was more important: living or the commission? I had to decide quickly. The major was awaiting a response.

"Was that extension for sixty or ninety days?" I queried.

As I was leaving the Orderly Room I stopped on the porch to put on my cap. The session with Major Williams had left me in a foul mood. An unfamiliar captain—Graves, according to the name tag—dropped his duffel bags beside the porch and headed up the steps. "Morning, Captain," I said politely. "You reporting in to the outfit?"

Captain Graves stopped and glared at me, not returning my friendly greeting. I wasn't sure what to do, so I just glared back. Finally, after several seconds, he broke the lingering silence. "Mister, don't they teach warrant officers to salute commissioned officers?"

I was momentarily taken aback by the question. It had

been months since I'd saluted a company-grade officer. In a cavalry troop such courtesies were normally suspended as a matter of practicality. There were so many captains, lieutenants, and warrant officers running around that nothing would get accomplished except saluting. "Yes, sir, momentarily slipped my mind," I replied as I snapped, and held, a picture-perfect military salute.

"Apology accepted," responded the captain as he returned my salute. "See that your memory works a little better in the future."

"Yes, sir," I replied while turning to leave. "By the way, sir," I said, and then I paused to ensure that I had the captain's attention.

"Yes?" he replied.

"When you get home to your mother this evening, you be sure to tell her that you got to salute a *real* soldier today."

Captain John Graves became the new Gun Platoon leader, thus providing a fortuitous aspect to my reassignment to the scouts. Subsequent events would also indicate that he was a man who formed lasting opinions of people based on initial encounters. The next day I began my transition training for the Loach. I dragged the training out as long as possible, but eventually the day of reckoning could no longer be postponed.

It was time for my first scout mission. A time to test my mettle . . . to see if I had the guts to stare down the barrel of an enemy machine gun from a distance of fifteen or twenty feet. Frankly, the notion was not particularly appealing. There ought to be a safer way to fight a war. I suppose it would be accurate to say that I was apprehensive about the notion of flying scouts, particularly given their longevity rates—or lack thereof. I was soon to discover that my apprehension was well-founded.

PART
THREE

■ ■ ■ ■ ■ ■ ■ ■ ■ ■ ■ ■

Scouts

9

■ ■ ■ ■ ■ ■ ■ ■ ■ ■ ■ ■ ■ ■

First Scout Mission

IT WAS OCTOBER 27. THREE DAYS AFTER MY PROMOTION TO
Chief Warrant Officer, CW2. More importantly, it was my
day of reckoning as a scout pilot. I had spent a sleepless
night, tossing and turning. After what seemed an eternity
the alarm clock mercifully began ringing at 0530 hours. I
gratefully shut it off; quickly, so as not to disturb Doc
Post's snoring. At least the alarm clock gave me a rationale
for being awake at such an ungodly hour. Shortly thereafter
I was seated in the mess hall, the breakfast a stopover en
route to the flight line for an 0700 departure. My symptoms
of a severe nervous condition weren't restricted to sleep-
lessness. I couldn't eat. The sunny-side-up eggs stared back
at me from the greasy tray. Across the table Eric Masterson
wolfed his breakfast as if there were no tomorrow. I forced
down some coffee and puffed on my Marlboro. And I contemplated the enigma seated across from me.

Chief Warrant Officer Eric Masterson was a couple of
inches taller than me and a year or two younger. He had
handsome features that undoubtedly attracted his share of
women. Curly brown hair. Dark brown eyes. Boyish in
appearance, yet mature in behavior. He was also a very
good scout pilot. Perhaps the best aeroscout ever. Certainly
the best one I ever knew: Kit Carson and Charles Lind-

bergh rolled into one. The VC were always located when Eric was doing the scouting. And he could make a Loach do things that were never intended by its designers. Fate had placed him in a position where his latent talents could emerge.

But there were other sides to Eric Masterson. He had acquaintances, but no friends. He allowed no one that close. Eventually this would change, but only after I successfully bridged all the hidden barriers that protected him from friendship. He killed mercilessly, yet he was compassionate. He followed orders, but only if he agreed with the orders. He drank at least a quart of bourbon a day, yet he was never drunk. He also showed no fear in the face of battle, and this bothered me most of all. It seemed to me that normal people showed concern when someone was trying to kill them. In short, Eric Masterson was an anomaly. And I, the scout newby, had been assigned as his wingman.

Prior to the relationship that would develop between us, the closest thing Eric had had to a true friend was the dog that he'd acquired at an An Khe bazaar, thereby saving it from the butcher's block. The dog is truly man's best friend. This is particularly so in a combat zone, where he provides faithful companionship and a constant reminder of what things were like in better times and better places. Will Rogers often said that he never met a man he didn't like. I don't think he was sincere. If so, he led a very sheltered existence. Had he said that he'd never met a dog he didn't like, he would have been much more believable.

Eric's puppy was ugly as sin and cute as the devil, and he quickly blossomed to more than a hundred pounds of frolicking friendliness. Eric named him Butch, although by consensus of those subsequently encountering the grown Butch in confined quarters, this was changed to Gaseous Ignaseous, or GI for short. GI had a severe gastrointestinal malady. To be truthful, it was necessary to wear your gas mask if you were unlucky enough to get cooped up with GI. He required lots of fresh air and open spaces. There was also the danger of an explosion from some uninformed person attempting to light a cigarette in his presence.

Doc Post, the flight surgeon, had tried every concoction

known to medicine to remedy GI's unsociable malady, but it was all to no avail. If he'd been afflicted with a gynecological malfunction, Doc would probably have been successful.

Eventually GI would provide Eric and me with the revenge we sought against Major Williams for a grievous slight that he inflicted on us. In the meantime, everyone struggled to survive in GI's presence. Eric refused to give up the dog.

"You'd better eat, son."

I resented being called son by a younger person, but I let it pass. "I know. But my stomach doesn't seem interested. A little nervous, I guess."

"What's to be nervous about?"

"You know. It's my first scout mission."

"Nothing to be nervous about. I wasn't nervous on my first mission."

No doubt, I thought as he paused to scoop up another mouthful of eggs. Mr. Cool. Mr. Icewater.

"No," he continued, "not on the first one. The second one—that's when I was nervous."

"Why?" I queried.

"Because of what happened on the first one," he replied.

At first I thought he was just making a joke at my expense. And maybe he was. On the other hand, one should avoid jumping to conclusions. "Why? What happened?"

"You ever heard the story that right before you die your whole life flashes past you?"

"Sure. Everyone has."

"Well, it's not true . . . at least not completely true," Eric said reflectively, as if he were visualizing a long-forgotten experience. "I flew wing on Tim Briggs that first mission. You never knew Tim. He was with 1/10th Cavalry." He interrupted his reminiscence to ask, "How many hours you got in the Loach?"

"A little over twenty, I suppose. There was the ten-hour transition, and then about another ten hours of ash-and-trash."

"Yeah, well, that's about right. By way of comparison, I had an hour and a half in the Loach before my first mission."

"But you're required to have at least the ten-hour transition."

"Exigencies of war. We were short on scout pilots and even shorter on instructor pilots. An hour and a half with a C 7/17 IP over at Pleiku was the best we could do. The point being that you have far less to be nervous about than I did. At least you've had some time with the aircraft.

"Anyway, I was flying wing on Tim Briggs. Being a newby to scouts, like you, I hadn't been assigned my own Loach yet. Magilla Gorilla—that wasn't his real name, of course; he just looked and acted like the cartoon character—was on R & R, so I was assigned his Loach. Later I learned that he'd written the Loach up his last two missions because it didn't feel right. Naturally, Maintenance couldn't find anything wrong with it. It was hardly a precise complaint."

Eric paused again to reflect, then continued. "I'm getting ahead of myself. Let me get back to the mission. We'd been flying most of the day. Must have gotten on to about three o'clock in the afternoon when it happened.

"I was doing left-hand orbits around Tim's Loach, keeping my door gunner trained on him. We were about five feet over the trees at fifteen to twenty knots. Large trees. Triple-canopy stuff.

"Everything was peaceful—somewhat boring, actually—orbit after orbit. Then all of a sudden: BANG! Something broke. At least I thought there was a bang. I could never be sure if I actually heard it or just imagined it.

"At any rate, I reacted. Reflexively. I closed the throttle and autorotated into the trees. Of course, only a couple of seconds passed between the bang and hitting the trees.

"But it was a very long two seconds, during which I thought I was going to die.

"So did my whole life flash before me? No. But two distinct thoughts did flash through my mind. The first one was: 'What a way to go. I didn't even get shot.' And the second one was: 'My God. What a big fucking tree!' "

"Then what?" I asked intently.

"Then we hit that big fucking tree. Next thing I know the helicopter's lying on the jungle floor with me and the door gunner still strapped in, and we're choking on red smoke—a smoke grenade went off in the cockpit when we hit the tree.

"The Loach came to rest on my side. In addition to the smoke problem, fuel's pouring out on the ground underneath me. And my door gunner is hanging in the air above me screaming, 'What happened?'

"Talk about an irrelevant question. We're about to go up in flames any second, and he wants to know what happened.

"I yell at him to get out. Have to do it two or three times before it finally penetrates.

"Finally he unbuckles his shoulder harness to climb out. Of course, as soon as he releases the buckle he falls right on top of me.

"Now he's down where he can see the fuel that's spilling out beneath me. There was no holding him back then. He nearly trampled me to death scrambling out of there. I was bruised for weeks."

"How'd you get out of the jungle?"

"We walked until we found a small clearing. Probably wasn't more than a couple hundred meters, but in that undergrowth it seemed like miles.

"The clearing was just large enough for Tim Briggs to squeeze his Loach in and get within about five feet of the ground. We jumped up on the skids and then climbed aboard."

As Eric paused I reflected on the story. Then I broached a sensitive question. "What caused the accident?"

"Well, I took a lot of kidding about Papa Tango—pilot technique. I think most people assumed that I just screwed up and hit a tree with my tail rotor.

"The accident investigating officer was a staff jockey from Fourth Division. A newby that had never flown in the field. He didn't believe a thing I said. Particularly since my door gunner couldn't corroborate the bang. Hell, I couldn't even be sure that I had actually heard a bang.

"Anyway, the jackass wrote me up for operating the aircraft in the dead man's zone—low altitude and low airspeed. He concluded that I had gotten into a Hughes tailspin and didn't have sufficient altitude to recover."

"But that makes no sense," I interrupted. "Scout tactics

require that we do most of our flying in the dead man's zone."

"True."

"And another thing," I continued. "You were making left orbits. You get a Hughes tailspin with right turns."

"Also true."

"You didn't just leave it that way, did you?"

"Welcome to the real world. He was the official investigating officer. It was his report. I later learned that the entire accident investigation could have been avoided by shooting the aircraft."

"What do you mean?"

"You pull your pistol out and put a few bullet holes in the aircraft. Then it's combat damage, not an accident. And that means no accident investigation."

"You're kidding."

"No. Another aspect of the real world.

"Anyway, for several weeks I replayed the accident in my mind. Trying to analyze the events from every angle. Trying to prod my memory into releasing just one more detail. Trying to be sure that I had acted, or rather reacted, correctly.

"For example, why had I closed the throttle? Obviously the engine was still running. Did the tail rotor fail? I couldn't recall any symptoms of anti-torque failure. And if the tail rotor had failed, I wouldn't have closed the throttle so quickly. I would have tried to control torque with the throttle and only closed it as a last resort.

"All I could tell the investigating officer was that I heard a bang and that for some reason I closed the throttle. The truth as I knew it, or at least as I thought I knew it. Not much to go on. And the door gunner couldn't even substantiate the bang. Maybe I had just imagined it. But I wouldn't have just closed the throttle for no reason. So. An enigma, you see. A mystery."

"That's the way it ended? As an unsolved mystery?"

"No. In accidents like this the army automatically ships the helicopter to Corpus Christi for teardown analysis. They're very intent on determining the real cause of an accident.

"It turns out that the main drive shaft was defective and

had snapped. That explained why I had closed the throttle so quickly. It also explained Magilla Gorilla's complaints that the aircraft didn't feel right and why Maintenance couldn't find anything wrong with it. It's not something they would be likely to catch.

"It seems that there was a whole batch of defective drive shafts that had gotten shipped to the field. In this case the army had a list of serial numbers and was recalling them. They just hadn't gotten around to mine."

"Did they correct your records?"

"Yep. Got a letter from the Pentagon—top brass. Directed that my records be corrected to reflect the true cause of the accident. They also enclosed a copy of a letter of reprimand for the investigating officer. Like you, they were less than impressed with his conclusions."

I reflected on Eric's story about crashing on his first scout mission. "So that's why you were nervous on your second scout mission?"

"Sort of."

"What do you mean?"

"Trees. Trees made me very nervous for quite some time. It was like getting back on a horse after you've been thrown. It took a lot of willpower to force myself to fly over trees again."

"Well, you obviously succeeded."

"Yes . . . yes, I did," Eric responded reflectively.

"So tell me. Were you nervous on your third scout mission?"

"Definitely."

"Because of the trees?"

"No. I had pretty much conquered the tree thing by then. It was because of what happened on my second scout mission."

We departed An Khe in our routine configuration for air cavalry operations: two Cobras, two Loaches, and a C & C bird. We headed into the rising sun, the AO lying thirty miles to the east. It felt strange to be clipping along the treetops in a Loach instead of cruising along at fifteen hundred feet in a Cobra or Charley Model. Of course, clipping the treetops was a much better test of aviator skills.

When we arrived at the AO I fell into a routine wing pattern on Eric's Loach: continuous left-hand orbits at twenty to thirty knots, keeping my door gunner in position to provide covering fire. This was the wing's primary purpose: to protect the lead aircraft. In addition, you had to scout for the enemy and fly the aircraft. This latter task could be particularly burdensome, since we operated in the trees. A momentary lapse of concentration and you'd be needing at least a new set of main rotor blades.

As the day progressed my nervousness began to subside. It was like stage fright: Once you actually got into the activity, the apprehension went away. I began enjoying myself, the challenges of mastering new skills overriding the inherent boredom of flying in monotonous circles. Before I realized it the day was half gone, and we returned to An Khe for lunch—the never-ending dried-out roast beef and reconstituted potatoes. I opted for the bootleg C-rations I kept hidden in my hooch.

After lunch we returned to the AO, continuing the task of trying to locate an elusive enemy. Given the terrain we were working in, it was a fairly futile task. The jungle canopy was triple depth here . . . massive. And it was at least a hundred feet from the tops of the trees to the jungle floor. A herd of elephants could have been wandering around down there and we'd never have known it.

I was about to point out to Eric the futility of scouting in this terrain when I was suddenly presented with new evidence that contradicted both my proposition and my conclusion, thus sparing me the embarrassment my naïveté would have created. I had never heard AKs that close before. It's a terrifying experience. And not just the first time it happens. It is not something you adapt to. It's always terrifying. The bullets don't ping like they do in the movies; they literally explode. Frequently to the accompaniment of shattering Plexiglas.

Eric shouted, "Receiving fire!" over the UHF and dropped a smoke grenade to mark the location for the gunships, which would already be rolling in hot. My door gunner simultaneously opened up with the M-60, peppering the area under Eric's Loach. I watched the nose of his Loach dip and swing right as he applied max power in an effort to vacate the area. I did likewise. It also occurred to me that there was a small weakness in our scout tactics: Nobody provided covering fire for the wingman. I had asked about that earlier. I'd been assured that ninety percent of the time Charlie went for the lead Loach, eight percent of the time for both Loaches, and two percent for the wing Loach. I took great comfort in these statistics. At least I did until the bullets started ripping through my Loach. Either Charlie hadn't studied the percentages, or this was one of those eight percenters.

As the rockets from the Cobras erupted on top of Eric's target-marking smoke grenade my door gunner, Jim Davis, suddenly slumped forward, and my Loach jerked violently. Then the flight controls quit responding. As the Loach fell toward the trees Eric's earlier recitation of his first scout mission flashed through my mind. Like him, I found that the moment before my impending demise was occupied by two thoughts. The first was: At least I was shot down. Strangely enough, the second thought was identical to Eric's: My God! What a big fucking tree! Also like Eric, I hit that big fucking tree. Then there was darkness.

I came back to consciousness slowly amid the acrid fumes of JP-4. As awareness returned I realized the Loach had come to rest on its right side. My wounded door gunner was suspended in space above me, apparently unconscious. The JP-4 was my immediate concern, as I had never had the desire to be the guest of honor at a barbecue; the fuel from the ruptured tank was flowing freely beneath me. The eight-day clock on the instrument panel showed almost two hours had elapsed since our departure from An Khe. That meant that it had been almost a half hour since we'd crashed. It also meant Charlie'd been looking for us for a half hour. Not surprisingly, I could hear no sounds of other helicopters. To my team members it must have seemed as if the jungle had simply swallowed my Loach. Official sunset would soon be on us, although the jungle floor was already bathed in darkness. We had to get moving.

I climbed awkwardly over Jim Davis and out the left door of the Loach. I rested briefly—the extraction process was exhausting—and then dragged him out the same opening. Balancing Jim on the doorway, I reached back in and grabbed one of the Willie Pete grenades that was hanging from the quick-release wire on the gunner's side of the Loach. I also grabbed the first-aid kit so I could tend to Jim's wound, time permitting. Dragging him away from the helicopter, I pulled the pin on the Willie Pete and tossed it back toward the Loach. Charlie wouldn't be salvaging anything of value from my bird.

Hoisting Jim to my shoulders, I moved awkwardly into the jungle. Behind us the Willie Pete burst, spewing forth its flaming phosphorous, and quickly ignited the free-flowing JP-4. The Loach disintegrated in a secondary explosion, sending a fireball to the tops of the jungle trees. Above the noise of the inferno I could hear voices in the jungle, the rhythmic singsong of the Vietnamese language. The fireball would bring them quickly to our position. My rudimentary escape and evasion training was about to receive its first real test. I thought of the poor little bunny rabbit I'd had to kill and eat during escape and evasion training back at Fort Rucker. I hoped Vietnamese bunnies were as cooperative.

As dawn's light began to grow stronger, signaling a change in shifts for the restless jungle, I staggered into the foliage between two huge tropical trees. My right boot failed to maintain traction in the slippery undergrowth, and—too exhausted to fight for balance—I fell heavily to the jungle floor. Still, I managed to use my body to cushion the impact of the fall on Jim, whom I was continuing to carry, sling-fashion. Shifting my position to ease the weight from my back, I rolled over and lay quietly, listening to the language of the jungle . . . a language I was learning to speak well.

The trees provided some shelter from the unseasonable drizzling rain. More importantly, they provided a place to hide from the VC patrols that relentlessly stalked the jungle pathways, presumably searching for us. As the assumed quarry, hiding had been our most important strategy. Armed only with a .38 and a Bowie knife, we sure as hell couldn't fight our way back to An Khe. Hiding was how we'd avoided the initial search when the helicopter went down: burrowing under the foliage and waiting for nightfall. Lying in the underbrush, we listened, petrified, as the VC excitedly discovered our downed and burning Loach and then began looking for its crew. That had been three days earlier. Since then we had traveled only by night and had avoided using the jungle trails. Unable to use the natural pathways, we found that traversing the thick undergrowth at night became a nearly impossible task. Distance was measured in feet, not miles. While scouts didn't carry maps, I knew that a southern course would eventually intersect with Highway 19, the main east-west road that ran through II Corps. Once there, we could hitch a ride on the first American vehicle that came by.

Using a procedure that had by now become automatic, I checked to be sure that no telltale signs pointed to our temporary hiding place—no broken twigs, no bent blades of grass, no footprints, no disturbed animal droppings—and then covered Jim and myself with dead leaves and brush. We wouldn't move again for twelve hours. The drizzling rain had stopped now, providing the VC with yet another advantage. Jim's wound was our biggest liability in this deadly game of cat-and-mouse. The bullet had hit him in the left shoulder, from the rear. I'd managed to get the bleeding stopped and had bandaged the wound. The immediate danger was from infection, and he was already running a high fever. The wound slowed us down tremendously. And carrying him sapped my strength. I was bone-weary tired. If we didn't cross Highway 19 soon, I'd have to consider leaving him behind and hope I could get back to him in time. I couldn't carry him much farther.

I felt a trickle along my left leg as the first of many insects began its trek along my body. The first day of this had been the worst. The temptation to kill them and scratch at the skin irritations had been almost overwhelming. But to do so meant movement and noise, however slight. I also knew logically that scratching would only provide a temporary respite. And the risk of discovery would increase, with the odds already stacked against us. After the second day with the spindly-legged creatures I mastered the log trick. Logs did not mind if insects crawled on them and bit them. In fact, they rather enjoyed it. It was a natural part of the life cycle. Logs were a source of refuge and nutrition for the insects. Soon I would once more become a log. Occasionally I contemplated the relationship between logs and snakes, but I did not allow myself to dwell on the topic. Snakes were not good. At least the insects repaid my hospitality by providing breakfast when the log came back to life. Jim refused to eat the little devils, but I had developed quite a taste for them. I'd even learned to prefer the flavor of some to others. But I didn't like the ones with the little furry legs. They tasted too much like butterscotch.

While I waited for the log to take over my being I could hear the distant enemy voices as they barked orders to restart the search. I knew their routine by now. It never changed—and it constantly brought them closer. They would come abreast through the jungle, about ten meters apart. Like us, the searchers were ignoring the natural pathways. Thus far we had managed to stay ahead of the VC patrols, but our fatigue-ridden lack of progress the night before would change that. The search was starting too close. It was inevitable that we would cross paths with the VC today. Whether or not they found us was another matter. We could only remain immobile and wait—and hope—and pray. Well, maybe not pray, I thought as I subconsciously tightened my grip on the unsheathed Bowie knife resting in my right hand. If praying had done any good, we'd still be aloft in the Loach. At the moment I was too tired to care. I gave in to the insects . . . and to sleep.

The rustling of leaves in the nearby undergrowth caused me to come instantly awake. I quickly nudged Jim to alert him to the approaching danger. Then I waited, listening and clutching the knife. My pistol was useless, since its noise would have been suicide. I could hear an enemy soldier moving closer and closer, using his rifle to probe behind each bush in his path. He was only a couple of feet away from us. Another probe with the rifle and he would surely strike pay dirt. Suddenly he stopped and spoke to a nearby companion, the singsong of the Vietnamese language incomprehensible to me.

The reason for the halt in the search became abundantly clear a few seconds later when warm liquid began trickling through the bushes as the soldier relieved himself. I closed my eyes as the warmth spread across my fatigues, the stench assaulting my nostrils. The downpour soon ended as abruptly as it had begun. The VC soldier spoke to his companion and the search continued, moving on past us. The relief I felt was almost overwhelming, the near encounter emotionally draining. Sleep quickly claimed me again.

When I awoke, near dusk, I mustered the last of my quickly ebbing strength, slung Jim over my shoulders, and continued our southbound trek. Around midnight I discovered that I was walking on pavement, not jungle foliage: Highway 19. Stumbling, I moved off the highway and back into the jungle. I located a hiding place that provided a good view of the road, as well as good concealment from probing eyes. Despite my exhaustion the remainder of the night passed restlessly and sleeplessly as I remained warily alert. I was too close to blow it now by relaxing. At 0700 hours the next morning I flagged down a westbound supply convoy, and we rode the fifteen miles back to An Khe, although I was sound asleep by the time the deuce-and-a-half began moving.

After much food and sleep my body returned to normalcy, and I was soon fidgeting to get back in the air. My first mission had not really demonstrated my potential as a scout pilot, and I needed to get my reputation on the road. I also had much to learn about being a scout pilot. Unfortunately, a major obstacle to getting back in the air confronted me: Since I had been involved in an aircraft accident, I was automatically grounded until cleared by a flight surgeon. This turned out to be a problem.

10

■ ■ ■ ■ ■ ■ ■ ■ ■ ■ ■ ■ ■

Man-eater

ONE OF THE THINGS AN ARMY AVIATOR FEARS MOST IS BEING grounded. This is particularly true for warrant officers, who are aviation specialists. Flying is virtually their only mission in life. Grounding means becoming a fish out of water. And everyone gets grounded for one reason or another. Most of these episodes are temporary, and the person returns to flying status in an expeditious manner (by the army's definition of expeditious, of course, which to a grounded aviator is akin to the speed of the turtle rather than the hare). Regardless of the length of the grounding, the aviator is mired in psychological muck; his wings have been clipped. He is not allowed to fly. He is a nonpilot, which is synonymous with being a nonentity. When the grounding occurs the aviator does everything possible to regain his true status quickly.

Unfortunately (to the aviator's way of thinking), some groundings are automatic. For example, if you're involved in an aircraft accident, you're medically grounded until cleared by a flight surgeon. Typically this is a minor inconvenience involving a rubber stamp. Such was normally the case in Delta Troop, since we had our own flight surgeon, Doc Post. Unhappily, the situation was not normal when I returned to Delta Troop after my first scout mission. I was automatically grounded because of the accident, and Doc Post had gone to Saigon to give a two-week course on using aspirin for the treatment of gonorrhea (an ineffectual treatment that Doc discovered one of our Australian counterparts applying as a self-treatment; however, Doc managed a two-week vacation out of it). Eric, whose flight physical had just expired, thereby grounding him, suggested that we should take action.

The nearest flight surgeon was at Camp Holloway, some fifty-odd miles to the west according to yon crow—an easy half-hour flight by helicopter. Unfortunately, there were no helicopters or crews available to make such an ash-and-trash run. Everything flyable was either flying or on standby or down for maintenance. This also added to our mental anguish. Delta Troop was into some heavy stuff, and Eric and I were relegated to being reluctant spectators. We decided to take matters into our own hands. As Mr. Spock says, "There are always alternatives." We would travel by ground.

However, such a solution was not easily implemented and required detailed planning. Traveling fifty miles on Highway 19 in a lone vehicle was not a low-risk activity. For one thing, there were constant VC ambushes of road traffic, particularly around Mang Yang Pass, a very nasty piece of terrain that we would have to cross. Because of the ambushes U.S. vehicles always traveled in convoys: safety in numbers. For another thing, we had no vehicle.

We solved both problems in typical scout fashion. With respect to the convoy, we had no idea how the army went about issuing convoys, so we opted for sheer bravado. We would travel solo and psych out the VC by pretending to be totally unconcerned about the possibility of an ambush. This would have the effect of making them suspicious of a trap. They would not attack such an easy and obvious target for fear that it was a decoy for a hidden reprisal force. Clauswitz would have been proud of us, our strategy utterly brilliant in its simplicity.

Obtaining a vehicle for the mission was the easy part. We simply went to the troop's motor pool, cranked up a three-quarter-ton truck, and drove off—with much gear meshing. The army was always misplacing its vehicles, at least on a temporary basis, so we figured our misappropriation would go undetected. Unless someone needed that particular truck and couldn't find it. If that occurred, we would have to paint a new identification number on the bumper and leave it parked somewhere inconspicuous. That would take years for the army to unravel: "Describe the missing vehicle, please," the CID investigator would say to the motor pool sergeant. "It was green—olive drab, actually—three-quarter ton, with 'U.S. Army' stenciled on it."

After leaving the motor pool we went back to the main troop area and outfitted the truck for our expedition. This consisted of putting two lawn chairs and a cooler of Budweiser in the back and commandeering two of our scout door gunners—one to drive and one to ride shotgun—Jim Braddock and Larry Anderson. Jim, being more forceful, elected himself driver. There were rumors that he wasn't completely sane, but you can't put much stock in rumors, particularly since everyone in scouts was generally considered to be mentally imbalanced. We also threw on enough armament to stock a small armory, and a PRC-25 radio. Eric and I donned our swimsuits, stretched out on the lawn chairs, began downing the Budweisers, and shouted, "Head 'em up and move 'em out." That meant "let's go" in scout lingo. The great plan was underway. An Khe was soon sprawling in our wake as we headed west on Highway 19.

Actually, our inane strategy wasn't half bad. That also means it was only half good. To be precise, it was three quarters good. We successfully negotiated the deserted stretches of Highway 19—pausing every few miles to visit the lonely outposts stationed periodically along the route—and nervously traversed the haunting and forbidding cliffs of Mang Yang Pass. We arrived at Camp Holloway around noon, had some lunch at the mess hall, took care of our business with the flight surgeon, and headed back to An Khe around 1500 hours. I was back on flying status, reborn as a whole and complete aviator.

The ride back was an even more cheerful resumption of our flamboyant beer-drinking excursion. By the time we crossed Mang Yang Pass headed back east our blood-alcohol levels had increased to the point of ensuring our invulnerability, assuming the truth of the adage that God looks out for drunks and other fools. We were about five miles east of the pass when the facade was violently stripped from our brilliant plan.

When we reached the valley floor the cavernous and deadly pass became a backdrop to our eastward trek. We were on the home stretch now, completing a brave journey that was the stuff of which legends are made. Once more the cavalry had demonstrated its wily mettle. We passed around more beers in a premature victory celebration.

Then the windshield disintegrated. In the rear of the truck Eric and I dived for the bed amid splintering wooden sideboards, which were being riddled by a hailstorm of automatic weapons fire. The attack was coming from the north, and I felt the truck surge as Jim Braddock floored the accelerator, swinging the steering wheel to and fro to disrupt the aim of the attackers. I expected him to make a hard right turn, heading into the jungle to the south of the highway, away from the ambushers. To my horror, he swung the truck to the left, and we went careening into the jungle to the north, headed directly for the Vietcong.

"Goddamn it, Jim!" I roared through the rear window of the truck, screaming above the din. "What the hell are you doing? Turn this thing around." The bullets continued their Swiss-cheese maneuver on the truck. The radiator began spewing steam, and the left front tire blew out. Eric and I bounced about three feet above the bed as the truck hit a ditch full force and kept rolling. The army procured their vehicular shock absorbers from the lowest bidder, depending on the resiliency of the human body as the real shock absorber; hard on the body, but good on a budget process managed with mirrors.

"The best defense is a good offense," Jim hollered back, firing his .45 out the window with his left hand while he clumsily steered the truck with his right. In the shotgun seat Larry Anderson had opened up with his M-60. Eric and I did our best to carry this Rat Patrol parody to fruition by blasting away with our M-16s and randomly tossing fragmentation grenades in every direction.

It worked. Braddock's suicidal charge completely confused the ambushers. In his naïve way Jim had executed the tactical maneuver known as the penetration, concurrently demonstrating that this maneuver is intuitive to the male of the species. We broke through the VC ambush, continuing our pell-mell plunge through the jungle, engine steaming and clanking. The enemy might have pursued us, but they would have had to have been wearing their cheetah shoes to catch us. They never got close. Our faithful and dying truck lumbered blindly through the jungle at forty miles per hour, blazing a new northbound trail as it went. Trees flying. Radiator steaming. Limping on three wheels.

Logic dictated that we wouldn't make it far before the engine seized. However, the motor was still steaming and chugging when we broke through a high stand of buffalo grass and found ourselves surrealistically suspended in midair as we plunged over the west bank of the Bong Sa River. For a moment frozen in time the truck struggled against the laws of gravity. Then it plummeted nose downward into a sandbar fifteen feet below.

The time-frozen moment had given everyone the opportunity to brace for the impact, a sudden stoppage that was cushioned by the soft sand. We sat there stunned—both from the crash and from the realization of being alive—as the rugged truck hissed its final throes. There were a few seconds of inactivity as we relaxed, exalting in our triumph over the deadly entrapment, adrenaline spent. Then simultaneously we moved back into action, realizing that we were still in a precarious situation: isolated in enemy territory, with potential pursuit not far behind us.

"Give me that PRC-25," I shouted to Anderson. He unstrapped it from the cab and tossed it down. Like us, it had miraculously escaped the encounter unscathed. I tuned in the troop's FM frequency, hoping to find one of our helicopters within range. I knew we were too far out to reach the troop, and they were the last people I wanted to talk to anyway. Our "rescue" had to be unofficial. Otherwise we would have to explain an illegally confiscated truck that now lay in ruins.

"Any aircraft, this is Blackhawk 12 on Fox Mike. Over." I waited. No response. I adjusted the squelch and repeated the call. Another pause. Then a weak reply that was barely decipherable against the background noise.

"Blackhawk 12, this is Blackhawk 34. Over."

The four of us exchanged glances, shared relief. A call sign in the thirty series also meant a Huey, which was just what the doctor ordered.

"Roger, Blackhawk 34. What's your location? Over."

"Three-four is just crossing Mang Yang Pass eastbound, heading for home port." The PRC-25 suddenly boomed clearly, signaling that Hawk 34 had cleared the pass. I readjusted the squelch, eliminating the background static.

"Roger, 34. Location understood. Can you pick up four passengers? We could use a ride back to the troop."

"Roger, 12. We're empty. Where are you?"

"We're about five miles north of you. On the river. Just follow the river until you get to a burning three-quarter-ton truck."

A pause.

"One-two, how'd you get a truck up there? There's no road."

"Let's just keep this off the record, 34. Ask me no questions, and I'll tell you no lies."

"Roger, 12."

Using our Bowie knives, we scraped the identification numbers from the truck's bumpers and then dropped a Willie Pete into the gas tank. Our faithful steed went to its final resting place accompanied by a huge fireball. A few minutes later the Huey picked us up—the crew displaying puzzled expressions but asking no questions—and we headed home, realizing that our adventure would have to remain a secret. The blackmail charged by the Huey crew for their silence was considerably less than the cost of a three-quarter-ton truck. After all, booze was cheap. The important thing was that I was once again a whole and complete person; the properly signed paper in my breast pocket attested to the fact that I was back on flying status.

The next day I saddled up my Loach and tried again, struggling nervously through my second scout mission. Eric had been right: It took a lot of willpower to fly over the trees again. Fortunately, the mission passed uneventfully, and my confidence in the aerodynamic properties of helicopters began to return.

Other missions followed, and I evolved into a scout pilot. I learned to read trail. I could track a VC through the jungle, virtually daring the enemy to shoot at me from ambush. As a wingman, most of my missions became relatively routine. It was usually the lead aircraft that carried the bull's-eye. I also learned to be especially careful with green enemy troops—NVA soldiers that had recently crossed the border into Vietnam—for they had not yet learned that they shouldn't shoot at the scouts (when they did, their world soon erupted). As they gained experience they learned better.

I had been flying wing for a couple of months when we got a mission that was truly out of the ordinary. It came amid a second confrontation with Captain John Graves, the Gun Platoon leader.

John Graves had somehow managed to acquire an electric skillet. The value of this utensil was inestimable, since it provided an escape from mess-hall chow or C-rations. Despite being afflicted with a somewhat stuffy personality, as indicated by my initial encounter with him, Captain Graves was a good officer and a good gunship pilot. But he did have two rather irksome quirks: He guarded his electric skillet with a passion, and he seemed to dislike me with an equal intensity. I don't know why he particularly disliked me. The initial saluting introduction didn't seem like a sufficient basis for forming a lifetime hatred. More than likely he just had me confused with someone else—someone from his childhood who'd tied him up and stuck him with straight pins.

While he protected the electric skillet with a religious fervor, Captain Graves was sufficiently kindhearted to allow the other pilots to use his skillet, with the proviso that it be thoroughly cleaned afterwards. And that meant cleaned to perfection. He had a detailed cleaning procedure that had to be followed step by step. No one was certain of the penalty for damaging or failing to clean the skillet, but we suspected that it would not be a pleasing experience.

One morning, having overslept, I was hurrying to the flight line, laden with gear, already late for departure. We were working an area southeast of An Khe that day, and Eric Masterson would be on my case for delaying the flight. I was already in a foul mood, having missed breakfast, and was not looking forward to Eric's chastisement. As I was rushing past Captain Graves's hooch he yelled at me and then came flying out of the door with his skillet in hand. Propelled by excessive force, the screen door banged fiercely against the wall of the hooch. He had obviously grabbed the skillet in haste because the cord and control unit were still attached. It was also obvious that someone had failed to clean the skillet. Dirty is not an adjective that would have adequately described the thing—pig-rolling filthy was more appropriate.

"Mr. Holley, why did you dirty my skillet?"

"I beg your pardon?" I responded, raising my eyebrows just a bit—but not enough to antagonize the obviously hysterical captain.

"Don't play dumb with me. Why did you dirty my skillet?"

"I haven't used your skillet, sir."

"Don't you know that the skillet is to be cleaned after it's used?"

"Yes, sir, I know that."

"Then why didn't you clean it?"

Pausing momentarily to contemplate his A = B therefore C = D logic, I attempted to point out the missing B-to-C connection. "Well, sir, I didn't clean it because I didn't use it."

"Aren't you a member of the Scout Platoon?"

"Yes, sir."

"Someone in the Scout Platoon used my skillet and didn't clean it."

"Well, when I get back from my mission I'll check around and see if I can find out who it was."

"Oh, no, you won't! Since you're a member of the Scout Platoon, and since they dirtied my skillet, you're going to clean it up right now," he said as he thrust the skillet at me.

I stared at him. "Sir, I quit pulling KP when I pinned on

warrant officer bars," I replied. "Besides, I'm already late for a mission."

"Mister, you didn't quit obeying direct orders. Now take this skillet and clean it. Right now! That's a direct order." Again he thrust the skillet at me.

By this time it was quite obvious that he was not going to listen to reason, and disobeying a direct order—even one as trivial as this—was serious business. I accepted the skillet while I pondered the situation. In addition to the KP issue, time was marching on, and an entire flight was waiting for me. Noticing a fifty-five-gallon fire barrel—filled to the brim with water—behind Captain Graves, I quickly sidestepped him and dropped the skillet into the barrel. Water sloshed over the sides as the skillet rapidly gurgled toward the bottom.

"Are you crazy?" the panic-stricken Graves screamed as he dived into the barrel to retrieve the electric skillet and its attached control unit.

"It was pretty dirty, sir. I thought I'd let it soak while I go fly my mission," I responded as I quickly headed for the flight line.

When I arrived at the revetments Eric chastised me as expected, although I no longer took his critiques very seriously. We'd been through too much together by this time, and our friendship had grown. I was almost as close to him now as his dog, GI. Besides, I was responsible for covering his butt in the AO. His chastisement had to be tempered by reality. By way of rebuttal I explained what had happened, attributing the entire delay to John Graves and relating the electric skillet episode. I omitted the part about oversleeping and already being late for the flight line when Graves had waylaid me. Eric seemed to enjoy the explanation—it was always enjoyable to have a strictly by-the-book RLO get his comeuppance—but cautioned me that I hadn't heard the last of John, particularly about the skillet.

As we departed the airfield Operations confirmed Eric's prediction: I was to report to the major when we returned. It occurred to me that Major Williams was a frequent user of Graves's skillet. I could be facing a kangaroo court. Technically, I figured I could beat the rap: I was still in the process of complying with Captain Graves's order to clean the skillet. As soon as it was through soaking—which should be by the time we returned—I fully intended to finish washing it. I'd pulled a lot of KP in my day, and I knew what it took to get pots and pans clean.

I fell in loosely on Eric's wing as we departed to the north. Once clear of the traffic pattern we swung southeast toward the AO, which lay some twenty-odd miles distant. The Loach was humming on all cylinders as I played "follow me" with Eric's Loach while he dipped in and out of the trees at a hundred knots. Over the previous couple of months I'd gained a lot of proficiency in the little bird. Like Eric, I could now make it do things that the designers at Hughes had never intended. The radios were constantly blaring with meaningless chatter, although my radio seemed to be fading in and out occasionally. We weren't very good at communications security. But then, we didn't really have to be. We were cavalry and therefore invincible. Normal security procedures were for mortal soldiers.

Arriving in the AO, I picked up my standard left-hand orbits around Eric's Loach. By this time I could pretty much have performed this routine blindfolded. It had become second nature. For once we got a break on the terrain: rolling hills and single-layer canopy. This was in marked contrast to the triple-layer canopy, mountains, and cliffs we usually worked in. With a single-layer canopy the downwash from the Loaches' rotors could be used to spread the foliage, giving us a clear view beneath the trees. This allowed us to function more as true scouts, rather than as bait.

After a half hour of scouting, during which my radios continued to function intermittently, Eric spotted three cube-shaped huts—about ten feet long on each dimension—camouflaged beneath the canopy. While Eric inspected the apparently deserted storage huts I moved down slope, following an obscure trail that I hoped would lead to the caretakers of the huts. Shortly thereafter I uncovered a barracks-style shanty hidden beneath the trees and built on short stilts. I reported the discovery to Eric, although it took several transmissions before he acknowledged comprehension. Mostly he just kept shouting, "What? Say again."

My radio problems seemed to be getting worse. I tried the UHF and got the same results. I didn't like scouting when communications were poor, but I didn't have much choice at the moment. We had to pursue our findings while the trail was hot.

There were no signs of life around the "barracks" I'd discovered, but the surrounding ground showed signs of use, like the Ho Chi Minh sandal prints around the porch. I flew in a slow circle around the thatch structure, inspecting it from all angles. As nearly as I could determine, there was only one door—poor planning on the part of the architect, but the VC didn't strictly enforce fire ordinances. There might have been a trapdoor in the floor, but I didn't think so. Charlie'd never expected us to find this building. And we wouldn't have if Eric hadn't stumbled on to the storage huts up the slope.

There was a good possibility that we'd trapped Charlie inside the building. If so, it was time to flush him out. Eric had joined me by this time, although our radio communications were nil, and had taken up a firing position to the east, covering the lone door to the hooch. I dropped a Willie Pete grenade on the thatch roof and then took up a firing position to the west, also covering the door. If Charlie came out, we'd have him in a cross fire.

A few seconds later the Willie Pete burst, showering the building with flaming phosphorous. About a minute later the entire hooch was ablaze, smoke billowing fiercely above the trees. Very quickly thereafter three black-pajama-clad VC came barreling out the door, coughing and rubbing their eyes, firing their AKs blindly. Eric's door gunner and my door gunner simultaneously opened up with their M-60s, ripping the three soldiers apart. We held our positions until the flaming hooch collapsed, no more VC emerging.

I fell in on Eric's wing as we moved back up the hill to the storage huts. I noticed that my electrical instruments were beginning to act erratically, moving gradually toward zero indications. I was obviously operating on battery power, which was being drained, rather than the generator. That's why the radio transmissions had been breaking up earlier, eventually fading away altogether. Now the instruments were going. I vaguely wondered how long the engine could continue to run operating only on battery power. While this was relatively benign terrain, it was not a good place for an autorotation, particularly from the dead man's zone. (As Joe Watkins would soon point out to me, a turbine engine does not depend on electricity to keep running. Apparently, I missed that point during flight school.)

I tried to get Eric's attention, motioning frantically, but he was intent on using his rotor downwash to blow the roof off one of the storage huts. Eventually he was successful, the roof giving up the struggle amid a barrage of flying straw. I was hoping that the huts would contain a weapons cache, but my hopes were immediately dashed. They were stuffed with newly harvested marijuana . . . curing. We began dropping Willie Petes on the three-thousand-cubic-foot stash. Even with the burning phosphorous the fire was slow to start. But once ignited it burned steadily. I watched a tear stream slowly down my gunner's cheek as the hallucinogenic smoke began rising in earnest from the three smoldering huts.

With the fires going strongly I finally got Eric's attention, and we headed for An Khe. By now it was time to refuel and have some lunch anyway. It had been a good morning. The Blues would be sent in to mop up the area, but not until Operations allowed enough time for the marijuana to burn completely. Fortunately, my Loach cooperated despite its deteriorating electrical condition, and I made it back to An Khe without needing to perform the anticipated-through-ignorance autorotation.

After lunch we returned to the AO, continuing to search for other treasures. We found only boredom. But events were taking place north of An Khe that would end up producing an exciting afternoon for us.

The village of Quan Song lay nestled in peaceful silence near the Bong Sa River. It was a small village with perhaps five hundred inhabitants. Twenty miles to the south lay the city of An Khe. A few of the villagers had visited the city on occasional trading trips, but most had never ventured beyond the confines of the few acres of jungle and paddies that defined their homeland.

Life was simple. The villagers were content. The paddies

provided their rice, and the river provided their fish. Nature provided the sun and rain to make the rice grow. They provided the labor to plant the seed and harvest the fruits of their efforts. Their communal way of life provided a harmonious existence. Internal squabbles were few, ambition and petty rivalries being virtually nonexistent. The village chief, Dhon So, was the ultimate authority, but in truth, authority was seldom needed. Mostly his duties consisted of ceremonial functions.

All was not idyllic, of course. There was a war going on. For the most part the villagers ignored the war, violence not being part of their nature, and they had little understanding of political ideology. Unfortunately, the war did not always ignore them. Most of the young men were gone, conscripted into whichever army happened to lay claim to them. Some had gone north; some had gone south. Few ever returned. The villagers did their best to hide the young men, to protect the village's heritage, but they were seldom successful.

And there were the forays by the Vietcong. Usually they sought food . . . and women. The villagers' stores of rice were frequently depleted. And the women would weep for many days. But even this the villagers had learned to accept. They did not understand, but they accepted. Occasionally the raids also brought torture and death—usually for the village chief, sometimes for his entire family. Dhon So was the third chief to rule the village that year.

Not all of the hardships that afflicted the village were caused by the war, however. For many years the villagers had maintained a peaceful coexistence with a tiger whose territory overlapped their meager acreage. They called the tiger Toc B'Long (Striped Prince). He tolerated this territorial sharing because on those occasions when natural game was scarce, their domestic animals provided a quick and easy meal. The villagers tolerated Toc B'Long because they had no choice. They were peaceful farmers, not hunters. Their primitive weapons and amateurish hunting skills could not have defeated his five hundred pounds of violent muscle artfully encased in gold, white, and black.

Very few of the villagers had actually seen Toc B'Long, even though he had been around for many, many years.

They had heard him. They frequently sensed his presence. They had seen his tracks. They had seen remnants of his kills. But he was wary of the two-legged creatures and their constant noise, and he maintained a phantomlike relationship with them. At least he had until recently.

Toc B'Long ended the lengthy quasi-symbiotic relationship with the villagers by killing and eating Dhon So's youngest daughter. Dhon So knew that other members of his village would soon meet a similar fate unless something was done quickly. Once a tiger turned man-eater it continued the practice. The tiger had to be killed before it struck again. Yet the villagers did not have the skills or the weapons to track down Toc B'Long and kill him. The grieving chief sent a messenger to the American army at An Khe requesting help.

I was tired. And hot. And hungry. I was completing my umpteenth orbit around Eric's Loach. It had been a long, boring afternoon. In retrospect, even the earlier electrical failure and the encounter with the VC didn't seem all that stimulating. I was getting to the point where it took AK-47 bullets hitting my Loach to get me excited. The VC that morning hadn't even come close. There was a time when simply being aloft in a helicopter had been an exciting event. This was the type of afternoon that caused one to look forward longingly to Miller time. Although I was not eagerly anticipating the inevitable electric-skillet confrontation with Major Williams and Captain Graves. Another half hour or so and we would be calling it quits. No more bad guys today. Then the call came from the C & C ship, postponing Miller time.

"This is Hawk 36. Our mission has been diverted. We're taking the scouts to hunt for a pussycat. Some locals have a man-eating tiger terrorizing their village. Head north, heading 330. It's the village of Quan Song on the Bong Sa."

I monitored Eric's "Roger, Hawk 34" as I pulled the torque near redline and moved in on the tail of the lead Loach. I eased off on the power as the airspeed hit one hundred knots. Treetops brushed the skids as our Loaches sped northward.

"Say, Lead, you got any idea about how to hunt a tiger?" I spoke over the FM frequency that was reserved for the scouts.

"Sure," Eric responded. "You stake out a goat, and when the tiger comes for it you shoot him. Didn't you ever watch "Jungle Jim" when you were a kid?"

"Good strategy. I didn't know you carried a goat as part of your basic load."

"All theories have flaws." Eric paused momentarily and then continued, referring to his door gunner, who was not known among the scouts as a mental giant. "But I do have Jeffrey."

"You wouldn't stake out Jeffrey?"

My query was greeted by silence. Finally I repeated myself. "I said, 'You wouldn't stake out Jeffrey?' "

"I heard you the first time. I'm trying to decide if it would work."

"You can't stake him out. What if the tiger got him?"

"Oh, I wasn't worried about that. I was just wondering if the tiger would want him.

"I think I'll give him the old tiger-stakeout IQ test," Eric said, flipping Jeffrey's FM receiver switch on so I could monitor the "test."

"Jeffrey." No response. "Jeffrey," he repeated.

Jeffrey suddenly came to life, "Yo. You called, Boss."

"Yes, Jeffrey. I called. I have a question for you."

"Hey, man. You got questions, I got answers. Fire away."

"Now this is a serious question, Jeffrey. Your entire future could depend on your answer. So I want you to take your time and think very carefully before you answer. Okay?"

"Sure, Boss. No problem."

"I want you to imagine that you're in this situation. You're tied to a tree in the middle of a clearing in the jungle, and the only weapon you have is a knife. In the distance you can hear a tiger roaring. As you listen you can tell that the tiger is moving closer. What do you do?"

"Whoa! That is a toughy. Let me think a minute."

Silence hung heavily in the air as Jeffrey contemplated this perplexing dilemma. Eric and I both maintained radio silence, not wishing to interrupt his ratiocinations. Finally Jeffrey broke the lingering silence. "Say, Boss, am I allowed to ask questions?"

"You're allowed one question, Jeffrey," Eric responded patiently.

"Okay. Well, how am I tied? I mean, am I trussed up real good or what?"

"There's a rope that's tied around one of your ankles and then tied to the tree. Like a leash."

Again silence ensued. After two minutes Eric turned off Jeffrey's FM receiver switch and spoke to me. "He flunked. I'll have to think of something else."

By this time our Loaches had intersected the Bong Sa River, and we began following its course upstream. Occasionally shots could be heard from the riverbanks as we raced past, but we paid them no heed. We rounded a bend in the river, and the village of Quan Song came quickly into view. Just as quickly it was behind us.

"Lead, you got any idea where to start looking for this tiger?"

"Yeah. We'll start at the elephant grass near the river. That's where he's supposed to have been hanging out."

Arriving at the elephant grass area, we began a standard search pattern, zigzagging back and forth through the tall grass, moving between the river and the overhanging cliffs. After about fifteen minutes our efforts were rewarded. Eric was the first to spot the man-eater. Then we all got a look at the majestic creature.

"There he is!" Eric bellowed over the radio, urging his Loach toward the tiger and kicking right pedal to give his gunner, Jeffrey, a better shot. The tiger, who had been napping peacefully near the river, was startled into panicked action by our approach and began racing through the elephant grass, heading for the rocky high ground above the river. Eric knew we'd never get him if he reached the rocks. There was too much cover, too many places to hide. In the wing Loach I swung a wider orbit, getting my ship in position for a shot.

In the lead aircraft Jeffrey tracked the tiger through the M-60's sight and then pressed the trigger. The M-60 bucked once, then fell silent, a round jammed in the chamber.

Meanwhile the tiger continued its race against death. There was no time to clear the weapon.

"Gun's jammed," Eric shouted over the radio, breaking left to provide a clearer shot for my Loach. My gunner, Dave Gomez, opened up. I had a quick view of the bullets erupting around the tiger. Then it disappeared back into the elephant grass, and we all lost sight of it.

"Did you get it?" Eric queried.

"Couldn't tell for sure. We only got off one burst before we lost it in the grass," I responded.

"Okay. Let's go back into a search pattern."

"Roger," I replied as I picked up a standard left orbit around the lead Loach. I continued the orbit for five minutes, becoming more and more puzzled as Eric led the search away from the rocks and zigzagged through the grass, gradually moving toward the river. Finally I could no longer maintain my silence.

"Say, Lead, what are you doing?"

"I'm looking for that damn tiger," Eric replied in an exasperated tone. He knew there would be hell to pay if we didn't get the tiger now. We might even have wounded it, making the villagers' situation worse.

"Want some advice?"

"I'm always interested in your pearls of wisdom."

"Well—and please keep in mind that I'm no professional tiger hunter—I think we should be going in the other direction."

"Why should we go the other way?"

"Because that's the way the tiger went. I think we're more likely to find him if we look where he is."

"Impeccable logic. Why in hell didn't you say something sooner?"

"I thought you knew what you were doing. You sounded so authoritative when you said 'Let's go back into a standard search pattern.' I said to myself, now there's a leader—a man I would follow straight to hell. Of course, with your sense of direction, I suppose we'd end up in heaven."

"Okay, wiseass. I get the picture. You lead, I'll wing."

"Roger," I responded as I moved my Loach back to where we had shot at the tiger. As the downwash from the rotor blades spread the tall blades of grass beneath us we were able to make out dark stains on the ground.

"We've got a blood trail," I announced as I began following the trail to the east. After a few minutes we reached a shallow creek, which flowed through a rugged crevasse in the earth's surface. Its steep banks were overgrown with thick vegetation. Moving along the creek, we soon spotted the tiger. It was lying on a sandbar near the middle of the narrow stream, its head partially resting in the water. Dark pools of blood spread on the sand beneath the tiger.

"Bingo!" I exclaimed. "He's down. Looks dead from here. I'm going to land above the creek and let Dave go down and get him. You cover from the air."

"Roger. You tell Dave to be careful."

I maneuvered the Loach to a barely usable landing space near the top of the creek's bank. The rotor blades clipped leaves from the low-hanging branches as I cautiously let the helicopter settle against the sloping ground. After satisfying myself that the Loach wouldn't topple over I gave Dave his instructions.

"Dave, go down and bring the tiger up and throw him in the back."

Dave Gomez looked at me with a puzzled expression. However, he was not in the habit of questioning officers. And I did have a reasonably good reputation as a scout pilot, at least up to this mission. No doubt he decided that I must know what I was talking about.

As Dave began unbuckling his seat belt I had an afterthought. I recalled reading a comic book when I was a kid in which a cowboy shot a cougar and then tied the carcass to the saddle of his horse. After riding for about five miles the cougar suddenly came back to life; it had only been unconscious. I had a premonition of the tiger coming back to life in the back of our Loach. That could cause some serious problems.

"Wait a second," I said as I pulled out my pistol and handed it to Dave. "First thing you do is shoot him in the head a couple of times. Even if he looks dead as a doornail, you shoot him anyway." There would be no danger of the tiger coming back to life after getting a couple of my special bullets in his head.

"Okay," Dave replied as he took the pistol and then disappeared into the undergrowth.

I waited nervously in the helicopter. And waited. And waited. Still there were no shots from the creek bed. I impatiently watched the clock on the instrument panel as its hands crawled around the dial. Five minutes passed. Then ten. Goddamn, I thought, I give him a simple set of instructions, and somehow he's managed to screw it up. If he brings that tiger back without shooting it first, I swear I'll court-martial him.

After another five minutes the foliage near the creek bank began to stir, followed by the emergence of Dave, pushing his way out through the leaves and branches to struggle back to the Loach. He had a fierce expression on his face, and his flight suit was soaked with sweat.

Without getting into the helicopter Dave reached in and plugged his helmet into the intercom. In a voice struggling for control he shouted at me, "I got two things to say to you, Mr. Holley. Number one, I ain't man enough to handle five hundred pounds of pussy by myself. I realize that may come as a shock to you. I hate to admit it myself. But it's the truth."

Tossing my pistol back to me, Dave continued, "And number two, next time we go out to fight a war, load your goddamn pistol."

While I had been awaiting Dave's return Eric had reported our situation to Operations. The major had been ecstatic. I naïvely thought his enthusiasm was directed at our success, having thwarted a real and terrifying danger to the Vietnamese peasants. In two hours we had done more for "winning the hearts and minds of the people" than all of the G-5 operations put together. I was wrong. His enthusiasm was otherwise motivated.

Soon a Huey arrived with four strong pallbearers, and they loaded up the pussycat. At the direction of the major the scouts were diverted to another "urgent" mission. By the time we got back to base the tiger had been skinned, and the hide had been shipped off to Alabama, where it would become a parlor rug for the major. The only real advantage to his euphoria regarding the tiger was that in the excitement, he forgot about Captain Graves's electric skillet. I'd dodged another bullet.

As a token of his appreciation the major presented Eric and me with a tiger tooth. Not one each. A tooth, singular. To be shared between us through perpetuity. We were virtually overcome with gratitude. We discussed various possibilities about how we would go about this tooth-sharing business, finally concluding that the matter was too complicated. We decided to forget the sharing and just flip a coin; winner would get the tooth. I flipped, Eric called, Eric won. I suggested that to make it a truly fair competition we should go for best two out of three. Eric declined, stating that the only way I would get the tiger's tooth now was over his dead body. He bought a gold chain at the PX, on which he mounted the tooth, and he displayed it as a permanent trophy around his neck. I suspected his motive for doing this was more to aggravate me than to adorn himself with jewelry.

Although I was disappointed about the lack of a trophy, bagging the tiger was an exciting memory of my tenure as a scout wingman. Eventually I would move up to the lead position, and eliminating the man-eater would become relatively unexciting; tigers don't shoot back. There were always those nasty statistics to be considered: Ninety percent of the time Charlie aimed for the lead Loach. My promotion to scout lead did not come about in the usual manner, however. Of course, with Major Williams, things seldom occurred in the expected manner.

John Larkin seemed more upset about the major cheating Eric and me out of our tiger trophy than we were. He brooded about it for several days and then announced his brilliant plan for killing two birds with one stone: avenging the tiger trophy and solving the problem of Eric's dog, GI. By this time even a disconsolate Eric had reached the conclusion that GI had to go. Our olfactory systems just couldn't take it any longer. However, this presented a problem. We all liked GI and wanted him to have a continuing humane existence. But once GI let forth with his infamous exhaust system, any potential new owner would probably insist on immediately returning him to Eric or giving him to the Vietnamese for supper.

In Delta Troop, when you thought of gas, two things came immediately to mind: GI and Major Williams. This was the cornerstone of John's idea, a match made in heaven. However, to avoid GI being returned when the major discovered GI's malady, the transfer of ownership had to be done in such a way that the major would never consider giving GI back. This was the more brilliant part of John's plan. We would hold an awards ceremony and present GI to the major as a token of our appreciation for the outstanding leadership he had provided to the troop. We would also tell him that Gaseous Ignaseous was so named in honor of the major's theories on using gas in guerrilla warfare.

The subsequent ceremony was conducted in a manner befitting the finest traditions of the military. The major's acceptance speech was quite emotional, emphasizing that we were the finest group of pilots he'd ever had the privilege of leading. He did not mention that we were the only group of pilots he'd ever had the privilege of leading. At one point the speech was slightly disrupted by GI choosing an opportune moment for an extreme passage of wind, to which the major responded in a commanding manner, "Calm yourself, Ignaseous." Fortunately, the ceremony ended prior to another outburst.

From that moment forward GI and the major were inseparable. This created something of an administrative bottleneck within the troop, since the first sergeant and his clerks would periodically have to perform an immediate evacuation of the Orderly Room. The amazing thing was that Major Williams never gave any indication that he was aware of GI's affliction.

Once I attended a conference in the major's office at which GI was comfortably curled at his master's feet. Within minutes everyone in the office, with the exception of the major, was struggling for air and had tears streaming down his face. The major never gave any indication that anything was amiss. This in itself seemed to be quite a mystery. No normal human was capable of deliberately ignoring the chemical onslaught to which we were being subjected. Later I mentioned this to Doc Post, my roommate, and he cleared up the mystery: Major Williams had a dysfunctional olfactory system; he had no sense of smell. Doc had discovered it while giving him his flight physical.

We had little time to celebrate our dog revenge. The G-2 fellows, via their uncanny abilities to read tea leaves and crystal balls, had determined that increased enemy traffic was taking place across the Cambodian border, near Ban Me Thuot. Delta Troop was sent to work the area. We had also gotten a brand-new Loach fresh from the docks at Qui Nhon, and it had an unpleasant surprise in store for me.

11

■ ■ ■ ■ ■ ■ ■ ■ ■ ■ ■ ■ ■ ■

Team Leader

IT WAS THE THIRD DAY OF THE MISSION. I DEARLY LOVED C-rations, but after three days they could begin to wear you down. The whole troop hadn't come to Ban Me Thout. We were operating teams in three-day shifts. Our team would be returning to An Khe that night, and a replacement team would arrive the next morning. The major, of course, came and went as he pleased. Dissatisfied with our lack of success thus far, he had arrived earlier in the day to personally provide our C & C. His Huey was loaded to the hilt with cases of gas. The NVA were obviously unaware of the foe on their trail, else they would have raised their white flags and the war would have ended.

We were quartered at an isolated field airstrip located a couple of miles from the thriving metropolis of Ban Me Thout. "Quartered" didn't really mean we had accommodations. The Holiday Inn was booked. The only bright spot in our little camping trip was the absence of rain. Monsoon season hadn't yet arrived, and we had our helicopters to sleep in . . . or under. But you had to be careful about the under part because of unfriendly creatures of the night. Most people only tried sleeping under the helicopters once. This was when you envied the Huey crews. It was tough to stretch out in a Loach or Cobra. Once, after spending the night in a Loach, one of our pilots had to be shipped to Japan for chiropractic treatment.

After three days in the field under such primitive conditions everyone became irritable. The lack of food, sanitation facilities, and sleep compounded themselves. The most common expression became "Fuck you." This, of course, was vehemently uttered by a wild- and bleary-eyed creature with a three-day growth of beard who was in possession of a variety of loaded weapons.

Perhaps the worst part of a three-day outing was the smell. This was particularly acute within the confines of a helicopter, even with the doors off. Right Guard showers could only do so much. The army had, of course, provided us with a portable field shower. It was very impressive— four heads. They should also have provided water to go with it.

I finished choking down my breakfast of C-ration beef and potatoes and began preflighting my new Loach in preparation for the day's activities. It was doubly new. My regular Loach had developed an oil-pressure problem the evening before, and Maintenance had flown this one in as a replacement during the night. It had come to us fresh from the shipping docks at Qui Nhon, shiny as a new dime. It wouldn't be that way for long. The cavalry was tough on its equipment. Poor little Loach.

Eric Masterson joined me as I finished the preflight. "Everything okay with the new Loach?"

"Seems okay. But it's got an extra switch in the cockpit."

"What kind of extra switch?"

"I'll show you," I responded. I took Eric to the cockpit and pointed out the mystery toggle switch, which was labeled FUEL PUMP.

"Looks like they've added an electric fuel pump," Eric observed brilliantly.

"Yeah. Do you think I'm supposed to fly with it on or off?"

"On, I guess. Why would they put it in if they didn't want you to use it?"

"Okay. Your guess is as good as mine." That might have

been true. If it were, subsequent events would demonstrate that we were both poor guessers.

"Where's the AO today?" I asked Eric.

"About twenty minutes away. Right on the border . . . Duc Lop. G-2's noise detectors were real active last night."

"That doesn't give the Cobras much time-on-station."

The Cobras were the limiting factor in our time-on-station. After they were loaded to the gills with ammunition they could only carry a half load of fuel. This limited our missions to about an hour and a half. This also resulted in our bladders becoming conditioned to operate at hour and a half intervals.

"*Xinh loi,*" Eric responded with a shrug of his shoulders. "Let's saddle up. The major's running the show today, and we wouldn't want to keep him waiting."

The flight to the AO was uneventful, although this was the part I always liked best. Two Loaches zipping through the trees at a hundred knots; two Cobras in loose trail at fifteen hundred feet; and a C & C Huey at twenty-five hundred feet, struggling to keep up with us. The Huey provided navigation instructions for the flight. Frequently those instructions had the Cobras and Loaches on a circling wild goose chase to keep them from running off and leaving the Huey.

We began performing a routine search of the AO using a zigzag pattern from east to west to east, gradually shifting from the northern part of the AO to the southern part. Back and forth. Dull. Boring. I noticed that the needle on my fuel gauge seemed to be dropping abnormally fast. I decided to keep a close eye on it.

After about fifteen minutes of zigzagging my door gunner spotted movement near the wooded area to our right. The terrain we were working was made up of heavily forested areas surrounding a lot of small clearings. I called Eric on the radio and had him fall in on my wing while I checked out the movement. It turned out to be a huge bull elephant, all by himself. This was suspicious. The NVA and VC used elephants as pack animals. A lone elephant suggested that it was being used for this purpose. I flew closer, trying to determine if the animal had any pack strap markings. The elephant looked up at me with apparent curiosity, then continued to graze. I did not have a lot of experience with elephants, but this did not seem to be the behavior one would expect from a wild creature.

Eric and I decided to turn the problem over to the major. "Blackhawk 6, this is Blackhawk 12. Over," I called over the radio.

The major immediately responded, "This is 6. Over."

"Roger, 6. We've got a single elephant down here. Over."

"Roger, 12. Understand a single elephant. Is it pink? Over."

"We can't tell for sure. It seems tame, but we can't be certain about pack strap markings. Over."

"Understood. Stand by for instructions. Out."

While we awaited the major's decision Eric and I decided to climb higher, searching the surrounding forests for an elephant herd. Perhaps our elephant was not a pack animal but had simply strayed from the group. Finally we spotted a herd meandering through the forest about a half mile away. We flew closer to investigate. The herd paid no attention to us. Nor did our lone elephant seem to fit with this group. There was a lot of forest between them.

"Blackhawk 12, this is 6. Over."

"Roger, 6."

"We've received instructions from Squadron to shoot the elephant. Over."

"Onc-two, wilco."

I returned to the lone elephant and positioned my door gunner for a good shot. The elephant looked up at me. Large, innocent brown eyes. I wished he wouldn't look at me. I called Eric on our secret Fox Mike frequency.

"Eric, you really think we should kill it?"

"No choice, Wingman. Do it."

"Roger," I said, and I gave the go-ahead to my gunner. The sudden burst of the M-60 split the air. I flinched with the impact of the bullets as the elephant slowly began to crumple, first to its knees, then to its side.

"Stampede!" Eric cried out over the radio.

The distant elephant herd had begun stampeding through the forest, leaving a huge swath of crushed timber in its wake. Amazingly, it was not stampeding away from us but was racing pell-mell for the clearing where our dying elephant lay on its side, the trunk occasionally and weakly sweeping back and forth.

At the edge of the clearing the herd suddenly stopped, clinging to the shelter of the trees. The lead elephant came forward slowly, appearing to survey the situation, and moved cautiously to his downed comrade. They spent a few seconds together "conversing," with the lead elephant frequently glancing up at my helicopter. Then the leader returned to the herd, stopping briefly at the edge of the clearing to give me a final dirty look, and stampeded the herd back through the forest, away from the danger.

With the surreal elephant episode still haunting me I fell in on Eric's wing as we resumed our search pattern. I was still concerned about the rate at which the needle in my fuel gauge was falling. I decided to time the drop to determine how much time on station I had remaining. Five minutes later I had the answer: at my present rate of fuel consumption the engine would flame out in twenty-five minutes. Our AO was twenty minutes away from the refueling point at Ban Me Thuot. That was obviously cutting it close, even if I left immediately. This was very peculiar. We hadn't been gone long enough for me to be so low on fuel. I called Eric on the secret frequency to check on his fuel status.

"Blackhawk 14, what's your fuel status? Over."

"This is 14. I'm a little under a half tank."

"Roger. I'm down to twenty-five minutes. Something peculiar here. We're going to have to head back."

"Understand, 12. But you make the call to the major."

"Thanks a lot, 14." I switched to the UHF radio and called the C & C. "Blackhawk 6, this is Blackhawk 12. Over."

"This is 6. Over."

"Roger, 6. I've got a fuel consumption problem. I'm going to have to head back for refueling. Over."

"This is 6. That's not possible, 12. You've got plenty of fuel left."

"No, sir, I don't. I'm down to twenty-five minutes."

"Standby, 12."

I monitored the radio as the major called the Cobras to check on their fuel status. As expected, they still had a half hour left on station.

"Twelve, this is 6. Over."

"Roger, 6."

"Everybody else has plenty of fuel. Over."

"Sir, I can't help that. I'm not flying everyone else's helicopter. This one is running out of gas . . . quickly. Over."

"You sure you topped it off?"

"I'm sure. It was to the brim when we left Ban Me Thuot."

"This is very peculiar, 12."

"Yes, sir."

"All right. We'll go back early. But I need five minutes more."

"Sir, that's cutting it very close. We're twenty minutes from Ban Me Thuot. Over."

"Five minutes, 12. Out." The major terminated the discussion with finality.

For the next five minutes I occupied myself more with monitoring the fuel gauge than with scouting. Finally the hands on the clock passed the magic numbers. But still there was no call from the major. When the twenty-minute fuel light illuminated I decided to initiate the call myself.

"Six, this is 12. Over."

"Roger, 12."

"Sir, it's been more than five minutes."

"Another five minutes, 12. We're liable to find something any minute."

Or any year, I thought. "Sir, my low-fuel light just came on. I really need to head back."

"I'll tell you when to leave, 12. Out."

My door gunner gave me a nervous look. I smiled at him encouragingly. We continued flying the search pattern, looking for the elusive enemy. The folks at G-2 must have been smoking something strange when they sent us to this AO. We had found no evidence that the enemy was using this part of Vietnam. Finally the major broke off the search, and we headed for Ban Me Thuot. If my fuel calculations were correct, I'd never make it. Eric fell in on my trail to escort me. I risked a scout nosebleed and climbed to two thousand feet. If the engine quit, I wanted plenty of altitude to play with.

Fifteen minutes later the fuel gauge was registering zero. My petrified door gunner was engaged in some sort of ritualistic, hysterical behavior in which he kept pointing to the fuel gauge and then crossing himself. Finally he pulled out a small magnet and held it against the glass on the fuel gauge, trying to urge the needle back toward the full side. It didn't seem to help. In the distance I could see Ban Me Thout, still five minutes away. A small clearing passed beneath the helicopter. It was the last potential safe landing area between me and the airfield. It was solid forest from there on. If the engine quit, it would mean crash landing in the trees. Another bout with the trees was not an appealing prospect.

I had a decision to make: take the risk that the fuel gauge was sufficiently inaccurate to allow me to cross the forest and make it to the airfield or set the helicopter down in the clearing and have some fuel flown out. The latter course of action could cause serious damage to my aviator reputation. Running out of gas was the number one taboo for a pilot.

I opted for embarrassment rather than potential disaster, lowering the collective to begin a descent and a 180° turn back to the clearing. A few seconds later the engine quit. I nervously guided the floating Loach to an autorotative landing in the small clearing. As we sat in the Loach waiting for the Huey to return with some fuel Eric provided covering fire. The fuel arrived quickly, and we were soon airborne again. The rest of the day's mission passed uneventfully, and a tired team headed for An Khe at sundown, our three days completed.

Back at An Khe that night we first attended to bodily needs—hot food and hot showers—and then I sought out Maintenance to inquire about the mysterious new electrical fuel pump. I finally located Joe Watkins, our maintenance officer, on the flight line, immersed in the task of tracking the rotor blades on a Cobra. Joe was about nine hundred years old, but he acted much older. And he didn't like me. I'd mowed some trees with a Charley Model once, and Joe had had to replace both main rotor blades. In Joe's mind, damaging a rotor blade was akin to child beating.

"Hello, Joe," I said cheerfully.

He responded with a dour look. I returned his non-smile. "What do you want?"

"I had a question for you about that new Loach . . . the one with the electric fuel pump."

"What about it?"

"Well, I ran out of gas in it today."

"Did you hurt the Loach?" he queried excitedly.

"No. The Loach is fine."

"With your piloting skill, that's amazing."

I chose to ignore the sarcastic comment. Joe had never flown a combat mission. Consequently, he couldn't understand why protecting the aircraft was not always our top priority. "Yeah . . . well . . . the point is that the fuel consumption rate was inordinately high."

"Did you turn the fuel pump off after you started the engine?"

"No. Why should I?"

"Because it's only to be used for priming the igniters during engine start. If you leave it on after that, you'll have a high fuel consumption and could run out of gas."

"How was I supposed to know that?"

"It's in the operator's manual."

"There wasn't an operator's manual in the Loach."

"I know. It's on my desk. I needed to read up on the new fuel pump. It'll be back in the Loach tomorrow."

I thanked Joe for his thoughtfulness and then headed for an evening of relaxation. Unbeknownst to me, it was not going to be a run-of-the-mill evening, nor was it going to be very relaxing.

We had a variety of recreational activities available to us. The most common nighttime entertainment was to watch a movie at the troop's theater and then play poker at the troop's Officers Club. This, of course, was accompanied by a lot of drinking. Booze was cheap in Vietnam, a little over a dollar a fifth for the good stuff. The cavalry tried to make the war profitable on a personal basis via alcohol consumption. The way we figured it, every time we drank a fifth of booze we made a profit of three or four dollars. If our tours of duty had been longer, we'd all have become millionaires.

Eric and I opted for one of those movie and poker nights. We strolled to the theater together, along with a fine bottle of Wild Turkey. We left for the theater early and sober but arrived late and somewhat less than sober. John Wayne had already destroyed half the Japanese army by the time we got to the theater. In the darkness we quietly found empty seats and settled back to see how the Duke would handle the other half of the opposing forces. The seats were not particularly comfortable—wooden benches mounted on tiers of concrete—but we had a good angle to the screen.

Three quarters of an hour and three quarters of a bottle later we began to have concern for the Duke's safety. The Japs had him pinned down, and they'd called in an air strike to finish him off. Things didn't look good for the home team. Wave after wave of enemy planes dived in, strafing and dropping bombs. The screen was virtually alive with fiery explosions. It was so realistic that the theater seemed to shake whenever a bomb went off.

"Damn good war scene," I whispered to Eric, although whispering was unnecessary. The exploding bombs were so loud that I could have yelled without disturbing the audience.

"About the best I've ever seen," he responded. "The screen even seems to be getting holes in it."

"Interesting. I wonder how they're getting the stereophonic effect with only one speaker. Must be a new recording technique."

Eric and I would have continued discussing the technical merits of the film, but we were rudely interrupted by the theater's lights being suddenly turned on, accompanied by yells of "Incoming! Incoming!" A panicked crowd began stampeding for all exits. Eric and I hit the floor, seeking protection behind the concrete tiers. Scout pilots had a higher panic threshold than most folks. At least when they were too drunk to run. Very quickly we had the theater to ourselves.

"Why do you think they all ran outside?" I asked Eric as the theater's walls continued to shake from the mortar attack.

"Beats me. It seems a lot safer in here than running around out in the open."

"Wonder how the Duke's doing."

"Can't tell. The lights are too bright."

We continued sipping our whiskey, awaiting the end of the attack and the return of the movie projectionist. Five minutes later the mortars stopped abruptly. We decided to conserve our energy by remaining on the floor until the rest of the people returned and got the movie going again, or until we ran out of Wild Turkey. A few seconds later the rear door of the theater stealthily swung open, and four black-pajama-clad VC quickly entered and moved up the aisle toward the projector. From our hidden vantage point we saw them begin to dismantle the projector.

"I'll be damned," Eric whispered. "Those little fuckers mortared us just so they could come in here and steal our projector. The nerve of them. That's damned discourteous."

"What do you think we should do?"

"Are you kidding? We've got VC in the open. We go hot."

"Uh . . . Eric. There's twice as many of them."

"Yeah, but they're small."

"Their guns aren't. You want to take on four AK-47s with our .38 pistols?"

"Reasonable odds. Besides, we've got the element of surprise on our side. You ready?"

Oh, shit, I thought, quietly cocking my .38. I hoped my special bullets were as good as the Special Forces claimed. Before the action could commence, another thought occurred to me: "Say, Eric. Do you think we'd be doing this if we were sober?"

He looked at me, perplexed. "Now how the hell can I tell you that when I'm obviously drunk? Ask me again tomorrow."

"If there is a tomorrow."

"Must you always be such a pessimist? Let's go. You take the two on the right; I'll take the two on the left. This'll work out just fine. Trust me."

Oh, Lord, I thought, why did he have to say that?

As Eric stood up to challenge the VC I remembered a

portion of my infantry training—one grenade will get you all—and moved to the right, putting distance between us.

"All right, you varmints. Stand easy," Eric drawled. It would have made Gary Cooper proud.

This produced a pregnant pause in the action. The reaction was coming. It was just a question of when and what. The four VC froze, taking in the situation, expressions of surprise changing to looks of fierce determination. Frankly, I didn't think they were as overwhelmed by us as Eric had expected them to be. They quickly answered both the when and the what by releasing their collective grip on the projector and going for their guns. Shit . . . shit . . . shit. Where was John Wayne when you really needed him?

I drew down on one of my targets, pulling off the first shot a split second ahead of Eric. I drilled the projector dead center. I knew right away that the Special Forces hadn't over-billed my bullets; the projector was finished . . . with one shot.

As we dived for the floor Eric kept yelling, "Not the projector, damn it. Shoot the VC." But in truth, his aim hadn't been any better than mine. And now AK-47 bullets were careening all over the place. We kept our heads down, clinging to the protection of the concrete tiers, occasionally risking a blind pistol shot back in the general vicinity of the enemy. The concrete provided good shielding from the VC's direct fire. Our biggest danger was getting hit by a ricochet. Or running out of ammunition. I only carried two bandoliers of spare bullets. I figured that eventually someone would be coming to see what all the shooting was about. After all, this was cavalry country, and the cavalry always came racing to the rescue, even when they were rescuing the cavalry.

"Eric," I bellowed over the hubbub, "I've got to tell you, this wasn't the best idea you've ever had."

The VC finally maneuvered their way back to the door from which they had entered—crouching, firing, moving. Escaping our entrapment, they vanished into the night as quickly as they had come. Silence descended on the theater.

Eric and I rose cautiously from our bulletproof firing positions. "How many do you think we got?" he asked.

* * *

We had moved into the second stage of entertainment, playing poker on the patio outside the troop's Officers Club. It was a beautiful night, full moon and soft, cooling breeze. Inside the club drunkenness prevailed, highlighted by the Dance of the Flaming Assholes. Outside the club drunkenness also prevailed, the Wild Turkey continuing to flow freely. The poker players included Eric and me, Dave Horton, John Larkin, a lieutenant from the Gun Platoon, and a newby—a Wobbly One named Butch Henderson. Six players made a good game, and newbies always provided fresh meat. The game was straight poker, nothing wild. Dave Horton was the current dealer. His choice of jacks to open, trips to win had built a huge pot.

"Open for a quarter," Eric said, starting the current round of betting.

Everyone matched the quarter until it got around to the newby. "Raise a quarter," he said.

I rechecked my cards, a pair of deuces and a pair of treys. They hadn't mysteriously changed their spots since the betting began. However, there was too much invested in the pot to back out now. That was the problem with trips to win. If no one had trips or better, the pot continued to build until there was a winner. If you dropped out along the way, you could remain a spectator for a long time. "Make it another one," I said, deciding to test the mettle of the newby. Besides, I had a feeling about this one. Sometimes you can just feel it when you're going to win, thereby ignoring rational approaches to the game.

Finally the pot was correct, and Dave said, "Cards?" Everyone took three except for me and the newby, who took one each. That meant he was drawing for a full house, straight, or flush. It also meant he didn't have trips—at least not yet. Unless, of course, he was a lot smarter than I figured, in which case he already had trips and held the fourth card as a decoy to build the pot. I didn't think so. Nor did I bother to check the card I had drawn. It wouldn't have made any difference in the way I was going to play the hand.

Eric checked, and the newby bet another quarter. I matched it and raised. This betting contest continued until we reached the three-raise limit, at which point I called. Everyone tossed in his cards—no trips—except the newby, who proudly displayed three aces. Butch was obviously smarter than I had figured; he'd held on to a decoy to build the pot. Still without looking at my cards I placed them face up on the table. The immediate reaction confirmed my feeling about the pot. Poor Butch. He literally turned white as he stared at the full house.

"Well, Butch," I said, "it's kinda like they say about the Dallas Cowboys: sometimes it's better to be lucky than good." I scraped in my winnings.

Eric began shuffling the cards to deal the next round when we were suddenly interrupted by incoming mortar rounds, our second attack of the evening. The VC must have been hacked off about the movie projector. They'd probably had their little hearts set on watching that John Wayne movie.

"Damn VC!" I shouted to the heavens as I scooped up my winnings and headed for the bunker, twenty meters away. "Just when I was on a winning streak."

"Shut up and get in the bunker," Eric said. "One win hardly constitutes a streak."

Instead of getting inside I dodged to one side to avoid getting trampled by a stampeding Joe Watkins, our maintenance officer, who came flying out of a nearby hooch clad only in underwear, combat boots, and a steel pot. Joe was deathly afraid of mortars, supposedly because he'd been hit by one on his first tour. As I dodged to the side he attempted to make the ninety-degree turn to go into the bunker but overshot and landed in the barbecue pit, half-cooked pieces of chicken and hot charcoal flying in all directions. Not being a single-trial learner, Joe had yet to miss the barbecue pit during a mortar attack. This would be his fourth or fifth purple heart.

Inside the dank bunker we took seats on the benches that lined each wall. Fortunately, the Wild Turkey had not been left behind. In the dim candlelight we took a head count.

"Where's Butch Henderson?" I asked. I'd begun to develop a fondness for the young fellow. He showed promise as a poker player.

Nobody responded.

"Did you see him, Eric?"

"Last I saw him, he was picking up his money. I thought he was right behind us." Eric passed the Wild Turkey over.

As usual, the attack lasted about a half hour and we straggled out to resume our interrupted festivities. I went by my hooch to check on my roommate, Doc Post, and then returned to the club.

"He's dead," Eric said as I walked up to the poker table.

"Who's dead?" I responded.

"The newby. Butch Henderson."

"How the hell could he be dead? He was just sitting right there with us. The mortars weren't even that close."

"Apparently he went back to his hooch to get his pistol."

"Why in hell would anybody run through a mortar attack to get a goddamn pistol? What the hell would you do with it anyway? The damn VC aren't going to attack while mortar rounds are coming in?"

"You're preaching to the choir. Who knows what goes through the mind of a newby?"

"Dumb. Just plain dumb. What a waste."

"Yeah, well, *xinh loi.*"

I shrugged. "You're right. *Xinh loi.*"

"You ready to continue the game?"

"Naw, this kinda puts a damper on it. Let's do some serious drinking."

"Good idea."

We headed inside.

A half hour later I was at the bar, continuing my elbow exercises with the Wild Turkey, when a hand tapped me politely on the shoulder. I turned around—or should I say wobbled around—to encounter Major Williams.

"Mr. Holley, may I speak to you privately, please?"

"Certainly, sir," I responded, although it came out more like "Shertainly, shir." At this point in the evening's festivities I claimed no responsibility for the accuracy of the articulation. I was only responsible for what I intended to say, interpretation being the responsibility of the hearer. I followed the major outside to the patio, where he selected an isolated bench to sit on.

"Sit down, please," he said, motioning me to sit near him on the bench. I sat down, my suspicions aroused by his fatherly demeanor. He was behaving out of character.

"Mr. Holley, I wanted to tell you that I was extremely impressed by your performance today."

Aha, I thought, so that's it. His ass would have been grass if I'd damaged the Loach. "You mean running out of gas, sir?" I asked innocently.

He seemed flustered. "Well . . . no . . . not exactly. That's part of it, of course. But not in any negative sense. I was speaking more generally. You demonstrated excellent judgment."

I wasn't sure where or when I'd demonstrated this excellent judgment. It seemed to me that excellent judgment would have been to ignore his order to remain on station, and return to Ban Me Thuot before I ran out of gas. But who was I to dispute his conclusion? If he wanted to believe that I had shown excellent judgment, then so be it. "Thank you, sir. I appreciate that."

"I also want you to know that you'll be flying lead scout from now on. I'll inform your platoon leader."

I wasn't sure if this was reward or punishment. Wing was much safer than lead. Maybe I could figure out a way to lead from the wing. "Yes, sir.That's a great privilege."

The major seemed pleased by my response, pausing to digest it. Then he continued, "Oh, one other thing . . ."

"Yes, sir?"

"I've decided to approve your application for a direct commission. I'll be forwarding the approved application to Squadron tomorrow."

I hated to burst his bubble—he appeared so thrilled with himself for bestowing all these "honors" on me—but it seemed necessary. "I've decided to withdraw my application, sir."

He seemed crestfallen. "But . . . but . . . why?" he sputtered.

"Well . . ." I struggled to express my decision. "Well, since our last discussion on the topic, a lot has happened to me. I've changed. Maybe it's maturity. I don't know. Right now I'm just not interested in the commission—not sure that I really should be a commissioned officer—and it wouldn't be fair to me or the army to go ahead with it."

"Oh, I see," he responded.

"Will that be all, sir?"

"Yes . . . I suppose."

I rose to leave.

"But Mr. Holley, if you change your mind, come and see me. I don't agree with your decision."

"I will, sir," I responded, and in deference to his uncharacteristic attitude I added an equally uncharacteristic "and thank you."

True to his word, the major moved me to the lead position. Two days later I flew the first of many missions as scout lead. I soon discovered that no matter how often I cleaned the windshield, I couldn't remove the indelible bull's-eye. However, we soon had a somewhat unscheduled break in the action: It was time for the holidays. But Christmas wasn't like the ones I'd experienced back in West Texas.

12

■ ■ ■ ■ ■ ■ ■ ■ ■ ■ ■ ■ ■ ■

Happy Holidays

THE SEASON TO BE JOLLY PASSED SLOWLY AND UNEVENT-
fully, at least with respect to the VC. A quasi-truce had
been in effect. Basically, it was an informal agreement: You
don't bother us for a week, and we won't bother you. Of
course, the Tet Offensive of the previous holiday season
was still fresh in everyone's mind, and we all wondered if
the North Vietnamese would provide a sequel. We chose
to ignore the possibility, enjoying the quasi-truce while we
could and letting the future worry about itself.

This strategy worked out well, and things progressed
smoothly . . . at least through the first day of the truce,
Christmas Eve. But Victor Charlie had nothing directly to
do with the problems that the quasi-truce produced. They
were entirely our own doing. Once again, Pogo was proved
right: we met the enemy, and he was us. Our Christmas
Eve party got a little out of hand. It probably would have
gone unnoticed in south Chicago, but we were in the midst
of a civilized combat zone. Although his patience seemed
to ebb as the evening progressed, the major was, in all
fairness, relatively broad-minded about the party, particularly since his hooch was adjacent to the troop Officers
Club and he'd toddled off to bed early to get a good night's
sleep.

As the party progressed the major, on several occasions, stormed into the club, admonishing us to hold down the noise. With each of these interruptions the warnings became progressively stronger. We finally got around to the last straw around one o'clock in the morning—Christmas morning, actually, although we weren't aware of it by this time.

That was when we decided a turkey shoot was in order. An expedition was dispatched to find a turkey for a prize, and the rest of us set up a firing range. Unfortunately, it was inside the club, against the rear wall. This provided about a fifty-foot range to the targets. One disadvantage of the improvised range was that the rear wall of the club also formed the side wall of the major's hooch. But we'd taken this into account in our calculations; our "range safety officer" assured us that he'd never once seen a .38-caliber bullet penetrate half-inch plywood from a distance of fifty feet. In retrospect, he should have been cross-examined more thoroughly. The turkey-finding expedition not having returned, we decided to proceed in their absence. An I.O.U. would suffice if a winner was declared prior to their return. We decided on a rapid-fire contest, six participants with six shots each per round.

The first six contestants lined up and began blasting away at the targets. Admittedly, this produced some noise. But I've heard more on a routine day at an artillery base . . . and we were celebrating. The next six contestants had no more than gotten their revolvers drawn when the major went roaring past the door screaming, "Incoming!" and dived into the mortar bunker. This produced a reaction remarkably similar to the effect of lightning striking a herd of milling longhorns. The stampeding herd landed as one in the bunker, but with sufficient presence of mind to include plenty of Wild Turkey and Jack Daniels in the chuck wagon.

When the major eventually figured out what had happened he retaliated by restricting us to our barracks for the remainder of the holidays. We thought it was mighty narrow-minded of him, particularly after he'd gone around yelling wolf like that.

The restriction to barracks proved to be the longest six

days of my life. Most of the other pilots at least had a roommate to help while away the hours. My roommate was the flight surgeon, Doc Post, and even the major couldn't restrict him. Doctors enjoyed a sort of diplomatic immunity, reporting through a separate chain of command. All I had for company was my ever-faithful Wild Turkey. I'd done some thumb-twiddling since joining the army, but that six days capped it.

By the time January 2 rolled around I was chomping at the bit, raring to get back in the saddle. The current and chronic personnel shortage in scout pilots assisted me in this regard. For the next three weeks I flew nearly every day, only occasionally taking a day off to rest. I seemed to have an irrational compulsion to make up the time lost during the holiday lull.

I developed a reputation for finding the bad guys, a reputation second only to Eric Masterson's. I also developed a reputation for coming back from these encounters relatively unscathed. A few bullet holes here and there, but nothing serious. Except to Joe Watkins, of course. I seemed to have developed a sixth sense for finding the enemy and then beating him to the punch, getting my Loaches out and rolling the Cobras in before Charlie went hot.

Reality didn't always square with the reputation, however. Like the day in late January when Major Williams convinced Division that the Cav could kick ass in An Khe Valley, a no-man's-land to the east. As was to be expected, gas formed the cornerstone of his plan. The division commander provided the major with four CH-47 Chinooks fully laden with canisters of gas. Delta Troop would locate the bad guys, and the Chinooks would gas them. A wonderful plan, to be sure.

"I've got a trail. Stick tight," I spoke over the FM to George Taylor, my wingman. George had flown wing on me before, and we worked well together. During my tenure as a scout lead I never did have the luxury of settling in on a regular wingman. It seemed we were always short-handed on scout pilots and we had to rotate the duty as best we could. Eric's transfer to the Slicks hadn't helped our personnel shortage problem either. But he'd paid his dues in scouts—five hundred hours or six months was the unwritten rule—and had opted for safer duty for the duration of his tour. I figured he was bored stiff.

I began cautiously following the elusive trail ever deeper into the jungle, farther and farther into the no-man's-land of An Khe Valley. Actually, no-man's-land was a misnomer; it was Charlie's land. The rugged, heavily forested mountains surrounding the valley had on several occasions proven themselves to be impenetrable by U. S. forces. At least the potential cost of penetration had been deemed excessive. Thereafter we ignored An Khe Valley, and its inhabitants ignored us. Now the major had us tinkering with Pandora's box.

The trail I was following began at the valley floor and edged its way up the mountainous wall that defined the northern border of the valley. Bloodhound style, I tenaciously followed the path as it snaked over higher toward the north. That sixth sense I'd developed began ringing my doorbell . . . urgently. I finally opened the door to see what was so important that I had to be interrupted in the middle of the chase.

The message was simple: It was too easy! The same thing had happened to the Blues the day Dave Horton had accidentally injected himself with the morphine. I'd followed this trail through dense jungle for over two miles and hadn't lost it once. I fancied myself to be a pretty good scout by this time, but no one's that good. I wasn't following this trail. It was following me.

"Hold your position," I radioed to George while I appraised the situation, making a 360° pedal turn. High ground on three sides, the only low ground back the way we'd come. We were getting pretty well boxed in. If this was a trap, the VC should be about ready to spring it. The important question was: Why? Why would the VC want to ambush the Loaches? We weren't up against naïve enemy soldiers, fresh across the border from North Vietnam. Such behavior was expected from green troops. But the occupants of An Khe Valley were seasoned veterans, and they wouldn't lure in Loaches without a reason.

In the C & C Huey the major was directing this operation personally, under the watchful eye of the division commander, who was observing gas warfare in action. I didn't like what I was feeling and decided to share my suspicions with the major. "Blackhawk 6, this is Blackhawk 12. Over."

"This is 6. Over."

"Roger, 6. I'm a little worried about this trail I've been following."

"Why's that, 12?"

"I think it's phony. Charlie's deliberately luring us deeper into the valley. I think we're walking into a trap."

"Nonsense, 12. Charlie's not stupid enough to deliberately tangle with the cavalry. And even if he did, we'd have him right where we want him."

It was easy to be macho from 2500 feet. At ten feet machismo is less compelling. I started to point out that his comment was somewhat lacking in logic, referencing the Blues' fiasco back in August, but he continued, thereby thwarting the opportunity. "Twelve, you get back on that trail and stick with it. We're going to flush old Charlie today!"

"Wilco. Out," I responded reluctantly. Switching to the FM, I told George to go Romeo. Romeo was an unauthorized, secret frequency that we used for private conversations. "George, I don't like it, but the Old Man says we've got to stick to this trail. You be on your toes and don't relax for a second."

"Wilco, 12," George replied from the wing.

Once more we began following the sucker trail, the hair on the back of my neck bristling. Fifteen minutes later I spotted the AK. It was luck, actually—a fleeting glint of sunlight off a blackened barrel nestled deep in the trees. Where there was one Charlie there would be more. Since Charlie didn't suspect he'd been spotted, I didn't react immediately. I set up the reaction. I intended to be an unappreciative guest of honor at Charlie's party.

"George, hold your position. When I yell *now*, I want you to throw a smoke grenade and then immediately vacate the area. Break right. We'll rendezvous to the east. You got all that? Over."

"This is 17. I copy. I take it you've spotted something."

"Roger. Stand by." Switching to the UHF, I called the lead Cobra. "Blackhawk 26, this is Hawk 12. Over."

"This is 26. Over."

"Roger, 26. Do you have my position pinpointed?"

"Roger, 12."

"In about five seconds I'm gong to be receiving fire. Please send some rockets. Over."

"Two-six is inbound."

I pointed out the target to my gunner, re-tuned to the FM, and shouted, *"Now."*

Simultaneously my gunner opened up with his M-60 and George Taylor's gunner dropped smoke. I suddenly realized how Mrs. O'Leary's cow must have felt when she tipped over that lantern. Who'd ever believe that such a small action could produce such a violent reaction? What ever happened to equal and opposite? We got the opposite, but there was no equal about it.

Every tree within fifty meters suddenly sprouted AKs that began spewing forth their messages of death. I was vaguely aware of the sounds of heavy-caliber machine guns opening up from farther along the cliffs. But these things are hard to sort out amid exploding Plexiglas. Fortunately, both George and I were already pulling max power for a right break when we lit the fuse. That was our saving grace. That coupled with ten-pound rockets hitting the trees almost instantaneously. Even so, George ended up with more than a dozen bullet holes in his Loach. I topped him with twenty-three, not counting the shrapnel holes from the Cobras' rockets. Sometimes the Cobras cut it a little thin.

George and I headed our wounded Loaches back to An Khe, our part of the mission complete. We'd found Charlie. Now someone else could worry about what to do with him. En route to An Khe we passed the four gas-laden Chinooks, outbound for the valley. Only one of them would return. Chinooks made nice, big targets for .51-caliber machine guns.

Later in the day Division inserted a battalion of infantry into the valley. It was quickly followed by another and another, until finally a full brigade was committed to the battle for the valley. Three days later Division had to make a decision: commit another brigade or close Pandora's box.

In an unusually wise decision they opted for the latter course of action, and the remnants of the brigade were withdrawn. The division commander attributed the successful operation to Major Williams's brilliant use of gas and rewarded him with a DFC, for valor above and beyond the call of duty.

For the next six weeks or so the scouting missions were relatively routine. I got the impression that Division was licking its wounds and was deliberately sending us to look for Charlie where he wasn't. If so, that strategy ended abruptly on a Monday in early March.

13

■ ■ ■ ■ ■ ■ ■ ■ ■ ■ ■ ■ ■ ■ ■

Mondays

FOR A MONDAY THE DAY STARTED OUT ALL RIGHT, WITH THE exception of the typically gloomy monsoon weather. During monsoon season we scheduled our flying to occur during the breaks between downpours and this strategy worked out pretty well. Of course, you still got wet and muddy. You never went anyplace without your rubber poncho, but since it extended only from your head to your knees, you were always soaked from the knees down.

I finished the preflight on my Loach and then headed to the mess hall for breakfast. I still had an hour till ETD. We would be heading for LZ English today, a large army encampment northwest of An Khe, to assist the brigade in a sweep of its AO. Our primary job would be to search and cordon a couple of large villages southeast of English. The scouts would cordon the villages, keeping the inhabitants inside, while the Blues performed a hut-to-hut search.

At the mess hall I filled up my tray with polyester eggs and then took a seat by Stan McDonald, the Blues' platoon sergeant, who was enjoying a cup of after-breakfast coffee. Stan had been back from the hospital in Japan for several months now. This tour had obviously taken its toll on him; he appeared to be twenty-five going on fifty. The mess hall was quiet, with few occupants at this early hour. We were ahead of the crowd. The principal noise came from the steady monsoon drizzle striking the tin roof of the mess hall.

"Morning, Stan," I said as I sat down.

"Morning, Mr. Holley. You leading the scout team today?"

"Yep. Going to ferret out the bad guys so you Blues will have some real war stories for when you get home."

"Please. I've got enough war stories already."

"Yeah, but most of your platoon doesn't."

"Ain't that the truth. Scares hell out of me, having so many green troops to depend on."

"Well, we were all green once."

"Yeah, but it's the quantity of green that bothers me. Poor odds."

"How many slicks are we taking?"

"Four. Seven Blues per slick."

"Are you familiar with the villages we'll be working?"

"Naw. This will be my first time to work that part of II Corps."

"It's a collection of several adjoining villages that make up one huge village."

"Have you worked the area often?"

"Several times. Working that village is getting to be a monthly ritual. Usually, though, we don't take our own Blues. Normally Brigade provides the grunts."

"You figure we'll find anything?"

"Not a chance," I responded with confidence. "I think the army works real hard at sending us to look for the bad guys where they aren't. If they really wanted to find them, they should let the scouts tell them where to look. They'd be so busy fighting alligators they wouldn't have time to drain the pond."

"I know what you mean. It gets pretty frustrating."

"Yeah. Today will be a blow-off. At least you'll get to conduct body searches on a lot of pretty Vietnamese girls."

"Not my cup of tea," Stan replied.

"Well, it's the closest thing to excitement you're likely to see today. In fact, it's going to be so quiet that I'm taking a half-virgin door gunner."

"What in hell is a half-virgin?"

"It's a local idiom that I just made up. I'm taking Frank Marsh from the Lift Platoon as my gunner."

"How come?"

"He's bored. This is his second tour as a Huey door gunner, and he wants to see what it's like as a scout gunner. I promised I'd take him along the first chance I got."

"Yeah, well, you better hope that today's as quiet as you say it's going to be."

"Not to worry. He's a good man and has a lot of experience in slicks. It's not like he's never been shot at before."

"Sure he's a good man. And sure he has lots of Huey experience. However, providing fire from a slick is not the same thing as shooting a VC that's eyeball-to-eyeball with you. In a Loach he'll be closer to the enemy than he's ever been before. That makes a big difference."

"You could be right. Not much I can do about it, though. I'll just have to keep an eye on him."

"Is your wingman carrying a good gunner?"

"Yeah . . . Murphy."

"Well, that should help if you get in a jam."

"Maybe," I responded, my lack of enthusiasm evident.

"Why maybe?"

"Mr. Fisher is flying my wing."

"Oh, shit!" McDonald exclaimed in astonishment. "You've really got the deck stacked against you."

Stan's reaction regarding Jerry Fisher as my wingman was understandable. He'd been with Delta Troop longer than any of us and had a great ability for doing paperwork. He had a virtually nonexistent ability to fly a helicopter. Consequently, he'd been the troop's administrative officer for the past eighteen months. Unfortunately, Jerry felt that the war was passing him by, and he had his heart set on being a real combat aviator. In truth, the war was passing him by . . . at the request and with the gratitude of his fellow aviators, who felt that the skies were a lot safer with him on the ground.

Unfortunately, Jerry pled his case to Major Williams and, after hinting about going over the major's head regarding misuse of army assets, was subsequently assigned to the Scout Platoon. This would be his third mission. I would be his third lead man. The first two had not yet returned from the hospital, each of them having been shot down. Fortunately, we would be working a quiet AO. Jerry would have to work real hard to get me shot down.

"Well, like I said: It's a zip AO. The Blues will be the only ones getting any action today, and that will be from searching the peasants."

"Are you always right about these things?" McDonald queried.

I remembered a similar question that I had posed to John Larkin. It seemed like a long time ago. "About as often as John Larkin," I responded, then I quickly changed the subject so Stan couldn't probe further. "You taking Old King along today?"

"Sure . . . although we don't have much say-so in the matter. King kinda does what he wants."

King was a German shepherd that hung out with the Blues. He'd been given to us by some LRRPs we supported. King was a veteran of several tours in Vietnam and had the battle scars to prove it. Mostly he just sort of hobbled around now, having gotten too old and crippled to go on LRRP patrols.

But Old King had trouble accepting the fact that time had passed him by. To compensate for his lost glory days he insisted on pretending that he was still a member of the LRRPs. Every time the Blues went off on a mission he would jump on board the Huey and ride to the LZ with them. Usually he would fall asleep en route, but as soon as the skids bounced against terra firma he would leap out, race around the LZ two or three times, then jump back on board as the helicopter began its departure.

Having Old King show up for his helicopter rides was as predictable as clockwork, but it was also clear that his age was rapidly overtaking his energy. His forays around the LZs were becoming slower, and his sleeping periods were becoming longer. Sometimes he slept right through the landing.

"Well, say hello to the mutt for me," I said, rising to leave.

"I'll do that. But you watch yourself out there today. You're playing with poor odds."

* * *

At 0700 hours the flight departed for LZ English—two Loaches, two Cobras, and four slicks. Since all of the slicks were being used to transport the Blues, the lead Cobra would function as C & C today. Consequently, the Gun Platoon leader—my buddy, Captain John Graves—was flying the lead Cobra. Dave Horton was his wing. After we crossed An Khe Pass I risked yet another scout nosebleed and climbed to a thousand feet so we could enjoy the lush scenery during the forty-five minute flight. Shortly thereafter a flock of large birds crossed my path. They dodged left, right, and down as we passed through them at a hundred knots. Crossing paths with a flock of birds was not an unusual happening. I was always amazed at their uncanny ability to avoid being struck by the helicopter.

Ahead, three stragglers were furiously flapping their wings, trying to catch up with the flock. As our paths intersected, two of them zagged down and to the right. The third bird initially zigged up and to the left, discovered himself to be alone, and immediately opted for the group decision, zagging down and to the right. By this time, of course, the particular airspace he chose to reenter was occupied by my Loach. This was a classic example of zigging when he should have zagged. It also indicated that the uncanny ability to avoid being struck by a helicopter is not inherent in all birds.

The windshield shattered on the door gunner's side of the Loach. Actually, only part of it shattered. The bird created about a one-foot-diameter hole as it came through. Blood and pieces of bird were plastered all over the inside of the Loach and on Frank Marsh, my door gunner. Frank immediately hunched over as if in pain.

"Are you all right?" I screamed over the intercom. Since we were still doing over a hundred knots, the wind was creating a lot of background noise as it rushed through the hole left by the bird. Frank didn't respond. Instead he began making frantic gestures while hunkering still lower in his seat.

"Hey! I said, are you all right?" More frantic gestures. More hunkering. Soon he would be down to the floor. He tried to talk on the intercom, but the rushing wind drowned out his voice. I decided the bird must have injured him when it came through the windshield.

"Should I head for the hospital?" I screamed. He covered his ears. Perhaps it wasn't necessary to scream. I repeated my question, lowering the decibel output considerably. "Should I head for the hospital?" He shook his head emphatically from side to side. This represented real progress.

"Then get back into your seat and sit down." Again he shook his head emphatically from side to side. The bird must have addled his brains. By this time he was nearly on the floor of the helicopter. I wasn't sure what I should do. The flight school curriculum hadn't covered berserk door gunners.

While I watched in amazement he curled himself into a tiny little ball on the floor of the helicopter, using his entire body to shield his microphone. Then he reached behind him and, with his hand, pushed down the push-to-talk switch located on the floor of the helicopter.

"Slow the fucking helicopter down," he said, articulating the words very precisely.

"What?" I responded. There was still quite a bit of background noise coming from the wind on his side of the helicopter.

"Slow . . . the . . . fucking . . . helicopter . . . down," he repeated with immaculate enunciation.

I slowed the helicopter to thirty knots. The rest of the flight began speeding away from me. Amazingly, the background noise of the wind rushing through the helicopter immediately died off. Frank Marsh uncurled himself from the floor and sat back down in his seat.

"You ever try to talk in a hundred-knot wind?" he screamed at me.

I chose to consider this a rhetorical question. Instead of responding, I called Maintenance and had them dispatch a replacement Loach to meet me at LZ English. Joe Watkins, our crotchety old maintenance officer, made some unkind remarks, but the new Loach would be delivered posthaste. I didn't know it then, but Joe would have more opportunities to cast disparaging remarks in my direction before the day was over.

* * *

The villages we were to search and cordon were located a few miles southeast of LZ English. They were actually three interconnected villages forming a single large village about two miles in circumference. Other Brigade assets were being used simultaneously to search other villages in the area. Jerry Fisher held a 45° angle off my right wing as we continually circled the perimeters of the villages. Our job was to ensure that no one left the villages until the search was completed. We'd been on station about an hour. In another fifteen minutes I'd send Fisher back to refuel. When he returned I'd go back for fuel. The Cobras would follow the same routine. This way we maintained constant—albeit limited, for short time periods—coverage for the Blues as they did their hut-to-hut search.

Occasionally a group of mama-sans tried to break out of the village—probably from general fear of having their homes invaded in such a manner—but a few warning shots from Frank Marsh's M-60 would send them scampering back. As I had predicted, it was turning out to be a zilch mission. At least it was until John Graves called me from the lead Cobra.

"Blackhawk 12, this is Blackhawk 26. Over."

"This is 12. Over."

"Roger, 12. We just spotted a possible bad guy jumping into an old bomb crater about seven hundred meters northwest of you. Over."

"Roger, 26. We'll check it out."

I tucked the nose of the Loach down, picking up airspeed, and headed northeast. "Are you on my wing?" I queried Jerry Fisher over the Fox Mike. He gave a positive response.

The bomb crater was easy to spot: a six-foot depression about thirty feet in diameter, overgrown with vegetation. It was in an open area, pocketed with clumps of bushes, about fifty meters from a tree line. I approached the crater from the left at high speed. As I came abreast of it I made a hard left turn, coming to an abrupt halt at a five-foot hover about ten meters away from the crater, positioning my door gunner for a clear shot. Blackhawk 26 had been correct: There was a bad guy crouched inside the crater. My sudden approach had caught him by surprise.

"Blackhawk 26, this is Blackhawk 12. I've got one bad guy in the crater. He's wearing green fatigue pants and a blue shirt. He's carrying an AK-47; he's swinging it around toward me; he's reaching for the trigger; he's releasing the safety catch. . . ."

At this point it occurred to me that my half-virgin door gunner might not fully understand the duties of his job. I decided to clarify the matter for him: "Shoot, goddamn it!" I screeched over the intercom. This did not produce the desired response. He immediately threw his M-60 to the floor of the helicopter and covered his face with his hands. For heaven's sake, I thought. Simultaneously I received a call from Dave Horton in the wing Cobra.

"One-two, you've got more bad guys in the bushes to your rear."

This warning caused my pucker factor to increase considerably. If I had had the time, I would have pondered over what my wingman was doing. After all, part of his job was to cover my six o'clock position. However, I was more immediately concerned with the VC in the bomb crater, whose index finger was beginning to tighten on the trigger of his AK-47. A fraction of a second before the AK erupted I snatched the collective up under my armpit and jerked the cyclic into my stomach. Fortunately, my chicken plate prevented me from injuring my abdominal area, and the helicopter abruptly jumped rearward. The full magazine burst from the AK took out most of the instrument panel and windshield. Almost immediately every bush in the vicinity began shooting at my Loach.

I roughly swung the helicopter's controls to and fro, theoretically dodging bullets as I vacated the area. My silent wingman provided no covering fire, and I later learned that his M-60 had jammed on its first firing burst. The Cobra's ten-pound rockets began bursting around my Loach, forcing the VC to break off their attack and race for the protective cover of the nearby tree line. Frank Marsh, having recovered from his initial shock at being face-to-face with an armed enemy soldier, apparently decided that my frantic control movements were indicative of an epileptic seizure.

He reached over to my side of the Loach, trying to grab the controls. After a brief wrestling match he retreated to his side of the aircraft.

By this time the VC's attention was focused on their own escape. After reaching a relatively safe distance and determining that my Loach was still in a flyable condition, I positioned myself to observe the after-battle. One of the Cobras was still completing its initial run, targeting three VC that had stopped at the edge of the tree line. The Cobra came lower and slower, definitely a not-by-the-book gun run. The three VC raised their AKs, targeting the Cobra, which by now was only fifty meters away and actually approaching a high hover. The Cobra was a sitting duck, its guns were remaining silent. Suddenly its rocket pods ignited in a salvo burst, spewing forth all of its remaining rockets. The still overweight and hovering Cobra shuddered from the back blast and then began a slow break to the right, gradually increasing airspeed and altitude, to resume a normal attack pattern. The three VC had disintegrated in an explosion of dirt, rocks, and jungle foliage at the rate of about eight rockets per VC. This was known in the trade as an overkill.

In the meantime, the slicks had moved the Blue Platoon from the village to the battle area, where they began the task of pursuing the VC that had gotten away. Stan McDonald gave me a thumbs-up as he gathered the Blues near the edge of the tree line. Then they disappeared into the jungle. I placed a call back to Maintenance at An Khe, requesting that a replacement Loach be sent to LZ English. I had lost another windshield and taken several rounds in the engine compartment. Joe Watkins said some very nasty things. He was not pleased with me. I also called Operations and had them ship out a replacement door gunner. At the moment, there wasn't much I could do about replacing my wingman.

I headed for LZ English and awaited the replacement Loach. I checked out the old Loach while I waited. Some of the bullets had come very close. There were holes within a few inches of my head. I gave the Loach a kiss on the nose and promised that I would never treat it badly again. Its quick response when I had jerked the controls rearward had been the difference between a near miss and a hit. The poor thing had more bullet holes in it than we could accurately count, including two in the engine. It would be a while before the old girl would fly again. I hoped my trusty steed didn't become a hangar queen.

By the time I had finished my third box of C-ration beef and potatoes the new Loach arrived, and we headed back out. Since the Blues were still pursuing the bad guys from the earlier encounter, the village search and cordon was put in a holding pattern, and Brigade diverted us to a recon mission north of LZ English. This was not a thrilling assignment; it was Butch Cassidy and the Sundance Kid territory. We weren't exactly going where no man had gone before, but we were going where no friendlies had gone before without suffering casualties.

As we entered the rugged, mountainous, triple-canopy terrain to begin our search for the enemy I was thankful that I had decided to replace Frank Marsh with an experienced scout door gunner, Jim Braddock. This was really nasty terrain, and we weren't likely to receive any prior warning if we found any bad guys. Braddock hadn't flown with me before, but he was known to be a competent and fearless gunner. I knew the fearless part was true, based on the time he had driven the truck when Eric and I went to the flight surgeon at Camp Holloway. On that occasion he'd also demonstrated a certain amount of mental instability by charging the VC, but being a bit loony wasn't a discriminating attribute among scouts. Jerry Fisher still represented a weak link as my wingman, but it was a shortcoming I would currently have to live—or die—with.

Unfortunately, this AO was not a free-fire zone. That meant that unless we were receiving direct fire from the enemy we had to receive permission from higher headquarters before we could shoot. Whoever came up with that policy had never flown scouts. When you were eyeball-to-eyeball with the enemy you weren't likely to be involved in a case of mistaken identity.

After about an hour of a slow search pattern through the cliffs and overhangs of the mountainous terrain we struck pay dirt. As we hovered slowly down the side of a mountain we abruptly came to an opening in the canopy that revealed a large cave with a patio-like entrance, the end of which formed the edge of a two-hundred-foot cliff. Three VC were sunning themselves on the patio, their weapons stacked nearby. In a free-fire zone they would have been dead meat. I requested permission to fire.

"Blackhawk 26, this is Blackhawk 12. I've got three bad guys in the open. Request permission to fire. Over."

"Roger, 12. Are they armed? Over."

"Their AKs are stacked nearby. They will be armed in the very near future. I think it would be to the army's economic advantage if we engaged them before that happened." The army continually emphasized that its aviators were valuable properties, each of them representing more than a quarter-million-dollar investment in training costs. I was intent on being a good portfolio manager for the army.

"Roger, 12. Stand by. Out."

The C & C would relay the request to Brigade, which would relay it to Division. Then the process would be repeated in reverse, probably accompanied by requests for additional information rather than the desired permission to fire.

In the meantime, the VC had behaved in a puzzling manner. The fact that they had been caught with their pants down and were still alive had left them confused. They calmly got to their feet, keeping wary eyes on my helicopter, and slowly—I guess to keep from startling us into violent action—walked into their cave. They had not taken the extra time that would have been necessary to retrieve their weapons. From the relative safety of their cave they peered out, talking among themselves. Finally one of them—he must have drawn the short straw—came out and retrieved their weapons. He continued to look at me, puzzled, as he made his way back to the cave.

"One-two, this is 26. Over."

Thank God, I thought. Finally I'll be able to shoot. Now that the VC had their weapons and the protective cover of their cave they were not likely to remain passive for long, particularly since they had a sitting duck hovering above the entranceway.

"This is 12. Over."

"Roger, 12. Brigade requests confirmation on the number of bad guys. Over."

You've got to be kidding, I thought. Who the hell cared exactly how many there were? "Three, goddam it! Three. One . . . two . . . three. Over."

"Good copy, 12. Stand by. Out."

While this was taking place the three VC, now fully armed, wandered back out of the cave and stood on the patio, occasionally pointing their AKs at us in a feinting gesture while they discussed the confusing situation among themselves. I was determined not to provoke them until I had permission to fire. He who shot first was likely to win this engagement.

Suddenly one of the VC shouted angrily, gestured at my helicopter, and then raised his AK to his shoulder, aiming at the gunner's side of the aircraft. Oh, shit, this is it, I thought as I turned my head to warn my gunner, Jim Braddock. To my horror, Braddock was prominently displaying the uplifted middle finger of his left hand to the VC. The reason for their unexpected anger became patently clear.

"Put that finger down," I yelled at Braddock over the intercom. "Holley Rule Number One is: Never give the finger to someone who is pointing a rifle at you."

Braddock reluctantly lowered his finger. The VC responded in kind by lowering his weapon, and we returned to our previous state of tenuous truce. I figured that the presence of two Loaches rather than one was probably what had kept the VC from firing on us thus far. They knew they couldn't get both of us without suffering casualties. Then it occurred to me that I hadn't seen Fisher's Loach in quite some time. He should have been holding at my four o'clock position.

I did a quick 360° pedal turn looking for Fisher, my rotor downwash pummeling the VC with leaves and dirt. He was nowhere in sight.

"Blackhawk 14, this is Blackhawk 12. Over."

"Roger 12, this is 14. Over."

"Where are you?" I queried.

"I'm about a quarter mile from you, along the river. We spotted some more of those long-beaked birds. Over."

Flabbergasted would not have served as an adequate description of my reaction to the wandering Fisher. However, before I could articulate an appropriate response the same

VC as before began shouting again and once more pointed his AK at the gunner's side of my Loach. This time he released the safety catch on the AK.

Given the orientation of the VC's weapon, I suspected that Braddock might have suffered a short-term memory lapse and repeated his attempt at communicating with the VC via sign language. Glancing over at the gunner's side of the aircraft, I discovered that I was incorrect. His nonverbal gestures had gone beyond the sign-language stage. Braddock had dropped his trousers, turned around in his seat, and plastered his butt against the windshield. I felt that I might be losing control of the situation.

My immediate concern, however, was the VC's finger, which was tightening on the trigger of his AK. I kicked right pedal, immediately placing the rear of the helicopter toward the enemy a split second before the weapon erupted in a stream of bullets. The familiar sound of bullets penetrating the thin skin of the helicopter pushed me into further action. All three AKs were firing now, the helicopter's engine taking the brunt of the punishment. The Loach began to lose power as I dropped over the cliff, gliding toward the river several hundred feet below.

Skimming the treetops, I abruptly encountered Fisher's Loach heading back to the cliff. Narrowly averting a collision, I coaxed my Loach on toward the river. With luck I would make the water—water was always preferable to trees when it came time for a forced landing—and maybe find a sandbar to sct the Loach down on. The instigator of the current crisis, my now-terrified door gunner, was frantically struggling back into his pants. Dying with your boots on was one thing; dying with your pants off was quite another.

"Blackhawk 12, this is Blackhawk 26. Over."

The radio call served as a reminder that I'd been too busy to inform the C & C of our current situation. "This is 12. Over."

"Roger, 12. You have permission to engage the enemy. Over."

"Roger, 26. Be advised that the enemy failed to cooperate while awaiting the permission to fire. I'm currently looking for a forced landing area near the river. Over."

"Understood, 12. We have you in sight and will follow you in. Out."

As the river loomed closer I watched the steady rise of the needle on the engine temperature gauge. It was going to be a close race. I eased the power, trying to achieve a compromise between altitude and loss of power. It didn't help much. I broke over the trees at the edge of the river-bank and made a quick turn into the wind. God's gift to mankind awaited me: a sandbar. I executed an autorotative landing and breathed a sigh of relief as I cushioned the skids onto terra firma. Then I turned my attention to my door gunner.

"Braddock, Holley Rule Number Two is: Never, ever moon someone who is pointing a rifle at you."

At the troop Officers Club that night I was less than popular in some quarters. For example, John Graves, the Gun Platoon leader, wasn't speaking to me. He'd wanted to court-martial Dave Horton for violating protocol on gun runs and also for overtorquing his Cobra. I wrote Dave and his copilot up for a medal. This didn't set well with Graves. It would make a court-martial impossible. Even the army didn't both punish and reward a soldier for the same action. And historically, medals for valor took precedence over courts-martial for bullshit. I figured Graves would cool off in a few days. Probably sooner if I'd also written *him* up for a medal.

No one seemed upset that I had written Braddock up for a medal, too. They felt that his actions were clearly valorous. In my opinion, they were also clearly stupid, but it's a fine line. Citations never read: "Confronted by deadly enemy fire from all quarters, this soldier distinguished himself above and beyond the call of duty by stupidly exposing himself to bodily injury." Such things were just not good for morale.

No, they didn't mind the medal for Braddock or, except for Captain Graves, the medal for Dave Horton. It was the medal for Jerry Fisher that caused the heavy flak.

"Are you crazy?" Eric Masterson barked at me. "Writing Fisher up for a medal is the dumbest thing you've ever done." Other pilots had joined the noisy discussion, encouraged by the free-flowing bourbon, and they were unanimous in their agreement with Eric's assessment of my action. I just smiled calmly as Eric continued his rampage.

"The guy not only does everything wrong that can possibly be done wrong, but he gets you shot down twice in the same day. Plus, he got his first two leads shot down. He's batting over a thousand. And that's not supposed to be possible. And you write the guy up for a medal. It's absolutely absurd."

"Eric," I responded, "what does Jerry want more than anything else in the world?"

"That's no secret. He wants to be a real combat aviator. That's how we got stuck with him in the scouts."

"Correct. Now, wouldn't you say that having a DFC is prima facie evidence that a pilot is a real combat aviator?"

"Well . . . yeah . . . I suppose so," Eric responded, his tone beginning to soften.

"Okay. Number one: Regardless of competence, Jerry performed courageously today. I didn't write him up for being competent. I wrote him up for being courageous. Number two: When Jerry gets his DFC he'll no longer need to prove that he's a real combat aviator. So what do you think he'll do?"

Eric mulled the question over momentarily. "He'll probably go back to being admin officer."

"Bingo. You win a kewpie doll from the third shelf. And that means that the hostile skies of Vietnam will become safe again."

Eric's prompted prediction came true. Jerry Fisher received his DFC and never flew another scout mission. It was the first time the scouts had thrown a going-away party for a pilot who'd only been with us for a week. It was a rip-roaring success. Everyone was deliriously happy, including Jerry. He'd always wanted to be a hero. Now he was not only a hero, but a very popular fellow.

However, I didn't have much time for recovering from the aftereffects of the party. I'd been in country for eight months, and it was time for some overdue rest and recreation, better known as R & R. Eric Masterson, John Larkin, Dave Horton, and I headed for An Khe Airport, where a C-130 took us to Cam Ranh Bay, the embarkation/debarkation point for R & R. Our intent, as well as the army's plan for us, was to laze away five days at our respective destinations so that we could return, filled with vim and vigor, to retackle the task of destroying the enemy. Our good intentions began to unravel shortly after our arrival at Cam Ranh Bay.

14

■ ■ ■ ■ ■ ■ ■ ■ ■ ■ ■ ■ ■ ■

R & R

DESPITE THE LINGERING HANGOVER FROM FISHER'S GOING-away party, I greeted the new day with enthusiasm. It was an absolutely beautiful day, the weather atrocious. Soon I would be seeing civilization again—at least some semblance of civilization. Nothing could dampen my excitement. The simple concept of tasting real food again after eight months of C-rations and reconstituted potatoes had my epinephrine flowing. At the moment I was on my way to the Orderly Room to arrange ground transportation to An Khe Airport, which was about five miles away. The other members of the R & R quartet—Eric, Dave, and John—had assigned me the task of arranging transport.

"Morning, Top," I said as I entered the Orderly Room, intentionally letting the screen door slam behind me. Top couldn't stand for the door to slam.

"Don't slam the door," the first sergeant shouted, as an afterthought remembering to throw in a "sir".

"Sorry, Top," I apologized, "my exuberance got the better of me. I'm headed out for R & R."

"Congratulations," the first sergeant responded unenthusiastically. "That should improve Mr. Watkin's maintenance report for a few days. What can I do for you?"

I ignored the barb. "There's four of us. We need a ride over to An Khe Airport."

"I'm afraid you're out of luck. The only thing left around here is the major's jeep. Everything else is either gone or down for maintenance."

"I reckon the major's jeep will do just fine."

"No sale. The major doesn't allow anyone to use his jeep. He could be called to Higher Headquarters at any time."

"Wait a minute, Top. You don't understand. The C-130 leaves in an hour."

"That's a tough break. You can ask the major if you want. But you're wasting your time."

"Can't hurt to try," I responded, heading for the major's office. At my knock the major beckoned me to enter.

"Sir, can we borrow your jeep for a few minutes?"

"Absolutely not."

"But sir, there's four of us that have to get to An Khe Airport within the hour."

"See the first sergeant. He'll fix you up."

"I already talked to the first sergeant. There's nothing available except your jeep."

"Wrong. That means there's nothing available. Nobody uses my jeep but me. No exceptions. Reschedule your R & R. You're dismissed, Mr. Holley."

"Yes, sir," I responded, leaving the Orderly Room. Outside I considered my alternatives. Since ground transportation wasn't available and we were too far inland to consider water transport, that seemed to leave air transportation as the only viable option. I headed for Operations and filed a flight plan for local-area orientation. It was a tight fit, all four of us and our luggage, but twenty minutes later I landed the Loach at An Khe Airport. Jerry Fisher had agreed to see that the Loach got back home and my flight plan got closed out. He owed me.

Cam Ranh Bay was a huge metropolis of a military installation. Thousands upon thousands of straphangers performed the demanding combat task of getting soldiers to and from their myriad destinations. In this bureaucratic humdrum of activity en-route soldiers would often have layovers of two or three days while they awaited their turns for transportation. Sometimes the transportation never came. The missing-in-action rolls could probably have been trimmed considerably if the army had done a thorough check of the transient billets at Cam Ranh Bay. Some of those folks had been there for quite a while.

The four of us soon learned that despite the destinations specified on our R & R orders, we were unlikely to get to our intended destinations before our R & R leaves expired. Consequently, we opted for taking the next R & R plane we could get on, regardless of destination. The good part was that the four of us would be spending our R & R together. The bad part was that the first R & R plane we could get on would be in two days . . . maybe.

The maybe related to how well we could circumvent the system. Any soldier quickly learns that the army can be prodded to move a bit faster. You just have to find the right button to push. Like the time back at Fort Hood when we'd landed at the Fort Sam Houston heliport and needed transportation to the VOQ. Post Transportation told us it would be a couple of hours before they could provide a ride. Dixon Thorpe, a new Wobbly One but with prior service as a staff sergeant, picked up the phone, announcing that he was Colonel Thorpe and demanded immediate transportation. A military taxi arrived five minutes later.

I figured our best bet for improving our timetable was to start with the transportation officer. He turned out to be a young captain, Harry Fletcher. The important thing was that he was wearing the silver wings of an army aviator, a comrade in arms. I had a feeling we were on our way now.

"Hi, Captain."

The captain glanced up from the schedule he was busily revising. Despite my fresh fatigues, I presented a somewhat battle-worn appearance. It takes more than a shave and a haircut to cover up eight months in the boonies with the cavalry. At any rate, I thought I detected a look of sympathetic understanding, even respect, in the captain's eyes.

"What can I do for you, Chief?"

"To tell the truth, sir, you can get me and my three buddies out of here."

"Are you coming or going?"

"Going. To anywhere."

"Been in the field long?"

"Eight months."

"That's quite a while. How come you're just getting around to R & R?"

"Been having too much fun to take a break."

"Right. Let me see your orders."

I handed them over, and the captain began checking his schedules. "There's no way I can get you on an R & R flight until day after tomorrow."

My disappointment showed.

"However," he continued, "I've got a C-130 cargo flight tomorrow morning. It'll make a refueling stop in Taiwan, and you can get off there. You interested?"

"Hell, yes," I said, beaming.

"It'll be a long flight."

"Who cares? At least it'll be moving."

"Are any of you squeamish?" the captain queried.

"I don't reckon. We're cavalry. That kinda makes you immune to being squeamish. Why?" I asked suspiciously.

"Oh, it doesn't really matter," he responded. "Tell you what. You and your buddies go see the billeting officer and get some bunk spaces for tonight. Then come over to my quarters about nineteen hundred hours. We're having a little party."

"That's mighty kind of you."

"*Nada*. It's not altruistic. In this lousy job I don't have many opportunities to shoot the breeze with fellow aviators. By the way, the name's Harry . . . Harry Fletcher."

We encountered several amazing things at Captain Harry Fletcher's party. The first was the quarters: a condominium complex. War was truly hell on support personnel. We were the only outsiders, and we stood out like four wolves in a herd of sheep. The rest of the guests were residents of the apartment complex—a varied concoction of straphangers, including an ample supply of the opposite sex. Real round-eyes. We didn't get to see many of those in our neck of the woods. Another amazing thing was the food. These people actually had fresh vegetables. I pigged out. I didn't mean to. It was just one of those things that couldn't be stopped. I think I was suffering from acute beriberi, and Mother Nature was trying to correct the deficiency.

It was a great party. I was having the time of my life. Just sitting in a corner eating BLTs and sipping bourbon. Nobody bothered me. Eric, Dave, and John were mingling, mostly chatting with the female guests. At the moment I preferred the sensory stimulation of my BLT. It was true bliss. At least it was until this horrible person intruded, ruining the entire evening.

At first I thought she was just trying to be polite. A lot of people are like that—they think if you're not jacking your jaws, you're not having a good time. I was mistaken about her intent, though. Politeness was the last thing on her mind. She was a Berkeley-trained free-lance journalist spoiling for a one-sided philosophical debate regarding the wrongness of the Vietnam War.

For twenty minutes she ranted at me, spouting her propaganda. I pretty much tried to ignore her. I figured that if she wanted to be a pacifist, that was her business. Frankly, I preferred being a pacifist myself. But someone kept shooting at me, and that made it difficult. Anyway, I figured philosophy's philosophy. Why waste your energy arguing about it? I continued munching my BLT and sipping my bourbon. I was being quite tactful, not letting her stinging barbs penetrate. Then Ms. Garbage Mouth finally managed to find my button.

"History will show that the real heroes of the Vietnam War were the ones who refused to fight and went to Canada instead."

"Lady—and I use the term loosely—you're full of shit. The real heroes are dead."

"That's a stupid thing to say."

"It may be many things, including plagiarized, but it's not stupid. It's a quote from Audie Murphy."

"He's just a lousy actor and a warmonger."

That did it. Some things were sacred to me: Roy Rogers, Gene Autry, John Wayne, Gary Cooper, Alvin York, Audie Murphy. Play heroes and real heroes, but sacred nevertheless. I struggled to maintain control. What I really wanted to do was to pick up a tomato and smash it into that smart mouth. Jimmy Cagney would have done that. But I couldn't. It would have been a violation of the Code of the West. So I stifled the emotional impulse, settling instead for a witty "Fuck off, bitch." I was quite imaginative with verbal comebacks.

This rebuttal was amazingly effective. In a huff, she departed . . . to go in search of another warmonger I supposed. I didn't stick around to find out. The discourse had put a damper on the party. I headed for the Cam Ranh Officers Club to do some serious drinking. Unfortunately, a half bottle of Wild Turkey later, my mood still hadn't improved. Deep down I knew there was an element of truth to the Berkeley woman's comments. But the middle of combat was no place for such moral philosophizing. Too much thinking at the wrong time could be hazardous to your health.

I gave up trying to improve my outlook on life with the Wild Turkey and returned to the transient billets to get some sleep. Tomorrow would bring another day. And an early airplane. And Taiwan.

Our C-130 departed at 0500 hours the following morning. True to his word, Captain Harry Fletcher got us on board. We soon discovered why he had asked if we were squeamish: It was a body bag flight. Well, we weren't, and the other passengers didn't seem to mind the extra company. Four and a half hours later we landed at an air force base in Taiwan. I never got the name of it. As we disembarked the crew chief pointed toward an airport exit and said, "That way." We followed his directions and soon found ourselves on the street.

"Wonder what happened to customs," Eric said.

"Who knows?" John responded. "And who cares? Let's grab a taxi and find a hotel."

Dave waved at a taxicab that was roaring past. It immediately did a 360° turn in the middle of the busy thoroughfare and screeched to the curb. The first thing that we learned about Taiwan was that the taxicab drivers had apparently been trained in Japan as kamikaze pilots.

After traveling for only a few blocks, watching the scenery and the local inhabitants whiz by, we temporarily shelved our tourist intentions and concerned ourselves with survival. We missed several dozen people by less than a half inch; drove on every side of the street, including some sides that didn't exist; and crossed over several sidewalks at full speed. Finally we headed full blast down what seemed to be an alley. To the casual observer this had the appearance of providing temporary safety, the alley being so narrow that it had to be a one-way thoroughfare. There was no way two vehicles could pass each other. This illusion was quickly shattered by a passenger bus, manufactured circa 1930, approaching from the opposite direction. As he had done several times in the past few minutes, our driver once again demonstrated that the laws of physics can be illusory, squeezing the cab between the bus and the curb without even slowing down

After what seemed an eternity we were deposited at the entrance of a popular local hotel. By this time we were all suffering from nervous exhaustion. Four brave lads, each of us having faced the VC firing gauntlet with never a flinch, were turned into quivering jelly by a routine Taiwanese taxicab ride.

The days and nights went quickly in Taiwan. Mostly we ate and slept. There were fresh vegetables and meats, and we did our best to stockpile such luxuries. One night we went to an Italian restaurant and had tacos. The Chinese must have confused something when they translated the international menu. On another night we had a minor brush with some Nazis, but they backed off before the situation escalated. It being a small world, Dave Horton also had an encounter with a flight-school nemesis who caught up with him in a Taiwan nightclub.

The four of us were sitting at the bar, lapping up whisky and beer about as fast as the pretty Chinese barmaid could refill our glasses, when Dave was suddenly spun around on his bar stool by a powerful hand that had abrasively gripped his shoulder. His leg banged into John, sitting at the adjoining bar stool, causing beer to slosh on to John's shirt. The powerful hand belonged to a powerful body whose face was wearing a fierce expression of displeasure. While no introductions were offered at the time, gentlemanly etiquette being temporarily suspended, Dave and John later explained that the offending individual was Warrant Officer Bob Snyder, ex–Green Beret and former flight-school classmate. Mr. Snyder was definitely exhibiting an unfriendly attitude. I suspected Dave might be in a bit of trouble.

"I've been looking for you for a long time, Horton."

If Dave was surprised by the unexpected encounter, he did an excellent job of hiding it. Coolly he responded, "Well, well. The amazing Bob Snyder. Long time no see."

"You've got a big mouth, Dave."

"Actually, my dentist says it's rather small . . . makes it difficult to work in," Dave replied.

Observe prime maxim, I thought: First engage brain, then mouth. Dave should not be further irritating this person. Apparently Dave had similar thoughts. He quickly continued in a more conciliatory manner, "Why do you say that, Bob?"

"That's *Mister* Snyder to you," replied Snyder, emphasizing the Mister.

"Well, what seems to be the problem, *Mister* Snyder?"

I was impressed with Dave's diplomacy. Had I been in Dave's place, I would probably have been unable to avoid continuing to refer to this character as Bob. But then, I thought back to some of my own encounters and decided that I, too, would have managed an extreme level of diplomacy. It's a foolish man who forces a fight he can't win.

"I'm going to take you outside and whip your butt," Snyder said sarcastically as he grabbed the front of Dave's shirt to pull him from the bar stool. Very intellectual way to describe a problem, I thought.

John intervened by placing his hand on top of Snyder's.

"Stay out of this, Larkin," responded Snyder. "This is between me and your buddy."

"Oh, I don't care about your beef with Dave," John said nonchalantly. "I'm more concerned about my beef with you."

Snyder looked puzzled. "What are you talking about?"

"See this wet spot on my shirt—the one that smells like beer? When I sat down here I was wearing a clean, dry shirt. Now it's all messy and smells like beer. I can't stand messy shirts, *Mister* Snyder." He stared directly at Snyder, a smile on his lips.

Snyder returned John's stare while he pondered the situation. It was well known that John had passed up a boxing scholarship and a potential shot at the Olympics to enlist for flight school. Apparently opting for prudence, Snyder finally released his grip on Dave's shirt with the warning, "You got lucky this time, Dave. But our paths will cross again."

As Snyder left we turned back to the bar. "What'd you do to him?" John asked.

"I have no idea," Dave replied with an impish grin that suggested a certain insincerity.

"Sure. And bears don't potty in the woods. Come clean."

"Well, there was a rumor about Snyder back in flight school."

"Yes?" prompted John.

"Seems he'd been dating this girl from Weatherford, Joyce Atkins. You may remember her."

"Joyce Atkins? She the one that drove the maroon Camaro?"

"That's her."

"Sharp . . . very sharp! What'd she ever see in Snyder, anyway?"

"Who knows? Women's minds work in mysterious ways, and all that stuff. Anyway, that's part of the rumor. She broke off the relationship."

"How come?"

"Supposedly she heard from a very reliable source that Snyder had a social disease."

"Social disease! You mean clap?"

"Well, as I understand it, the specifics were never mentioned. Personally, I think lack of social etiquette is a dreadful disease."

John looked quizzically at Dave and took a long pull on his beer. "Say . . . didn't you end up dating her a few times?"

Dave abruptly changed the subject by yelling at the barmaid to bring another round.

* * *

Too soon it was time to return to Vietnam. Due to our unusual method of arriving in Taiwan we had no return transportation. The first order of business was to find a military transportation office, which we did. Unfortunately, it came fully equipped with an individual named J. Joseph Peabody III. Such a name indicated that twice before the world had been afflicted with a J. Joseph Peabody. It is a testament to the world's persistence that it has survived such an onslaught. After a thorough check of all regulations Mr. Peabody concluded that since we hadn't come through customs we therefore weren't in Taiwan, and he bade us good-bye.

Since Uncle Sam couldn't be counted on for assistance with our transportation problem, we opted for the obvious solution: We hailed a Taiwanese taxicab and told the driver we wanted to go to Vietnam. It cost us forty dollars apiece, including air fare, but five hours later we landed at Saigon Airport. From there we hitched rides on helicopters, gradually continuing a northward journey until we arrived at An Khe.

No one seemed to notice that we were a couple of days late getting back. However, we weren't given time to recuperate from our exhausting R & R trip. The next day we were back in the saddle again. But it was a couple of days afterward that my Loach let me down. John Graves, the Gun Platoon leader, had made a deal with some grunts for some skin flicks. We would get three first-run flicks; the grunts would get a ride in a Loach. Since Captain Graves was still miffed at me for, among other things, screwing up his court-martial of Dave Horton, he felt that I was obligated to perform this service to redeem myself. So I did. Unfortunately, neither Graves nor the grunts got what they bargained for.

15

■ ■ ■ ■ ■ ■ ■ ■ ■ ■ ■ ■ ■ ■ ■

Skin Flicks

IT WAS A QUIET AFTERNOON IN DELTA TROOP. I WAS WHILING away the time, enjoying the unexpected leisure with a game of Spades in our makeshift Officers Club. It was mid-afternoon. My scout team was on standby for the day. This late, it was unlikely that we would be called out. More importantly, I was up about fourteen dollars. A solitary Major Williams sat at his reserved table in the far corner of the room, ignoring us while he sipped a glass of cognac and worked on some papers. The major frequently used the club as his second office.

Captain John Graves appeared in the doorway, noticed the major, and beckoned me very secretively to accompany him to the patio. Eric temporarily took my place in the card game while I followed John to the patio.

"What's up, John?" Calling him John was a test. He'd insisted that I call him Captain Graves ever since I had gotten on his bad side with the saluting affair. He didn't react to the informality, causing my suspicion index to rise a bit.

"I need a favor," he responded sweetly. My suspicion index jumped a notch higher.

"What's that?"

"I've made a deal with some grunts. They've got some

high-quality skin flicks they're willing to trade us for a ride in a Loach. The grunt sergeant used to be in scouts, and he's trying to get one of his guys to reenlist as a scout door gunner.''

"So . . . why me?''

"The sergeant wants a good sales pitch for scouts. I thought of you. Besides, I figure you owe me . . . about the Dave Horton thing.''

"I don't figure it that way. You were wrong, and you knew it. You've just got so much starch in your collar you won't admit it.''

"Okay. I admit it. I overreacted. Let's just look on this as an opportunity to kiss and make up.''

"That's reasonable, I suppose. But what's in the trade for me?''

"Why, you get to watch the skin flicks, of course.''

"I don't like skin flicks.''

"You're kidding," Captain Graves responded incredulously.

"No. It's a fact.''

"Then do it out of the goodness of your heart. *Esprit de corps.*''

"My reputation could suffer.''

"I doubt it. Your reputation is pretty impermeable. It would take more than one act of kindness to cause damage.''

"All right. I'll do it. But you owe me one.''

Graves smiled with pleasure as he shook my hand, his skin flick fantasies soon to be realized. "Great!''

"So when does this ride take place?" I asked.

"They'll meet us at the flight line in fifteen minutes.''

When I arrived at the flight line Captain Graves was waiting for me, accompanied by the sergeant and his two enlisted men. I took one look at them and thought, Oh, shit, my Loach will never get off the ground. The sergeant must have weighed at least three hundred pounds, and his men were well over two hundred each. And this weight was not attributable to muscle. These guys could have held their own porkers' convention. The OH-6 was designed to carry a pilot and three passengers, but not in the high density altitude environment of Vietnam. And certainly not if the passengers were suffering from chronic obesity.

Graves did the introductions: "Mr. Holley, this is Sergeant Thompson . . . Specialist Wilson . . . and Specialist Harrison." Graves was being so sugary sweet it made you want to throw up. We shook hands all around to show what good fellows we all were, then Sergeant Thompson said, "Mr. Holley, I understands that you's a real good scout pilot." His obesity had apparently affected his literacy.

"Well, I'm still alive. I guess that defines a good scout pilot," I replied modestly. Changing the subject, I spoke to Graves. "Could I talk to you alone for a moment?"

We moved out of earshot of the three passengers, and I said, "Are you crazy? That's damn near eight hundred pounds of beef on the hoof. How do you expect me to get the Loach off the ground?"

"Now, now. You're a talented pilot. I'm sure you'll manage," Graves responded soothingly. He had once read a book on applied psychology.

"Thanks a lot. Maybe I should take you along, too. Then we'd see how confident you really are."

Graves dodged the challenge. "Seriously, do you think you can get it off the ground?"

"It'll be close. But it can't be as bad as an overloaded Charley Model. Did I ever tell you about the time I went down in an overloaded Charley Model?"

"No. And I don't want to hear about it right now. You can tell me after I watch the skin flicks."

"It's a good story."

"I'll await your story with bated breath. Now get moving before the sergeant changes his mind."

"All right. But be sure and remind me to tell you the Charley Model story.

"Tell you what. I'll get the Loach out of the revetment, and then you load the passengers. I don't want to try to hover in the revetment with that much weight," I said as I headed for my Loach.

I cranked the Loach and then moved it into position on the dirt strip that ran between the rows of revetments. We normally took off from and landed on the dirt strips rather than the runway. That way we didn't stir up so much dirt taxiing around. Graves got the passengers strapped in and plugged their headsets into the intercom.

Prior to attempting the takeoff I did a hover check to determine available power. Along with the high density altitude and the weight of the passengers, I also had a crosswind condition to contend with. At least, what little wind existed was blowing perpendicular to the dirt strip and the runway. The Loach was able to hover . . . barely. The main rotor blades were coning tremendously, and the TOT needle approached the red zone. The takeoff was in the bag. I let the power down until the skids were just touching the ground and then eased the cyclic forward. We began bouncing along the ground, slowly gaining speed. Finally we bounced through translational lift, and the Loach was airborne.

Gradually increasing the airspeed, I turned east to pick up the river. It would provide good geography for a scout demonstration, and—more importantly—we were unlikely to encounter any VC this time of day. Along the way I gave a continual monologue on Scouting 101 to the passengers.

The potential scout door gunner had been seated next to me in the gunner's seat, and I concentrated the lecture on him, trying to give him a real feel for the exciting life and duties of the door gunner and the role of scouts in the cavalry. He didn't seem greatly impressed by the lecture. In fact, he seemed petrified with fear. It was difficult to get a response out of him. I figured he just wasn't used to dodging trees at a hundred knots. So I explained to him that when we were en route we went low and fast because it was really safer; the enemy had much less time to treat us as a target. I also explained that we seldom followed a geodesic route for the same reason. He just said "Uh-huh" and continued to hold on to his seat with both hands. For a black man he had mighty white knuckles. I explained to him that he didn't really have to hold on because he wouldn't fall out. He said "Uh-huh" and gripped the seat harder. I didn't seem to have much credibility with him.

By this time I had burned off enough fuel that I was within the operating constraints of the Loach, so I began hovering along the riverbank, pointing out trail signs and such. This went on for about half an hour. Then it was time for the grand finale. I pushed the airspeed up over a hundred knots and began whipping in and out of the trees along the riverbank, providing a running commentary.

"Now, a lot of times we'll be flying along en route like this and we'll see something that we need to check out in a hurry, or we'll get shot at, and we need to maneuver quickly to a particular position. The Loach is an incredibly maneuverable helicopter, and it really gives us an ace in the hole for such situations. For example, do you see that big tree going past your window?"

"Yes sir, I sees it," the recruit responded hesitantly.

"Okay, if we had spotted something there that we needed to check out quickly, I'd do this." I abruptly pulled the cyclic toward me and dropped the power, executing an aerobatic maneuver that put the Loach into a loop fifteen feet off the ground while not gaining altitude. Just before the aircraft turned completely upside down I threw the cyclic to the left and brought the power back in. This maneuver left us hovering in front of the tree that moments before we had been flying past at one hundred knots. My passengers were virtually speechless. To downplay my own skills in this demonstration I continued my dialogue as if nothing unusual had taken place, which from my point of view was the case.

"Now, another duty the gunner has to perform is to assist the pilot with monitoring the instrument readings. When you're scouting, sometimes the pilot gets busy and doesn't give them the attention they deserve. Monitoring the instruments is really very simple, because the important ones are all color-coded. You just glance at them occasionally to be sure that the needles are all in the green zones. You see," I said, pointing to each instrument as I spoke, "this one's green, this one's green, this one's red . . . uh . . . uh . . . this one's green." Oh, shit, shit, shit, I thought. My damn TOT's in the red, and here I am at a hover over trees.

I very carefully began easing the cyclic forward, hoping to get out of the dead man's zone and possibly clear of the trees before the engine quit. By nursing the power I was able to get fifty knots of airspeed and two hundred feet of altitude while maintaining the TOT in the yellow range. My passengers, not being complete fools, realized that something was amiss and were beginning to show some signs of panic. I attempted to calm them down.

"Now, gentlemen, as you can tell by this needle," I said nonchalantly while pointing at the TOT gauge with my left hand, "which was in the red but is now in the yellow, we've got a minor maintenance problem. Quite simply, it means that we're losing engine power, but that's nothing to get excited about. We just want to try to get back to An Khe before the engine quits completely."

This explanation did not produce the desired effect. If anything, it seemed to exacerbate the panic that was being displayed by my passengers. Obviously, they didn't understand the principles of autorotation, else they wouldn't be so excited. I explained this pinwheeling phenomenon to them. The fellow next to me unbuckled his seat belt, preferring to risk a leap into a soft tree. With much coaxing he finally put it back on.

Very slowly and apprehensively we covered the few miles back to the airport, the engine condition continuing to deteriorate. By the time we entered the traffic pattern for a straight-in emergency landing we were only a hundred feet above the ground. This was coupled with a very heavy load, a high density altitude, and a crosswind condition. This was going to be a tricky landing. There was not enough power to hover, which meant that the landing would have to be straight to the ground. However, if I went for a power-on landing and the engine quit in the dead man's zone, it would mean a sure crash. I decided to assume the engine was going to quit and opted for an autorotative landing. Because of the landing conditions I knew I would also get some ground run, so I decided to land on the dirt strip by the revetment area rather than the PSP runway.

I bottomed the collective, entering autorotation. Shortly thereafter the engine quit, thereby providing renewed testament to my brilliant judgment as a helicopter pilot. All things considered, I performed a mighty fine autorotative landing. As expected, I did encounter some ground run. Actually, it was a considerable amount of ground run, but who was counting? Captain Graves, who was standing by a revetment awaiting our return so he could consummate his skin flick deal, frowned disapprovingly as we skidded right on past him.

During this hectic few seconds I had been preoccupied with the landing, to the exclusion of attending to other matters . . . such as passengers. When the Loach finally came to a halt and the dust settled I turned to them to continue my narration of scout duties, only to discover that they were gone. Looking around, I observed the three of them racing helter-skelter down the paved road that led to the main post. They could have at least said thank you.

Through no fault of my own I had failed my golden opportunity to get back in the good graces of Captain Graves. We never saw or heard from my three passengers again, not that Graves didn't make every effort to locate them. He was bound and determined to get those skin flicks. He was also destined to fail. They shipped in a new engine for my Loach and had it up and running in a couple of days. The problem turned out to be an exhaust flange that had been improperly installed. This explanation exonerated me, except in the opinion of Joe Watkins, who insisted that I had somehow—the somehow remaining a mystery—managed to reverse the installation of the exhaust flange while I was flying the Loach. Anyway, I was airborne again in a couple of days, and a Ho Chi Minh sandal awaited my return to the battlefield. I was also to have an encounter with one of the dogs of war.

16

■ ■ ■ ■ ■ ■ ■ ■ ■ ■ ■ ■ ■ ■

War Dog

WE WERE HEADED BACK TO AN KHE, THE LOACHES SKIM-
ming the water of the Bong Sa River at a hundred knots,
when I spotted the Ho Chi Minh sandal. It was on a shallow
sandbar beneath about a foot of gently flowing water. This
piqued my curiosity, and I put the Loach into a scout emergency stop, bottoming the collective and pulling the cyclic
into my stomach. Just before the aircraft gave way to gravity at the top of the low-level loop I swung the cyclic hard
to the left and brought the power back in. This maneuver
left us at a three-foot hover above the lone sandal. Not
expecting the sudden stop, my wingman, Scott Banda, had
streaked on past and was now returning to take up his
protective orbit. I was about to call the C & C ship to
report my serendipitous discovery when he preempted me.
It was nice to know the team members upstairs were paying
attention.

"Blackhawk 12, this is 34. What've you got? Over."

"This is 12. I've got a sandal. Over."

"Say again. I must have misunderstood. Over."

"A sandal. Sierra, alpha, November, delta, alpha, lima.
Over."

"Roger. I guess I didn't misunderstand. One-two, it's

dinnertime. We're tired. We're hungry. And we're low on fuel. Do you really need a sandal? Over."

"But why is there only one sandal?"

"I don't know why there's only one sandal. Turn it over to Paul Drake of the Drake Detective Agency. Can't we go eat?"

"There's only one sandal because we surprised this guy, and he took off running for the west bank of the river. He *didi mau*ed so fast he lost one of his sandals."

"And how do you know that?"

"By the tracks. One barefoot, one with a sandal. Heading straight for the undergrowth on the west bank."

"Okay, 12, follow it up. But we've only got fifteen minutes of fuel to spare."

"Wilco," I acknowledged, positioning the right skid of the Loach over the lost sandal. Dropping the skid beneath the water, I momentarily applied power and forward cyclic, then reversed the control movements. While maintaining its stationary position the Loach did a nice little bow, snagging the rubber straps of the sandal over the skid. "Souvenir," I said to my gunner, Gary Poston, as we began following the tracks.

The undergrowth at the river's edge provided good cover and concealment for our fugitive. "Reconning by fire," I announced over the UHF as Gary began to pepper the thick foliage with a couple of hundred rounds from the M-60. Reconning by fire was a technique we used frequently in the jungle. The idea was, if you couldn't see Charlie, you might startle him into action. The typical reaction was that he started shooting back. Our efforts were greeted by silence, and I moved to the other side of the undergrowth, picking up a trail that moved upslope into the jungle, no longer able to follow Charlie's footprints.

We followed the path for about a quarter of a mile, the jungle foliage becoming progressively thicker. Then the trail opened into a small clearing. I was about halfway across the open space when I spotted the AK in the bushes to my left front. While I alerted my gunner, Blackhawk 34 chose this particular moment to prod me about our late dinner.

"Blackhawk 12, this is 34. That's enough. One VC gets to live another day. Let's go get some chow. Over."

I responded on the FM, to ensure that my wingman also got the message. "Three-four, this is 12. You better call for relief on station. Over."

"Why's that, 12?"

"Because the shit's about to hit the fan. Purple smoke's out. Target's fifteen meters north of it," I responded as Gary tossed a purple smoke grenade and then cut loose with the M-60. Simultaneously I pulled max power and broke right, my wingman's gunner firing beneath my helicopter. Everything went like clockwork. With one exception. My right break took me directly into the path of the main ambush Charlie had improvised. Rockets from the inbound Cobras began exploding to my rear as I encountered a hail of AK-47 rounds. The Loach shuddered from the impacts, the windshield disintegrating, but kept on flying, and I quickly broke line of sight with my hidden attackers.

"Main target is fifteen meters east of the smoke," I shouted over the FM, and then I concentrated on putting a little distance between us and the ambush site. Despite all the bullet holes, the Loach had not taken any critical hits. Arriving back at the river, I looked around for my wingman but didn't find him. I called him on the scout frequency but got no reply.

The radio traffic on the UHF was intense, everyone providing commentary as the battle progressed, so I called 34 on the FM. "Blackhawk 34, this is 12. Have you seen 19? Over."

"Negative, 12. Stand by," the C & C responded as he switched radios and broke in on the UHF traffic. "This is 34. Has anyone seen the second Loach? Over."

After a few seconds of silence Blackhawk 22, the wing Cobra, responded, "The last I saw of him, he'd broken away from the target, heading east."

"Roger," 34 responded. "One-two, did you copy? Over."

"Roger."

"One-two, we've just spotted some red smoke in that direction. About a hundred meters at your ten o'clock."

"Roger. I'm moving to check it out," I replied, putting the power to the Loach. After we topped a slight rise in the terrain the smoke was easy to spot. Very quickly we arrived over the area, and I used the downwash from my helicopter's rotor to spread the foliage for a look beneath the trees.

We had solved the case of the missing wingman. The crumpled Loach was resting on its side, riddled with bullet holes. The bloodied door gunner was dazedly sitting on the ground, back resting against the side of the wreckage, M-16 in hand. There was no sign of Scott Banda, the pilot. I motioned the wounded gunner to head west, toward the river. He made no effort to comply, whether because of his wounds or his state of shock. I alerted Blackhawk 34 to the situation, who in turn called Operations to send out the Blues.

"Well, Gary,' I said to my door gunner over the intercom, "looks like you get to play hero."

"What do you want me to do?"

"I'll hover down into the top of that tree. You hop out and climb down it. You did climb trees when you were a kid, didn't you?"

"No problem. What do I do after I'm down there?"

I pulled the Loach to a high hover and pointed to the west. "The river's right there, about a hundred meters. That's where I'll pick you up. Pop smoke when you get to the bank."

I dropped the Loach down into the heavy leaves of the large tree I had selected, chopping a few branches as I maneuvered as low as possible. As Gary was about to leave the helicopter I reminded him of the time factor. "Move as quickly as you can. Remember, the VC aren't far away, and I'm mighty low on fuel."

Then he was out and gone, scrambling down the tree. From the ground he gave me a thumbs-up, and I moved to the river to wait. Our relief on station had arrived to carry on the engagement until the infantry could get there to perform mop-up operations. The rest of the flight headed home.

As I arrived at the river my low fuel warning light came on, indicating twenty minutes of remaining fuel. I flew on across the river, finding a nice sandbar near the far bank, and landed the Loach. Shutting the Loach down, I grabbed my M-16 and headed for the jungle. I struggled up the steep bank and found a sheltered vantage point from which I could observe the far side of the river.

An anxious half hour later I spotted Gary's smoke and quickly cranked the Loach and headed for the pickup point. Gary helped the other gunner into the rear of the aircraft, buckled him in, and then climbed in beside me. After he donned his flight helmet I asked, "What about Mr. Banda?"

"Head shot," he replied by way of explanation.

I headed for An Khe, a light tail wind assisting the low fuel situation. An ambulance met us at the revetment area and quickly sped off with the wounded gunner. I had lost my first wingman.

I needed a hot shower, a hot meal, and lots of good bourbon. What I got was a cold shower, C-rations, and my turn as staff duty officer. For the next twelve hours I was in charge of Delta Troop. At least technically. The actual responsibility was to decide whether or not to wake up the Old Man if anything unusual occurred during the night. The problem with this responsibility was that in Vietnam the usual was unusual.

Bleary-eyed, I lifted my head from the duty officer's desk. Something had interrupted my catnap. Glancing at the clock on the far wall of the Orderly Room, I observed that it was a little after two o'clock in the morning on a long, boring night. I hated being duty officer. For the most part, it was a make-work job. In some sense it was like flying, though; it had its moments of stark terror.

Since the duty sergeant, Sergeant Phillips, appeared to be missing, I assumed the disturbance that had awakened me was his leaving to make the two o'clock rounds. According to my duties, I should have accompanied him, but Phillips was perfectly capable of making the rounds himself. John Larkin would not have shirked his duties and would have been out making the rounds. But John was a truly dedicated soldier and performed all his tasks with equal vigor, even the meaningless and trivial ones. I chose to pattern my behavior in such matters after Eric. I made an entry in the log, confirming that the two o'clock rounds had been made, and then put my head back down on the desk.

In a matter of seconds dreamland had me behind the controls of a Loach, coming to the rescue of a damsel in distress. I could sleep with the best of them. I was about to accept my reward for rescuing the fair maiden when the screen door burst open with a thunderous bang and Sergeant Phillips rushed in yelling, "Mr. Holley! Mr. Holley, come quick. It's an emergency!"

Through my cloud of sleep-fog I sprang immediately to my feet, spilling a stale half cup of coffee across the desktop. While I mopped up the mess Sergeant Phillips continued his report. "Sir, it's Sergeant Brooks . . . he's on guard duty . . . in the bunker on the perimeter."

"Yes? So far it doesn't seem to be much of an emergency."

"He's gone psychological, sir."

I pondered this proposition momentarily, not exactly sure of what constituted going psychological. "I see . . . gone psychological, you say?"

"Yes sir. He's gone completely psychological."

"Well, that does seem serious. Is there any immediate danger?"

"No, sir. They've got him all tied up now."

"Good . . . good. Has anyone been injured?"

"Not seriously. But he did bite one of the enlisted men when they were trying to tie him up."

"Well, that seems somewhat understandable. You get into a scuffle, sometimes you get bitten. Let's go check it out."

When Sergeant Phillips and I arrived at the bunker a fair-sized crowd had gathered despite the hour. Most of them had wandered over from other guard bunkers, drawn by the excitement. I immediately took charge. "All right, let's break it up. The show's over. You men get back to your posts." The onlookers departed reluctantly, and I entered the bunker.

Inside I found a wild-eyed Sergeant Brooks, bound tightly from head to toe. He was also gagged and was being watched closely from a safe distance by two enlisted men. "Thank God you got here, sir," one of them greeted me.

"We didn't know what else to do after we got him tied up."

"Look at this bite," the other man said, exposing the fleshy part of his arm and thrusting it toward me. A deep and bruising imprint of a human mouth had been forged into the arm. "That sucker bit the hell out of me!"

"That 'sucker' is a sergeant in the U.S. Army, and you will hereafter refer to him with the proper respect, Specialist," I admonished the man.

"Not anymore he ain't," the man responded.

"I think you're confused, Specialist."

"Well, sir, in this case it don't really matter what you think. He thinks he's a dog, and that's what counts. And I never met a dog that cares if you call it 'sucker.' "

"What do you mean he thinks he's a dog?"

"Just that, sir. That's what started the ruckus. All of a sudden Sergeant Brooks hops down on all fours and starts howling and growling and yelping and crawling around the bunker. At first we thought he was just pulling a little joke, but then the sucker bit me. It took several of us to get him trussed up like that."

"I see," I said. "Well, take off the gag."

"Not me. He's got mighty sharp teeth. I'm not getting close to him."

"Pansy," I retorted, moving over to remove the gag from Brooks, who began growling fiercely as I approached. "Good boy . . . nice boy," I spoke soothingly while patting him gently on the head. Brooks whined his appreciation, recognizing a dog lover. I gently removed the gag, and Brooks licked my hand in gratitude.

"Well, ain't that something," the specialist said. "You gentled him right down."

"I was raised in the country," I responded by way of explanation. I cautiously untied Brooks's feet and hands while continuing to pat him gently on the head, occasionally scratching him behind the ear. Brooks got up on all fours and began rubbing against my leg. I fashioned one of the pieces of rope into a collar, slipping it around his neck, and tied a second piece of rope to the collar.

"Well, that takes care of that," I said, handing the rope to the specialist.

"What do you mean, that takes care of that?" the specialist queried as he hesitantly took the proffered rope. "What are we supposed to do with him?"

"Oh, you just keep him here and pet him occasionally. Put out a bowl of water . . . and maybe some food scraps. If he isn't better by daylight, we'll call in the vet."

Due to my tour as duty officer I was scheduled to have the next day off. However, fate had me scheduled to fly anyway. The Fourth Infantry Division had stirred up a real hornet's nest near Dak To, and they were having to call for assistance from every unit in II Corps, our troop included. Fate also had me scheduled for a close encounter with an NVA marksman, but it was the Blues that would catch the brunt of the engagement. Major Williams had been promoted to lieutenant colonel and sent to the Pentagon. Somehow he'd managed to take GI with him. His replacement, Major Talbot, was an unknown quantity, and the troop was about to step into some of the fiercest fighting we'd encountered.

Eric Masterson's luck hadn't changed any since he'd won the coin toss that determined ownership of the tiger-tooth trophy. He was heading home on a Freedom Bird, rather than to Dak To in a Loach. The tooth continued to adorn his neck as we bade each other solemn farewell and made a date to meet at the Seattle airport when I got back to the States. I was glad for Eric, sad for me. My war would be much lonelier. But Victor Charlie was going to see that I wasn't bored.

17

■ ■ ■ ■ ■ ■ ■ ■ ■ ■ ■ ■ ■ ■ ■

Head Shot

IT WAS MAY 10, 1969, A DATE I WOULD NEVER FORGET. IT started off as an ordinary day—beautiful weather, clear skies and sunshine. In another time and place it would have been perfect weather for heading to the beach. I was in Stan McDonald's hooch sponging an after-lunch beer when the Blues' platoon leader rapped quickly on the door and, not waiting, came on in. Stan didn't like the message he brought with him. When the LT told him about the mission Stan explained in uncertain terms that it was utterly absurd to use Blue Platoon to reinforce an infantry battalion. The LT pointed out that what remained of the battalion wasn't much larger than a platoon now anyway. The Fourth Infantry Division had stepped into some hard-core fighting near Dak To. They were heavily outmanned by swarms of NVA regulars coming across the border from Cambodia. They were pulling in reinforcements from every unit in II Corps.

"Lieutenant, did it ever occur to anyone that if they're getting chewed up that badly, they might be using the wrong strategy? Maybe they should try cutting their losses short instead of pouring more fuel onto the fire," Stan argued.

The LT ignored McDonald's sarcasm. "Have the men at the flight line at 0600. I'll brief them prior to departure."

"Yes sir. But I still say it's downright stupid."

The LT departed, and Stan began packing his gear. He took extra care with the task, for he knew they would quite likely be jumping into some hot stuff. His gear carefully assembled, he swung the backpack on and buckled it down. Then he headed for the Blues barracks to get the men squared away.

I headed for the Ready Room for the pilot's briefing.

The new major gave the flight crew briefing personally, another indicator that we weren't going on a routine mission. We would be staging out of a rearming and refueling point about ten miles southwest of Dak To. To say that we were nervous would have been an understatement. Nobody liked working the Dak To area, particularly scouts. It was a main embarkation route from North Vietnam. This meant lots of NVA, as the Fourth Division was once again discovering. More importantly to us, it meant lots of inexperienced NVA soldiers who would shoot at scouts at every opportunity. Such naïve attacks lent credence to the air cavalry's tactical employment of aeroscouts, but it was mighty hard on the scouts and the Loaches.

In addition, the Tet Offensive of 1968 was still recent enough to be considered a current event, rather than a battle of historic note. In II Corps that engagement was virtually synonymous with the battle for Dak To. The fighting became so fierce that the gunships didn't even bother to take off. They just parked the helicopters facing west and fired across the Dak To runway. We didn't win that one—unless not losing equates to winning—but we held on to Dak To per se. The area surrounding Dak To continued to belong to Charlie and the NVA.

We were also using a heavy lineup for this mission: five slicks, three Loaches, and four Cobras. Four of the slicks would be used to transport the Blues; the fifth would serve as the C & C ship, with the Lift Platoon leader providing the honors. That bothered me some. He didn't have a lot of experience, and I had a feeling that this mission would end up needing all the experience we could muster. John Larkin, who would be leading the two teams of Cobras, must have shared my opinion. He'd loaded the gun teams with the most experienced pilots. He even dragged a disgruntled Dave Horton out of bed to fly as his own copilot. Dave was not pleased but was obliged through past favors to cater to John's whims.

As for the scouts, I would be rotating the other two Loaches, which were piloted by Sam Hawkins and Gary Botts. Sam was an experienced wingman who was being groomed to take over a lead position. When he was flying I would take up the role of wingman and provide training from that vantage point. Gary was an RLO who had been newly assigned to the scouts. When he was flying I would take up the role of lead and provide training from that position. If the mission turned out to be as hot as everyone expected, it was quite likely that my two assistants would receive the ultimate in on-the-job training.

The major's operations order had the scouts going directly to the refueling point, where they would await the remainder of the flight. The Hueys and Cobras would insert the Blues about twenty miles southwest of Dak To, where they would link up with the battalion from the Fourth Division. The battalion would be responsible for ground security at the LZ, and Larkin would use both Cobra teams to provide airborne support. After the insertion the Hueys and Cobras would rendezvous with the scouts at the refueling point, and we would begin our normal cavalry routine, using two Loaches, two Cobras, and a C & C bird. The four Hueys would remain on standby at the refueling point to pick up the Blues. The extra Loach and two Cobras would be rotated each time we came back to refuel. With this plan everyone got to rest except me and the C & C. I decided to ask for a raise.

I was sitting in my Loach, helmet off, awaiting crank time. Two rows of revetments over from me I heard McDonald yell "Saddle up" to the Blues, who were lounging near the flight line awaiting departure time. I'd watched their LT finish his briefing several minutes before. Now it was H-hour, time to take off. Following their routine loading plan, the four squads of Blues moved to their respective helicopters and climbed aboard. Old King, the retired LRRP German shepherd, hopped on board the lead aircraft.

The Hueys were parked on the taxiway, their engines running. According to SOP, Stan would be in the trail aircraft, Chalk 4, and the LT would be in the lead aircraft, Chalk 1. This way the loss of a single ship wouldn't take out all of the Blues' leaders. I put on my helmet and cranked the Loach. Following my lead, the two other scouts did likewise.

The hour-long flight to the LZ seemed to pass quickly. I did not envy the Blues. They were about to be inserted into hell . . . and they knew it. I'm sure they passed the time by contemplating their own mortality and the surprises that fate had awaiting them. I suspected that what little conversation occurred in the backs of the Hueys was mostly false bravado, coming from the less-experienced members of the squad. The older hands knew better: There was no bravado in a firefight, only a desperate scramble for survival.

Over the UHF Chalk 1 suddenly announced, "LZ in two minutes." From my trailing vantage point I could observe the entire flight, including the two teams of Cobras that were flanking the slicks. The Hueys began an abrupt descent as the Cobras suddenly forged ahead of the flight, rockets and guns blazing. It was show time.

Rather than adhering strictly to the briefing plan and going directly to the refueling point, I chose to watch the insertion. It would give me and my accompanying scouts an opportunity to familiarize ourselves with the layout before we began our screening operations. The other two Loaches picked up on my trail as I maintained a slow orbit a quarter mile from the LZ. This gave us a good view of the area, and the radios provided continual commentary for the visual action. I recognized John Larkin's voice and call sign as he provided directions for employing the gun teams.

"Hawk 21, this is Hawk 24. The good guys are in the trees on the east side of the LZ. Everything else is unknown. Your team covers the north and south. I'll hit the west," Larkin said over the frequency that was reserved for the Cobras.

"Roger, 24. I've got north and south. We're inbound. Take care of yourself now."

"Wilco. Out."

John began punching off ten-pounders toward the tree line on the west side of the LZ. In the front seat Dave began walking the 40mm along the same tree line. Larkin completed the initial run and swung the Cobra tightly into a left bank, rotor blades skimming the treetops, to enter the outbound leg of the racetrack pattern they were using for the gun runs. As John moved outbound his wingman turned inbound. The slicks were on short final for the LZ—a simultaneous four-ship landing—and had not taken any fire yet. So far, so good. It looked like it might be a quiet landing. Larkin turned back inbound as his wingman, Hawk 27, broke off his run.

"I'm taking fire from a .51-caliber," Hawk 27 shrieked over the UHF as he dropped his Cobra below the trees to break line of sight with the heavy-caliber weapon.

Taking in the situation, I realized that Larkin's Cobra was a sitting duck. He had no possibility of breaking line of sight with the enemy gun. His only defense was to provide a quicker offense than the enemy machine gunner. But a green line of tracers from the .51-caliber was already snaking a deadly path toward his Cobra. It was too late for him to shoot . . . or dodge.

The precision firing from the .51-caliber machine gun began ripping the Cobra apart. The skill of the enemy gunner was admirable. He had waited until the gunship was in its most vulnerable position before he opened up. Dave and John could neither return fire nor break line of sight with the machine gun, and their wing Cobra was still on its outbound leg. John and Dave must have cringed reflexively as the bullets tore through the cockpit. The noise must have been deafening as fragments of radios, instruments, and Plexiglas suddenly became deadly missiles. At some point the flight controls must have quit responding. The Cobra listed sharply starboard and plunged, smoking, toward the trees.

In the LZ the skids of the slicks were just touching the ground, and the Blues began scrambling off. Herded by McDonald and the LT, they made a serpentine dash for the eastern tree line. Thus far they had received no fire during the insertion, but for a few seconds they would be exposed and vulnerable. They were still several meters from the shelter of the jungle when the mortars began falling in front of them. Reflexively and instantaneously most of the Blues dived for the ground. Several of the newer members of the platoon were slow to react and paid the price. I could imagine the sounds of the exploding mortar rounds being joined by the inhuman shrieks of the wounded and dying men. Then the AKs and machine guns—hidden in the tree lines to the north and west—opened up, adding chaos to the chaos.

While the mortars had the Blues pinned down the enemy's guns concentrated on the four slicks, which were desperately trying to take off amid the fusillade. With mortars falling to the Blues' front, their escape path lay to the rear, to return to the helicopters. Several of the Blues began crawling back toward the slicks when the lead Huey, Chalk 1, suddenly exploded, scattering debris throughout the LZ. Two of the three remaining slicks soon met a similar fate. A crewman from Chalk 4 came running out of the inferno clothes ablaze. In his panic he raced straight for the enemy machine-gun positions. They aimed low, crippling him. He slowly burned to death, his shrieks of agony no doubt filling the air. Chalk 3 managed to get airborne. For a moment I thought he was going to make it. Then, engine smoking and sputtering, he banked sharply to the left and disappeared into the jungle to the west.

The enemy began walking the mortars in toward the remaining Blues. They were completely trapped . . . nowhere to either run or hide. Their only chance was to go forward quickly, to try to penetrate the wall of mortar fire that was steadfastly moving closer. The machine guns and AKs, having run out of helicopter targets, would soon begin turning their attention to the Blues, providing insurance for the mortars. The Blues timed their spurt for safety to take advantage of the infrequent lapses in the incoming mortar rounds, those short pauses when several tubes would be reloading simultaneously. When they judged such a lapse was about to occur the desperate Blues sprang to their feet and raced forward in unison, dragging their wounded with them. The expected lull in incoming mortar fire did not occur. The Blues had guessed wrong.

*　　*　　*

The insertion completed, in a manner of speaking, I took my Loaches to the refueling point. We were joined shortly thereafter by the C & C ship and the three remaining Cobras. In addition to the Cobra and four Hueys that had been lost, one of the returning Cobras had been badly damaged. Division gave us till noon to search for our downed crews, including Dave and John. If we didn't find them by then, we were to get back into the thick of things. During the search I alternated between flying wing on Sam Hawkins and flying lead for Gary Botts, switching roles after each refueling stop. We refueled three times before our twelve o'clock deadline arrived. Our search had been fruitless. Even though we had the approximate coordinates for where Dave and John had gone down, we could find no trace of them or their Cobra. The thick jungle canopy had simply swallowed them.

We took a lunch break before returning to our primary mission of providing perimeter security for the Division. I was on my third box of C-ration beef and potatoes when the Lift Platoon leader, Captain Davidson, began yelling at me for holding up the mission. I lived by a few simple philosophies, one of which involved going into combat on a full stomach. I ignored Davidson and finished my lunch at a leisurely pace, including the stale cookies and canned peaches, and then cranked my Loach and headed for the battle area.

Despite our finding heavy signs of NVA activity in the area, the afternoon passed uneventfully. At least it did until around four o'clock. Sam Hawkins, who was taking his turn in the scout rotation plan, committed an error in judgment that I was unable to correct before we had to suffer the consequences. Or, more accurately, before my door gunner and I had to suffer the consequences. The unit we were directly supporting was receiving sniper fire, and they requested that we try to locate the marksmen.

"Romeo Alpha 6, this is Blackhawk 15. Over." Hawkins was temporarily using his FM radio, which was normally dedicated for interscout communications, to coordinate with the infantry unit. Our interscout communications were being conducted on a shared UHF frequency. This worked out all right as long as no one else chose to use the UHF at an inopportune moment. Usually they didn't, recognizing they could be jeopardizing the scouts. But sometimes they got excited.

"Roger, Blackhawk 15, this is Alpha 6. Over."

"Roger, 6. I understand you folks are receiving some sniper fire. Over."

"Roger that. It seems to be coming from the trees to the northwest, across the clearing from us. We'd sure appreciate any help you could give us. Over."

"Good copy, 6. What's your location? Over."

"We're in the southern tree line of a clearing located at coordinates Quebec, Romeo, Yankee, Yankee, Sierra, Bravo, Delta, Delta. Over."

"Roger, 6. Wait one. Out." Sam switched to the UHF and gave the encrypted coordinates to the C & C. Scouts didn't carry a CEOI or maps. It was difficult to fly and read at the same time. It was also an unnecessary security risk, since scouts operated so close to the enemy. If they went down, the information could fall into the wrong hands. Sam followed the directions provided by the C & C, and moments later we were in the vicinity of the infantry.

"Romeo Alpha 6, this is Hawk 15. Over."

"Roger, 15."

"We should be in your vicinity. Do you have visual contact? Over."

"Negative, 15. But we hear you. Over."

"Roger, 6. We'll be moving into the clearing. Pop smoke on each of your flanks so we can pinpoint your location."

"Stand by, 15," Alpha 6 responded. Moments later he reported, "Yellow smoke's out on each flank."

In a few seconds the smoke began trickling above the treetops. Unfortunately, this did not allow us to pinpoint the position of the infantry. Yellow smoke began rising above every tree line in the area. I called Sam on the UHF. "Tell him to go to his alternate frequency and pop smoke again. But let us identify the color. He can confirm."

"Alpha 6, this is 15. We've got yellow smoke all over the place. Looks like you've got lots of company out here. Advise you to switch to your alternate frequency and pop smoke again. This time let us identify the color. Over."

"Understood, 15. Smoke's out, and we're switching frequencies. Out."

This time we got a virtual rainbow of smoke surrounding the clearing. Charlie was guessing. Sam picked the red smoke. "Alpha 6, I've got you as the red smoke. Over."

"Red smoke confirmed."

Finally we were making progress. Of course, I didn't feel very comfortable with the situation. It seemed obvious that we could choose any of the three remaining tree lines and immediately find "snipers." What these folks needed was a brigade of infantry, not scouts. I was contemplating this dilemma when the C & C called Sam on the UHF, presenting me with a more urgent dilemma.

"Hawk 15, this is Hawk 36. We just spotted three bad guys running down the dirt road to your south. They jumped into a clump of bushes on the east side of the road. About a hundred meters from you. Over."

Sam immediately headed for the bad guys while maintaining a continuous dialogue with the C & C. I was necessarily compelled to accompany him, while I sought to break into their conversation to point out that if the C & C could see the bad guys from fifteen hundred feet, we didn't really need to look at them close up and personal. The C & C should have had the Cobras rolling in hot. Unfortunately, the UHF frequency was blocked by Sam and the C & C, and the FM was blocked with ground traffic. I was temporarily incommunicado. I tried Guard but got a multitude of simultaneous responses from army and air force pilots all over Vietnam. I didn't recognize any of the voices. By then it was too late anyway. We'd arrived at the suspected area.

The clump of bushes did not provide us with a definitive clue for locating the quarry. It was like searching for a man wearing green fatigues on an army post. However, being the outstanding scouts that we were, we soon located the enemy despite the vagueness of the clue.

Or, more precisely, the enemy located us. Even more precisely, they located me. They let Sam's Loach go on past, then they emptied three magazines of AK rounds into my Loach from a distance of about fifteen feet. It was the fastest and slowest few seconds in eternity. Everything seemed to be happening in slow motion, yet with blazing speed. At the initial outpouring of automatic weapons fire my door gunner attempted to bring his M-60 to bear on the hidden soldiers, while I pulled the collective up under my armpit in an effort to break contact with them. Sam Hawkins began swinging his Loach around to provide covering fire. Then there was a loud bang in my left ear.

My last fully conscious awareness was of my instruments going into the red zone from the maximum power I had applied, and my door gunner flopping around in his seat, holding his stomach with both hands and screaming, "I'm hit!" I continued flying the helicopter automatically, breaking line of sight with Charlie, my door gunner continuing to writhe in agony.

I didn't completely lose consciousness, but I had no reasoning processes and no memory. Quite simply, I could not think. I felt that I should be doing something to help my door gunner, but for the life of me I couldn't figure out what it might be. I tried talking on the radio to solicit advice, but no one responded. Finally I set the Loach down in the first available clearing. Sam landed his Loach nearby and sent his door gunner over to assist us. Together we carried my door gunner over to Sam's Loach and laid him out on the floor, tying him in. Then I returned to my Loach and strapped in.

Sam kept waiting for me to take off. Since I was in the crippled Loach, he wanted me to lead so he could keep me in sight. I thought very hard about what I would do once I was airborne, but I couldn't come up with an answer. I couldn't remember where we were or which direction we needed to go. Finally I motioned to Sam to lead, and I fell in on his tail as he took off.

Twenty minutes later we landed at the hospital helipad at Dak To. While my door gunner was loaded into an ambulance I checked out the damage to my Loach. My foggy brain had begun to clear some by this time, but it would be another two hours before my memory completely returned.

While the Loach bore a strong resemblance to a chunk of Swiss cheese, I found no major damage to its flightworthiness. Later Joe Watkins would chastise me for flying the Loach home with a push-pull tube that had almost been severed by the gunfire. He would have chastised me for something anyway. Once more I had broken one of "his birds."

My loss of communications was explained by the bullet that had hit me. Prior to impacting my helmet, the armor-piercing round had passed through the ashtray in the passenger compartment—where it shed its armor-piercing jacket—and then severed my communications cord. It struck my helmet behind the left ear, shattering my microphone. Later, Doc Post dug the bullet out of my helmet. It had entered behind my left ear, circled my head, and then embedded itself in the styrofoam lining in the top of the helmet. Doc speculated that the bullet's passage through the ashtray had saved my life. This also suggested that smoking is not always hazardous to your health.

We headed back to An Khe, weary and battle worn. I used my door gunner's helmet for the return flight and plugged into the communications cord on the left side of the Loach. It made transmissions a bit clumsy but workable. Of the twelve helicopters that had left An Khe that morning, only seven would be returning, and two of those were badly damaged. We also no longer had a Blue Platoon, including the adopted LRRP retiree, Old King. While the Blues were en route to Dak To the Huey in which he was riding had hit a sudden air pocket at fifteen hundred feet and been buffeted rather severely. King was roused from his sleep by the jolting, which somewhat resembled the impact of the skids touching down on the ground, and immediately jumped out of the helicopter to run around the LZ.

More importantly, John Larkin and Dave Horton were missing in action.

About a week after my head shot we got word that Dave and John had been found by a South Vietnamese Army patrol. Their escape and evasion training had apparently paid off having managed to avoid the NVA for several tortuous days. John had been wounded when the Cobra was hit, but Dave refused to leave him behind, carrying him most of the way back to friendly territory. It reminded me of the time, on my first scout mission, when I carried Jim Davis out of the jungle. We also heard that the South Vietnamese

Army was quite unhappy with Dave. In his confused state of mind he had not recognized that the Vietnamese soldiers who found them were of the friendly variety. He heard only Vietnamese, and he'd been hiding from the Vietnamese for several days. The unwitting soldier who stumbled onto their hiding place got a Bowie knife plunged through his throat before Dave could be restrained and identities established. Since their tours were nearly finished by this time, neither Dave nor John returned to Delta Troop. John went to a hospital in Japan and then on to the States. Dave's Freedom Bird took the direct route.

Gary Botts, the new guy I had been training as a wingman, was quite upset by the scouting events he'd been exposed to at Dak To. He went to Major Talbot and explained that he'd spent twenty-six long and arduous years developing his body to its present state of perfection, and he had no intention of throwing all that work down the drain. At his request he was transferred to the Lift Platoon to fly slicks. I guess it never occurred to him that we had lost eight Huey pilots at Dak To and no scout pilots. Even though flying scouts was normally the more hazardous of the two occupations, you only had to get killed once to ruin the odds.

The Scout Platoon leader also informed me that my scouting days were over. There was an unwritten rule in the cavalry: six months or five hundred hours of flying scouts and you were transferred to a position with better prospects for longevity . . . like jumping Snake River Canyon on a motorcycle. I was approaching ten months and a thousand hours. When my six-months or five-hundred-hour milestone had passed I'd volunteered to continue flying scouts. I was enjoying it by then. Insanity ran in my family.

Anyway, the platoon leader felt that my head shot had come too close for the comfort of his conscience. He went to Major Talbot and had me reassigned as supply officer. I was now officially a clerk and an ash-and-trash pilot. Within a few days I had the supply paperwork in such good shape that the supply sergeant requested that I never set foot in the supply room again. The request was made politely . . . but firmly.

So I concentrated on the safe and routine task of flying

ash-and-trash missions. My first such mission involved picking up the chaplain from Blackhawk Firebase and bringing him to the troop to perform Sunday services. It wasn't really Sunday, of course. There were only so many chaplains available to cover a long circuit. However, the army guaranteed that the chaplain would arrive on Sunday, plus or minus three days. So whenever the chaplain arrived we pretended it was Sunday. On this particular "Sunday" I set out in a Loach to fetch the chaplain and his aide. In the process I was giving some stick time to a new scout pilot. I soon discovered that ash-and-trash missions weren't necessarily as boring as they were cracked up to be. Almost anything can be livened up with anti-aircraft fire.

18

■ ■ ■ ■ ■ ■ ■ ■ ■ ■ ■ ■ ■ ■ ■ ■

Scout Interlude

THE TROOP'S NEWEST WOBBLY ONE, DARYL HAMMONDS, was waiting for me when I arrived at the revetment area for my first official ash-and-trash mission. He needed to get some stick time in the Loach before he would be ready for operational scout missions. First you learned to fly the aircraft, then you learned to fly scouts. That was the rule. We would be going to Blackhawk Firebase, a distance of about thirty miles to the west, to bring the chaplain back for Sunday services. I tossed my helmet into the left seat and began preflighting the Loach.

"Sir, I've already done the preflight," Daryl spoke up.

"I should hope so. I'm just checking to make sure you didn't miss anything important . . . like the Jesus nut. And don't call me sir."

"Yes sir."

"Why're you carrying all that personal equipment?" The newby had a carbine, pistol, flight helmet, chicken plate, rations, and canteen. By comparison, I only had my pistol and flight helmet.

"I thought this is what we were supposed to carry."

"Maybe on a real mission. But this is ash-and-trash. There's no reason we shouldn't be comfortable. Throw that excess baggage in a stowage compartment."

"But the SOP says"—Daryl began protesting, but discontinued when he noticed my glare—"well, can I at least keep the chicken plate?"

"What for?"

"In case we get shot at. This is a combat zone, you know."

"Yes, but it's not a combat mission. Throw your stuff in the back. We're not going anyplace where we're going to get shot at. Trust me."

The newby didn't seem convinced, but he complied with my request. We cranked the Loach and headed for Blackhawk Firebase. He flew; I criticized. It took several miles before I could entice him to maintain a comfortable altitude. He kept wanting to get above fifty feet. Eventually he grasped the concept of a scout nosebleed, and we skimmed along Highway 19, clipping antennas off of jeeps and APCs. I pointed out the two artillery firebases, and their respective ranges, positioned at five-mile intervals between An Khe and the pass to the west, Mang Yang Pass. Then we entered the formidable pass, its steep cliffs flanking the helicopter as we sped along the valley floor. It had been the final battleground for many an unfortunate soldier.

As we approached the western edge of Mang Yang I took the controls and swung the helicopter up into the mountainous terrain to the north. A few seconds later I was hovering along the "graveyard," hundreds of white crosses that covered the slopes above the pass.

"What are those?" Daryl asked.

"Those are the graves of the last folks who tangled with the North Vietnamese. They're the graves of French soldiers, buried standing up and facing east . . . toward their homeland."

"There must be hundreds of them."

"At least. Although I hear this one's small compared to the one at Dien Bien Phu. I always like to swing by here when I'm in the vicinity. Helps one maintain perspective. It serves as a reminder that old Uncle Sam's probably got a tiger by the tail. Let's go get the chaplain. You've got the controls."

"I've got the controls," Daryl confirmed as he took over

the chore of flying the Loach. "How do I get there from here?"

"IFR."

"You want me to fly instruments?" Daryl asked incredulously. "I didn't know there were any electronic aids to navigation around here."

"There aren't. IFR: I Follow Roads. Go back and pick up Highway 19 and turn right. Blackhawk's the next firebase up the road . . . about eight or ten miles."

The chaplain and his aide were waiting for us when we landed at the Blackhawk helipad. Daryl stayed with the controls, engine running, while I got out and assisted them into the passenger compartment, checking to be sure that they were properly buckled in. We were also required by regulations to provide a passenger briefing prior to departure. The army gave us briefing cards to assist in this endeavor, but I preferred my own paraphrased version: "Gentlemen, do not fire any weapons without my permission. Do not unbuckle your seat belts without my permission. If we crash, do not leave the aircraft without my permission. Do not throw up in the aircraft without my permission. And after we land, do not walk into any turning rotor blades without my permission." I pointed to a nonexistent button on the back of the pilot's seat and continued, "And, most importantly, do not press that button without my permission. Are there any questions?"

"Yes, Driver, what does this button do?" the chaplain replied, pointing to the nonexistent button.

"That's the self-destruct button. It's so we don't fall into enemy hands. And don't call me Driver."

"What should I call you?"

"Sir will do nicely."

"Yes, sir."

I loved it when captains called me sir. "Very well, gentlemen. Enjoy your flight." I climbed into the left seat, accompanied by some strange looks from Daryl.

The return flight was uneventful. At least it was until we arrived back at Mang Yang Pass and dropped down its backside. As we crested the pass, dropping down into the valley on the eastern side at about fifty feet altitude and a hundred knots, we suddenly found ourselves in the middle of a convoy ambush. Vehicles were strung out, with several stalled and burning, along about a two-mile stretch of road. The ambush hadn't been in progress very long. The fighting was still intense, accompanied by the chatter of automatic weapons and exploding grenades. As soon as Charlie spotted our Loach they turned their guns on us. We represented an unexpected and prized target. Charlie loved to bring down a helicopter, even a small one.

"I've got the controls," I yelled to Daryl. The quickest route to safety appeared to be straight up. If we could get a thousand feet of altitude quickly we would be out of range of the small-caliber weapons. I pulled maximum power and brought the cyclic back into my stomach. The Loach shot skyward, trading airspeed for altitude. As I passed through a thousand feet I glanced back at my two passengers. They were both lost in prayer, their heads bowed and their hands clasped before their faces. I would have to add something about praying to my passenger briefing.

Suddenly black puffs of smoke began bursting around the helicopter. Son of a bitch, I thought. My wide-eyed copilot was staring in transfixed amazement at the tiny black cloudbursts. Not being certain of the range of the antiaircraft weapon, but figuring I couldn't outclimb it quickly enough, I bottomed the collective and pushed left pedal. This no-power, out-of-trim condition had the effect of causing the Loach to immediately plunge earthward, falling like a rock. It also had the effect of causing my copilot and passengers to grab on for dear life. The prayer services in the passenger compartment intensified. As the jungle rushed rapidly toward us I brought the power back in at the last possible moment, timing the maneuver to put us in a treetop-skimming, en-route condition for the continuing flight to An Khe. When I had the helicopter stabilized I said to Daryl, "You've got the controls."

"Roger, I've got the controls," he responded, his shaking hands grasping the cyclic and collective. "I thought you said I didn't need a chicken plate for ash-and-trash missions."

"You don't."

"You don't think you need a chicken plate when you're getting shot at like that?" he responded hotly.

"Oh, that wasn't really getting shot at. Wait till you have a few scout missions under your belt—then you'll know the difference. Hell, I've had friendly fire come closer than that."

When we got to An Khe the chaplain requested a different "driver" for his return flight.

My ash-and-trash missions generally settled into a dull and uneventful routine. At least for the most part. There were occasional exceptions. Like the day I had to ferry a Loach to maintenance support at Qui Nhon. Operations had decided to kill two birds with one stone by having the Huey IP, Mark Harbison, pick me up at Qui Nhon and give me a currency ride on the way back. Shortly after I arrived at Qui Nhon Airport things began going downhill . . . and continued going that way.

I led the two-ship flight into Qui Nhon Airport. On arrival, Ground Control provided specific instructions for taxiing to Hangar 8, our destination. The hangar was located west of the runway at the end of a long taxiway. I hovered up the taxiway toward the large, open bay doors of Hangar 8 while looking for a place to park the Loach. Mark parked the Huey alongside the taxiway and waited for me. His copilot left for parts unknown, since he wouldn't be returning with us.

When I was about fifty feet from the hangar I noticed a faint yellow line painted on the taxiway as it passed beneath the chin bubble. Holding my position to inspect it, I was barely able to decipher the faded, upside-down letters, which read: NO FLY LINE.

Well, I thought, since I can't get any closer, this must be where they want the helicopter parked. Turning the Loach parallel to the yellow line, I sat it on the ground and cut the throttle to flight idle. I took off my helmet and began filling out the logbook while I waited for the engine to cool down.

About this time a young captain came storming out of the hangar and headed toward me, obviously upset.

Thrusting his head inside the cockpit, he began screaming at me, "What's the matter with you? Can't you read?"

This appeared to be a rhetorical question, since the captain could see for himself that I was in the process of both reading from and writing in the logbook. Not realizing that he actually expected a response, I ignored the question and continued with my logbook entries. This did not ingratiate me with the captain.

"Mister, when a superior officer asks you a question, you answer him!" he shrieked.

"Sorry, Captain. I'm not sure I understood the question," I responded.

"First off, you address me as sir. I said: Can't you read?"

"Oh . . . yes, sir, it was one of the requirements to get into flight school."

"Don't you smart-mouth me. What does that say?" the now–red-faced captain screeched as he pointed at the yellow words painted in the taxiway.

I looked in the direction he was pointing and squinted my eyes real hard. "Sir, that says No Fly Line."

"Then why did you fly beyond it?"

"Beg your pardon, sir, but I didn't fly past it. As you can see, I'm parked right on top of it, not beyond it."

"Are you calling me a liar?" he screamed. "Do you know the penalty for being insubordinate to a superior officer?"

"Yes sir," I responded. "They send you to Vietnam."

"You pick this helicopter up and move it off of my yellow line, and then you report to me in my office."

Now, to tell you the truth, under normal circumstances I might have been more tolerant with the captain, but flying ash-and-trash for a couple of weeks had gotten me a shade on the irritable side. And here I was—perfectly innocent of committing the crime of flying past the no fly line, which incidentally belonged to the army, not the captain—being lambasted by a straphanger who got hot meals three times a day and stole his war stories from *Stars and Stripes*. Observing that the engine temperature had been stabilized for two minutes, I cut the throttle and killed the engine.

The captain exploded. "What the hell's wrong with you? Don't you know a direct order when you hear one? You crank this bird up and move it off my yellow line. I'm getting sick and tired of you warrant officers coming in from the boondocks and ignoring our rules and regulations. You may get away with your barbaric behavior out there, but this is civilization, and you'll damn well do as you're told."

I looked the red-faced captain in the eye and slowly pulled out my .38-caliber pistol.

"What are you doing?" he asked, a note of concern edging into his tone.

Checking the cylinder of my .38, I discovered that once again I had forgotten to load the pistol prior to takeoff. I began taking bullets out of my ammunition belt and methodically putting them into the cylinder.

"What are you doing with that pistol?" the captain repeated, taking a step backward.

"Captain, you got many rats around here?" I asked.

Momentarily caught off guard by the unexpected question, he responded, "A few."

"Just as I thought. I've observed these symptoms before . . . up around Dak To . . . terminal stages of hydrophobia."

The captain, still unsure of my intentions, stared at me as I continued. "Take my word for it, sir. It's too late for medical assistance. There's only one solution now." With a flick of my wrist I snapped the cylinder shut on the .38.

The captain jumped back from the Loach and scurried for the safety of the maintenance hangar. I put away my pistol, grabbed my gear, and headed for the Huey.

"What was all that about?" Mark asked as I climbed into the right seat.

"Fellow had hydrophobia."

"Aah . . . that certainly explains it. Well, let's do some emergency procedures here—they've got a nice runway and not much traffic today—and then we'll head back to An Khe. You've got the controls."

"I have the controls," I responded. I hovered the Huey back up the taxiway and then executed a departure. After flying the Loach for so long, the Huey seemed large and clumsy. It was like switching to a Cadillac after getting used to a Porsche.

As I turned downwind in the traffic pattern Mark said, "Make an extended downwind leg. I'll give you a hydraulics failure first."

"You're not supposed to tell me what the emergency is going to be, Mark. That's why they call it training. You're supposed to surprise me."

"Sorry. Sometimes I forget. I'll give you a surprise later. I promise."

I held the altitude at five hundred feet as the ocean sped rapidly past us. Most of the Qui Nhon traffic pattern was over water. Mark was looking out his side of the aircraft, watching the boats as I began turning into the base leg of the pattern. He reached over without looking and turned off the "hydraulics switch." The engine immediately quit. Mark had accidentally turned off the master fuel switch, which was located next to the hydraulics switch.

"Goddam it, Mark. Now look what you've done."

"Never yell at your IP," Mark replied. "You will always get a pink slip. I have the aircraft."

"You have the aircraft," I responded, relinquishing the controls. "You'll think pink slip if you don't manage to make the runway. The army'll make you buy this thing. You'll be on the installment plan the rest of your life. And furthermore, I don't relish the idea of an early-morning swim. That water looks damned cold."

"Boy, you're irritable today," Mark replied, and then he busied himself with trying to stretch the glide path of the rapidly descending Huey. Our altitude had been too low to attempt an aerial restart of the engine. The rotor RPM began to bleed off as Mark began milking it to increase the glide. We were still about three hundred feet from the runway and continuing to descend. For a moment it looked like Mark might just squeeze it out: We were only about fifty feet from the runway when the rotor RPM got too low to maintain lift and the Huey fell through. I had been right about the ocean water: It was cold.

The Huey hit the water belly first and then rocked violently forward before settling back. The jolt slammed me against my shoulder harness, which was locked. The aircraft began floating, but this wouldn't last long, as water quickly filled the bilge. The primary danger in ditching a helicopter is the main rotor, which is why you're supposed to roll the aircraft on its side. That way the water halts its spinning. Unfortunately, we didn't have enough rotor RPM to roll the helicopter.

Jettisoning the doors, we dived into the water and swam beneath the surface until we were well clear of the sinking Huey and its still-turning rotor. Gulping for air, we trod water and watched the bird sink to its final resting place. Then we swam for shore.

When the ash-and-trash routine became too dull I had a surefire method for relieving the boredom. I would go visit the Special Forces over near Pleiku, the ones that provided me with my special bullets. I could always find some reason to fly over to Camp Enari and get weathered in for a couple of days. Unlike some folks, the Special Forces were always glad to see me. Of course, they were probably glad to see anyone with a helicopter. The trade for their hospitality was to take a group of them up to ten thousand feet and let them jump out. I guess they got bored occasionally, too. Still, I could never understand why anyone would deliberately jump out of a perfectly good aircraft.

I arrived at the Special Forces camp about 1800 hours. They could always be counted on to provide a clean bunk for the night. I headed directly for their local bar, where I was greeted warmly.

"Hey, Chief, join us," one of the soldiers shouted to me as I entered. I recognized him from one of my previous visits as Jim Marcus, a sergeant first class on his third tour. He was seated at a table with four other members of the team. From their apparent revelry it seemed refreshment time had begun quite a bit earlier.

As they made room at the table for an additional occupant I pulled a chair over from an adjacent table and sat down. An attractive Vietnamese waitress in a miniskirt immediately served me a bottle of Wild Turkey. The Special

Forces did things right. "That's Nancy," Jim said, admiring her figure as she moved away. "She costs big bucks, but she's worth it."

"I can see why," I said conversationally. "How's the war going?"

"Oh, about the same as always. It used to be a better war. Inflation and politics are taking the fun out of it."

"Hear, hear," the other table members seconded.

"Say, Jim, did I ever tell you about John Harrison?" the soldier to my left asked.

"No, I don't believe you did, Carl," Jim responded. I was beginning to get the boys identified, there having been no introductions.

"Well," Carl replied, "John Harrison was in jump school with me back at Fort Benning. John was a big old boy, and tough. Not real smart, but he probably turned out to be a real good soldier. After all, being smart isn't necessarily a requirement for being a good soldier. His major drawback, though, was a speech impediment. When he got excited he stuttered to beat the devil, sorta like Mel Tillis.

"Anyway, we're up in the air for our very first real jump, about twenty of us cruising along at ten thousand feet in a C-130. We're all nervous as hell, except John. He's calm as can be. The green light comes on, and we all hook up and shuffle to the door. The jump master tells us to remember to count to ten and then pull our rip cords. Nothing to it. John, who was two soldiers behind me in the lineup, spoke up and said, 'Right, Jump Master. Count to ten and pull the rip cord.' Not a trace of a stutter, as there would have been if he were nervous. As for myself, I was as skittish as a cat in a room full of rocking chairs. I decided that John's veins must be filled with icewater.

"My turn came, and I stepped into the open doorway. Of course, there was no turning back at this point. You either jumped out or you were thrown out, so you might just as well pretend to be brave about it. I was determined to leave the aircraft of my own volition rather than by means of a forceful push from the jump master. I pried my fingers from the aircraft, closed my eyes, and jumped. After counting to ten I pulled the rip cord, and the parachute billowed open. I began floating earthward . . . man, what a rush.

"I guess John Harrison's nervousness didn't hit him until he stepped into that open doorway and was confronted by the reality of the situation. I later learned that it took four of them to throw him off the airplane, and he left claw marks on the door jamb.

"So here I am floating gently to earth, really enjoying the ride by this time, and I'm starting to concentrate on the landing, since I'm getting close to the ground, and a couple of seconds later John Harrison comes flying past me. As he goes by, I hear him counting: 'T-t-t-t-t-t-t-two . . . t-t-t-t-th-th-th-thr-three.' "

We burst into laughter. It was a good story. "Well, that's not a bad little tale," Jim said. "But let me tell you a good one, so you'll know the difference next time. It was a similar situation. We were airborne for our first jump. Unlike your John Harrison, Rodney Ford was clearly nervous and made no effort to hide it. But he was also a spunky little fellow.

"The jump master recognized that Rodney was rather frightened, so he provided him with an encouraging pep talk. When Rodney's turn at the door came the jump master says to him, 'Now remember, Rodney, you just count to ten and pull your rip cord. Nothing to it. Now, if for some reason your chute doesn't happen to open—and remember, Rodney, that hardly ever happens—you just count to ten again and pull your second rip cord. That'll release your emergency chute. It works just as good as your main chute. When you get to the ground there'll be a truck waiting to take you back. You got all that?'

" 'Yes, Jump Master,' Rodney says as he braces himself momentarily and then leaps into the wild blue yonder. He counts to ten and pulls his rip cord. Nothing happens. So he counts to ten again and pulls the rip cord for his emergency chute. Nothing happens. Then he looks down at the ground, searching the landscape, and says, 'Yeah, and I'll bet that fucking truck won't be there either.' "

According to the official soldier laugh meter, Jim's story had topped Carl's. While we recovered there was a momentary lull in the conversation. Nobody seemed eager to try to outdo Jim's yarn. Finally, the soldier across from me spoke up. I subsequently learned that his name was Terry. "Well, I don't know any funny stories, but I do know one interesting anecdote."

We suspected he might be setting us up. Whoever heard of a war story that wasn't funny? And *anecdote* was a pretty sophisticated word for a fellow that claimed to have a limited library of stories. We kept our guard up, not wanting to be suckered in too easily. Terry began his tale. "This one happened when I was in Africa, in the desert. I can't tell you what I was doing there, because it was classified. But there was about a hundred of us, and we were quartered in an old army post that used to belong to the French. Before we occupied it the post had been deserted for some time.

"Well, we'd been there about six months when we get in a new lieutenant as our XO. He was a pretty green pup and apparently had a strong glandular drive for members of the opposite sex. First chance he got, he pulled the first sergeant aside—so he could speak to him privately—and said, 'Say, Top, this is a pretty isolated post. What do the men do for . . . uh . . . recreation?'

"The first sergeant didn't exactly catch his drift and responded, 'Oh, we have movies in the evenings. And there's also Ping-Pong.' To which the lieutenant replies, 'Uh, Top . . . that's not exactly the type of recreation I had in mind.' This time the first sergeant understands. 'Oh, I get you, sir. Follow me. I'll show you.'

"Well, the lieutenant thought it was a bit peculiar for the first sergeant to be showing him this type of recreation, but since he considered it a vital piece of information he went along. The first sergeant took him down to the stables, which were deserted except for one stall in the far corner of the barn. Inside the stall was a camel, one of those with a single hump.

"'There she is, sir,' the first sergeant said. 'There's what?' the lieutenant responded, unsure of what the first sergeant was trying to communicate. 'There's what the men use for sexual recreation.' The lieutenant stared incredulously. 'First Sergeant, that's the most disgusting thing I've ever heard.' The first sergeant responded, somewhat surprised at the lieutenant's moral outrage, 'Oh, she's not so bad, sir. She kinda grows on you. When you've been here as long as us, you'll probably feel different.' The lieutenant stormed out, saying, 'I would never stoop that low.' The first sergeant called after him, 'But you don't have to stoop, sir. The camel does that.'

"A couple of months later the first sergeant was in the orderly room doing some paperwork when one of the enlisted men came rushing in shouting, 'First Sergeant, First Sergeant, come quick! There's a terrible ruckus down at the stables.' The first sergeant jumped up and raced to the stables. When he got there he discovered the ruckus was coming from the camel's stall. Inside he found the lieutenant, trouserless, trying to get a wild-eyed camel down on its knees.

" 'Lieutenant, what are you doing?' the flabbergasted first sergeant shouted. 'Well, you were right, Top,' the Lieutenant responded. 'When you've been here long enough, this old girl begins to look pretty good.'

" 'But sir,' the first sergeant says, 'we don't do *that* to the camel. We use the camel to ride to the village. It's about five miles to the south and has a real good cathouse.' "

When the laughter subsided following Terry's "interesting" yarn, Carl spoke up again. "Say, Larry, tell the chief that story about when your CO wanted a painting done of his wife."

"Jeez, I'd almost forgotten that one," Larry said reflectively. "Okay. Let's see now . . . this took place during my first tour in 'Nam. We were based near Kontum, and we'd fixed our area up real nice. One of our guys, Specialist Markarovich, was a pretty good artist, and he'd painted this great mural in the Enlisted Men's Club. Covered an entire wall. When the CO finds out about it he decides to have Markarovich do a portrait of his wife for a birthday present.

"The CO, Captain Andrews, calls him in and says, 'Markarovich, I saw your mural in the Enlisted Men's Club. Excellent job! I was wondering if you would do a painting for me.'

" 'Of course, sir. I'd be pleased,' Markarovich responded.

" 'Excellent! It's a portrait of my wife. Sort of a birthday present,' the captain said as he took a photograph from his wallet, fondled it lovingly for a moment, and then handed it to Markarovich, who carefully and professionally scrutinized the image of the captain's wife, a homely creature staring lifelessly at the camera from beneath a huge, wide-brimmed hat.

" 'She's a lovely woman,' the captain said. 'Quite a full figure, too. By the way, when you do the painting, leave off the warts. She's very sensitive about that.'

" 'Yes, sir. I can take care of that. Would you also like me to shorten the nose a bit?' Markarovich asked.

" 'Oh, no. That won't be necessary,' the captain replied, 'but leave off the hat when you do the painting. I never did like that hat.'

"Markarovich carefully reexamined the photograph before responding, 'No problem, sir. But I'll need to know the color of her hair and how she wears it.'

" 'Don't be absurd,' the captain retorted, "You'll know that when you take the hat off.' "

When we regained our composure, Jim turned to me and said, "Well, now, Chief, looks like its your turn. Surely you flyboys know a tale or two."

"Boy, I don't know, Jim. You guys are a tough act to follow."

"Now, now. Don't be shy. It's unbecoming."

"Well . . . there was a real interesting battle I got involved in a few months ago," I said reluctantly.

"Let's hear about it."

"Like I said, it took place a few months back. Up in An Khe Pass. You boys familiar with that pass?" The other occupants of the table nodded, so I continued my tale. "Then you know that's mighty nasty territory, real rough terrain, and it mostly belongs to Charlie. Well, we inadvertently stepped into a real hot spot. We got cut off and had no choice but to fight it out. Must have been five hundred or a thousand soldiers against three."

"Man, those are tough odds," Carl interjected.

"Tell me about it," I responded. "Anyway, we fought them off as best we could. I'll tell you, that was the fiercest fighting I ever want to take part in. It went on nonstop for nearly four days."

"Man!" Jim exclaimed. "That must have really been something. Three against a thousand, and you fought them for four days. Hell, that's better than the Alamo."

"I suppose so. Of course, we tried to get in some reinforcements, but we had lost contact with Division 'cause of being down in the Valley. The radios didn't have much range."

"Well, how'd you finally get away?" Carl asked.

"Oh . . . we finally wore them down and overran their position. But I'll tell you what: Those were the toughest three guys we ever had to fight."

Despite my entertaining interludes such as visits to the Special Forces camp, the troop managed to keep me busy with the ash-and-trash missions. There was always something or someone that needed to be flown hither or yon. Most of these flights were routine. There was, however, one noteworthy flight that occurred in mid–June. It involved a night resupply mission in the mountains near Mang Yang Pass during very bad weather. Since I was relatively low on slick time, Operations had assigned an experienced member of the Lift Platoon, Albert Davis, as aircraft commander.

I knew Albert, but I had never flown with him. He had a reputation as an excellent pilot, coupled with some strange personality quirks. In fact, Thoreau's "marching to a different drummer" didn't come close to describing Albert. He not only marched to a different drummer, he built his own drum.

In addition to this being a night flight, the weather was dreadful: rain, fog, and low-hanging clouds. Visibility was virtually nonexistent. Since heavy fog always hung around the mountains we were flying into, the weather there was likely to be even worse. The mission briefing had emphasized that the PZ, while large enough to accommodate a Huey, had a major drawback: a huge tree located right in the middle of it. We were cautioned to exercise due diligence to avoid the tree.

Despite the poor visibility, the flight to the PZ passed

uneventfully. Of course, the real test of our crashworthiness was yet to come. Because of his Huey experience, Albert was at the controls for our landing in the PZ. Through the rain and fog we could just make out the portable landing lights that had been erected in the landing area. Albert lowered the collective, initiating our descent. I concentrated on trying to locate the big tree in the middle of the PZ. It was a hopeless task. I couldn't see ten feet outside of the helicopter.

As the altimeter needle dropped lower and lower I kept hoping that Albert would call for the landing light. I was beginning to sweat. Preserving your night vision was one thing, but a tree that size had a kill probability of 1.0. Finally I could maintain my silence no longer.

"Albert, do you want the landing light?"

"No . . . not yet."

"Are you sure, Albert?"

"Yeah. I'll let you know when I need it."

Maybe Albert had forgotten about the tree. After all, he had a lot on his mind. "You do remember there's a big tree in the middle of the PZ, don't you?"

"Sure."

I began squirming as the Huey continued its relentless descent into what I was sure would be disaster. If possible, the visibility had become even worse. Based on the barometric altimeter reading I estimated our altitude at about a hundred feet off the ground, still descending, still blind. I concluded I was in the hands of a maniac. Later this opinion would be confirmed. I was about to pursue the issue of the landing light when Albert suddenly blared at the top of his voice, "Quick! Turn on the landing light!"

I flipped on the landing light. To my horror, the light revealed that big tree—not more than twenty feet in front of the helicopter and dead in our path. We were descending right into the top of it. Just as suddenly and loudly as before Albert shouted again, "Quick! Turn off the landing light!"

I guess Albert figured if he couldn't see the tree, it didn't really exist. I turned off the landing light, closed my eyes, and braced myself for the inevitable. Two seconds later the skids bounced to a landing on terra firma, and six infantrymen scrambled aboard.

I stared at Albert in amazement. There was absolutely no way we could have missed that tree. "How did you do that?" I queried, my voice reflecting my astonishment.

"Do what?"

"How did you miss that tree?"

"What tree?" Albert asked.

I didn't have time to pursue the implications of Albert's response, as he yanked the collective up under his arm for a maximum-power takeoff. We were airborne once more. With the mountains dead ahead he put the Huey into a hard right bank. Fifty feet off the ground we entered the thick clouds that were covering the mountains. We were now in a hard turn and completely reliant on our instruments. Albert suddenly shouted, "Quick! Take the controls!"

I grabbed the controls, assuming he must have become disoriented in the process of transitioning from visual flying to instrument flying. "I've got the controls," I responded, tackling the task of trying to stabilize the Huey into some semblance of a coordinated turn and climb out.

Albert began frantically going through the pockets of his flight suit, finally extracting his wallet. He thumbed through the wallet for a bit and then exclaimed, "Aha! There it is."

"Albert, what in the hell are you doing over there?" I wailed, my voice strained by the events of the last few minutes.

"I was just checking my instrument ticket. I couldn't remember if it had expired."

Shortly after the flight with Albert, Division decided to have Delta Troop swap places with Bravo Troop of the 7/17th Air Cavalry, which was located at Phan Thiet. They figured the respective changes in scenery would be good for the morale of both units. Being the troop's primary ash-and-trash pilot, I got in a lot of stick time during the move. And Division was right. The change in location was good for morale. At least it was for a couple of days. We were now located right on the ocean, in the southeastern corner of II Corps. And the natives were peaceful. Some of the members of Bravo Troop had filled us in on what a good deal they had set up. We were looking forward with relish to the serenity of an "unofficial" in-country R & R. Things were really looking good. Then Major Talbot got the natives stirred up.

Bravo Troop, which had been operating out of Phan Thiet for the previous year, had managed during the course of their occupation to establish a symbiotic relationship with the nearby villagers. Bravo Troop provided them with a marketplace for their lobster catches—at a quarter apiece, freshly delivered each morning—and also with a number of jobs, thereby further supporting the local economy. The villagers had never had it so good; Bravo Troop had never had it so good. The jobs that were provided to the villagers not only included the typical employment that was offered to the Vietnamese, such as maid and janitorial services, but real career-oriented positions . . . like security.

Bravo Troop actually hired the villagers to provide security services for them. While on the surface this seems ludicrous, it proved to be an excellent strategy. Not only did Bravo Troop get fresh lobster three meals a day, but they hadn't had a mortar attack since they'd occupied the place. No sappers, no firefights, no mortar attacks . . . and no guard duty. The villagers' security services were superb.

When Major Talbot arrived on the scene he immediately determined that Bravo Troop's arrangement had been lacking in military security. His first official act was to ban all villagers from the troop area. The lobster was gone; the guard duty was back. That night, the area we now occupied received its first mortar attack in over a year. And we received mortar attacks every night thereafter.

Major Talbot's second official act at Phan Thiet was equally absurd. Upon discovering that he was short of scout pilots, he transferred me back to scouts. In my opinion, this transfer was done in an arbitrary and capricious manner. I'd have volunteered to go back to scouts if he'd bothered to ask. But he didn't ask. He ordered. I began searching for a mechanism to communicate to him that the commanding officer had no right to behave as if he were the guy in charge—not when it affected an old scout pilot. Eric certainly wouldn't have tolerated such behavior, and he would have been very disappointed in me if I failed to retaliate. In the meantime, I was back in the saddle again.

19

■ ■ ■ ■ ■ ■ ■ ■ ■ ■ ■ ■ ■ ■ ■ ■ ■

Last Scout Mission

I WAS A BIT NERVOUS FOR MY FIRST MISSION BACK IN THE
scouts. I was pushing my luck, and I knew it. I was going
to be very disappointed if I got killed at this stage of the
game. Previously I had considered the maudlin lyrics of
"The Last Roundup," which was the scout theme song, to
be nothing more than an expression of bravado, a satirical
comment on the army's employment of scouts. Now I
wasn't so sure. The lyrics were losing their satire. "Sad-
dling up Old Paint for the last time tonight" was getting to
be seriouser and seriouser.

Technically, I had served my obligatory time in scouts,
as well as my obligatory time in Vietnam. I was now into
the sixty-day extension that Major Williams had forced on
me. Most of my friends were gone now, either rotated out
or in the hospital. The people I had relied on for so long
to keep me alive weren't around anymore, like Eric Masterson, Dave Horton, and John Larkin. Now I felt like the
Lone Ranger . . . without Tonto.

Today's mission had us doing routine cavalry operations
near Dalat, about an hour's flight west of Phan Thiet; two
Loaches, two Cobras, and a C & C ship. Dalat was famous
for its French culture and extensive rubber plantations. The

terrain in this part of II Corps was radically different from the mountainous jungles that we'd become used to working in. It was much more open and exposed, more like plains than jungle. We refueled at Dalat and then began our recon operations.

I soon discovered that I was seeing imaginary AKs and VC behind every bush and in every spider hole: short-timer's syndrome. I had to get a grip on myself, else my reputation as a steely-nerved scout pilot could be in jeopardy. Finally I was able to convince my brain that my eyes were playing tricks on it. I calmed down. Then one of those imaginary AKs opened up on me.

"Receiving fire, receiving fire! Smoke's out," I yelled over the radio as I broke right, my wingman's gunner firing under my helicopter to cover the break. Seconds later the ten pounders from the Cobras began pummeling the area. They were about two seconds slower than John or Dave would have been. And that could be a very long two seconds.

That sneaky son-of-a-bitching VC, I thought. Hiding down in a spider hole, poking his AK out, and putting a bunch of holes in my Loach. I was pissed off, my nervousness temporarily forgotten. There was nothing like a few bullet holes through the windshield to cause mental regression. I forgot about being a cautious short-timer. I was getting tired of being shot at by some soldier safely tucked in the sanctuary of a hidey-hole.

Soon the Cobras broke off their attack. They weren't really expected to be doing any real damage, their rockets and miniguns unable to penetrate the spider holes and bunkers. They were simply causing the VC to keep their heads down while the scouts vacated the area. Normally we'd have inserted the Blues at this point to mop up the area. But currently we had to operate without the Blues, their ranks still not replenished from the Dak To battle. When the dust settled from the Cobras' aerial bombardment I moved back into the area, heading for the spider hole from which Mr. Sneaky Charlie had fired on me.

"Sir, where are we going?" my door gunner, Ben Smith,

asked nervously over the intercom. Before I could reply the same question was poised by Blackhawk 33, the C & C.

"Blackhawk 12, this is 33. Where are you going? Over."

"I left something back there at a spider hole. It'll just take a minute to get it."

"What did you leave? Over," Blackhawk 33 queried.

"That damn sneaky son-of-a-bitch VC that just shot me up."

"Blackhawk 12, you stay out of there. I've called Division, and they're sending an infantry platoon to mop up. Over."

"By the time they get here Charlie'll be having supper in Saigon."

"Blackhawk 12, I say again: You stay out of that area. That's an order. Do you read me? Over."

"You're coming in broken and garbled, 33. I can't make out what you're saying."

"Don't give me that broken and garbled stuff. You stay out of there."

"Three-three, I still can't make out your transmission. I'll try again after we finish mopping up down here. Out." I turned the UHF off. He wouldn't dare call me on the FM.

"Blackhawk 12, you're not fooling anyone," Blackhawk 33 transmitted over the FM. "You better hope the VC get your butt this time, 'cause if they don't, it belongs to me when we get back to Phan Thiet."

"Unknown station, this is Blackhawk 12. Please refrain from transmitting on this frequency. You could get someone killed. Out."

While the debate with Blackhawk 33 was ongoing I had moved back into the area. There were lots of spider holes and several bunkers. I had a particular spider hole in mind. It took me a few minutes, but I finally spotted it, approaching it from the backside at a slow hover. I was pissed off, but I wasn't crazy. Charlie would have to show himself to get a second shot at me. And he wasn't about to do that.

I gave Ben Smith, my door gunner, his instructions and then inched the Loach up to the spider hole. We could see the muzzle of the AK protruding from the hole, but Charlie couldn't swing it around on us. Ben pulled the pin on the fragmentation grenade and dropped it into the spider hole. I moved the Loach back a few yards, waiting for the situation to develop. This was a lot like flushing ground squirrels back in West Texas.

About two seconds later the spider hole regurgitated the grenade. It came flying back out, straight up into the air. We were hovering within its burst radius. Oh, shit, I thought as I kicked right pedal, spinning the Loach's tail around toward the grenade. A split second later the Loach bucked from the concussion, metal fragments pinging its skin. Joe Watkins was going to have some more choice words for me when I got back to Phan Thiet.

The explosion also alerted Charlie's buddies to the situation. We began receiving sporadic AK fire from other spider holes in the vicinity. My wingman concentrated on keeping them pinned down while I continued to deal with Mr. Sneaky Charlie. I'd had enough of him. His shenanigans had caused a lot of damage to my Loach. This time I was taking no chances. If you wanted a job done right, you had to do it yourself.

"Ben, pull the pin on one of those Willie Petes and hand it to me," I said to my door gunner as I moved the Loach back into position behind the spider hole. He handed me a white phosphorous grenade, pulling the pin and carefully keeping the firing handle clamped down.

"How long's the fuse on these suckers?" I asked. The question was for didactic purposes, since I already knew the answer. Part of my job was to provide training to my subordinates.

"Two seconds, sir."

I released the firing pin and began counting, "One thousand and one . . . one thousand and two . . ." Ben's eyes suddenly grew quite large, and he covered himself with his arms, hunkering down in his seat. I continued counting— "one thousand and three"—and then heaved the grenade into the spider hole. I immediately jerked the Loach rearward to avoid the upcoming white phosphorous explosion. As soon as the grenade entered the small opening to the spider hole it exploded, sending plumes of white smoke streaking into the air. A shrieking and burning Mr. Sneaky Charlie soon followed. My wingman finished him off.

"By the way, Ben," I said to my still-quaking door gunner, "a Willie Pete grenade has a four-second fuse."

"Yessir," he responded, "but that's plus or minus one second. I included a safety margin."

The infantry platoon from Division finally arrived and began mopping up the area. Amidst deteriorating weather conditions we continued our cavalry operations in another area, searching for new targets. We didn't find any, and by three o'clock the weather had become so bad that we returned to Dalat for a final refueling. We slipped into the Dalat airfield right ahead of the rain and clouds. By the time we refueled, visibility was less than a quarter mile and dropping.

Blackhawk 33 had a decision to make: whether to spend a wet and rough night in the helicopters or try to make it back to Phan Thiet. The main problem with the latter option was the Loaches, since they weren't equipped for instrument flying. After much debate Blackhawk 33 reluctantly went along with the collective decision: We headed back for Phan Thiet. The agreed-upon strategy was to use two flights, the Cobras forming one flight and the rest of the helicopters forming the other flight. The Loaches would try to stay close enough to the C & C Huey, Blackhawk 33, to maintain visual contact. That way he could provide our navigation for the flight back.

The Cobras departed, followed five minutes later by the rest of us. I stuck to Blackhawk 33's tail, and my wingman stuck to mine. The tricky part of this strategy was to not lose sight of the aircraft in front of you while at the same time not getting so close that you were liable to run into him if he did something peculiar. We were also flying low level, Blackhawk 33 having opted for trying to keep the ground in sight in case the Loaches got separated. As long as we could see the ground, we could land and wait out the weather.

Things progressed smoothly for about five minutes. Then I received a garbled transmission from Blackhawk 33 over the UHF radio. This time it really was garbled: "Mumphety, mumphety, mumphety." I keyed my microphone to ask for clarification when the message suddenly became perfectly clear. The massive electrical power lines that served Dalat were racing toward me, perpendicular to my flight path. Over the radio I screamed, "Climb. Now," as I pulled max power and rammed the cyclic into my stomach. With my warning, my wingman had plenty of time to react. I, on the other hand, was in for a squeaker thanks to Blackhawk 33's garbled warning.

The power lines loomed closer and closer as the Loach ever so slowly gained altitude. I decided I wasn't going to make it. Of course, this represented a moot decision. I was committed, no other options available. It was all up to the Loach. Fortunately, the power lines were strung in a pyramid fashion, with fewer wires as the tiers went higher. That arrangement proved to be the difference between the Loach hitting or missing the wires. My skids cleared the lower tier by about two inches. As we moved forward and upward we cleared each successive tier by a slightly wider margin. Finally we hurdled the top wire, and I breathed a sigh of relief.

We had miraculously cleared the wires. We were safe! Then it occurred to me that I had perhaps celebrated too soon. We were now in a situation that could accurately be described as jumping from the frying pan into the fire. The wires no longer posed a threat, but I was now about three hundred feet in the air in a cloud bank, with no visibility. The position lights of the Huey had disappeared during my frantic climb over the power lines. Now I had a more enduring problem: I had to fly instruments in a helicopter that wasn't equipped for instrument flying.

"Blackhawk 14, this is 12. What's your position? Over," I asked my wingman.

"This is 14. I'm still on your tail. Just don't make any sudden moves. If I move back any further, I'll lose you."

"Roger, 14. 'Bout the only thing we can do is to try to climb over the top of this shit. We'll continue to climb and maintain a heading of 130°. Over."

"Roger the 130."

About fifteen minutes later we broke out on top of the clouds. We were a little over ten thousand feet. This was the highest I'd been in a helicopter since I experimented with my Mattel Messerschmidt back in flight school. Our

major problem now was to get back down to the ground . . .
in one piece. I continued heading southeast, knowing that
we would eventually reach the ocean. Hopefully, the cloud
cover would break up if we went far enough out to sea.
Then we could try dropping down below the clouds and
sneaking in under them till we got back to shore. A nice,
sandy beach would look mighty good right now. Of
course, there was also the fuel issue to consider. If we
were forced to fly too far offshore, we'd never make it
back to dry land.

After holding our heading for another forty-five minutes
I estimated that we were approaching the coastline, give or
take a hundred miles. There was still no indication that the
clouds were going to break up.

"Hawk 12, this is 14. I just passed over a hole in the
clouds. Over."

"Roger, 14. I'm swinging around to take a look." One
of the first things they taught you in flight school was never
to try to sneak through a hole in the clouds. They were
called sucker holes. Once you were into them they had a
knack for closing up, leaving you disoriented.

I peeked through Hawk 14's hole in the sky, a narrow
tunnel arcing gracefully to the ground. At the other end I
could see lights, dusk having overtaken us by this time. I
didn't have any idea who the lights belonged to, but right
now they looked mighty good regardless. Certainly preferable to sharks.

"Let's do it," I said to Blackhawk 14, bottoming the
collective and dropping into the hole. It turned out to be a
friendly hole. Five minutes later we broke through the bottom of the cloud cover, which was holding a two-hundred-
foot ceiling above Phan Thiet. The unknown lights that
we'd spotted turned out to be the airfield at Phan Thiet.
We nonchalantly parked the Loaches and headed for the
club. I was in dire need of a drink.

At the club I modestly accepted the free drinks that were
offered as tribute to my phenomenal demonstration of navigational skills. In repayment I provided my colleagues with
various tips for overcoming the hazards of adverse weather
conditions. Neither Blackhawk 14 nor I ever let on that we

didn't have the foggiest idea where we were when we dropped through the clouds above Phan Thiet.

The next day I was in my hooch, strategizing. A half bottle of Wild Turkey the night before had helped to clarify my thinking: I was not going to fly scouts again. At least not on this tour. Hence my dilemma: Major Talbot had already made his position clear by transferring me back to the scouts. He wasn't likely to back off from his decision. I wasn't going to fly scouts, and the major wasn't going to let me not fly scouts.

While I was contemplating plausible solutions to this problem I was half listening to the radio. Suddenly I gave it my undivided attention. It was a time of rumored troop withdrawals—Nixon's prelude to Vietnamization of the war. The announcer was requesting volunteers to transfer to the Ninth Infantry Division, which was being withdrawn to Hawaii. The only hitch was that you had to have been in country for at least ten months. I was slowly approaching thirteen. Another thought occurred to me: Thus far, all of the pilots from Delta Troop had received reassignment orders to Germany. I'd heard horror stories about those cold German winters. Cold weather headed the list of my dislikes, right up there with snakes. The Ninth Infantry Division, coupled with the warm beaches of Hawaii, sounded like the solution to all my troubles.

I immediately headed for the orderly room and turned in my transfer papers. Major Talbot was not pleased, providing me with a long lecture on loyalty to the troop. Nevertheless, he duly signed the request and forwarded it through channels. He also assured me that I would be appropriately occupied while the transfer was pending.

20

■ ■ ■ ■ ■ ■ ■ ■ ■ ■ ■ ■

Freedom Bird

AT FIRST I THOUGHT THE MAJOR HAD UNDERGONE A DRA-
matic personality shift, exhibiting a kindly heart buried
deeply beneath his despotic exterior. This erroneous impression developed when I discovered that, rather than being
assigned scout missions while my paperwork was pending,
I was shifted back to flying ash-and-trash missions. However, the handpicked-by-the-major missions that I would be
performing suggested an element of vindictiveness associated with my request for transfer. The first of these involved transporting four enlisted men to Cam Ranh Bay to
catch their Freedom Bird home, going on to Qui Nhon to
drop the Huey off for badly needed repairs, and bringing
back a Loach that was being released from maintenance.

I began to have suspicions about the major's good intentions when I checked the logbook on the Huey during my
preflight. One of the main rotor blade grip reservoirs had
been written up for leaking, and the battery wouldn't hold
a charge. I climbed on top of the slick to check the reservoir, to the accompaniment of impatient grousing from the
scheduled passengers. The problem, from their perspective,
was that this was the only available aircraft, all others either on higher-priority missions or down for maintenance.
If I grounded it, they would miss their departure out of

Cam Ranh. I was in danger of moving to the top of the least-popular-pilot list.

To my chagrin, the transmission housing was splattered with heavyweight oil, and one of the grip reservoirs was empty. This alone was not sufficient cause for grounding the aircraft, since the length of time it had taken for the draining to occur was also critical. But it was certainly not a cause for celebrating. Empathizing with my passengers' circumstances, I figured there would be a minimal risk provided I could shut down at Cam Ranh, check the reservoir, and, if necessary, fill it prior to flying on to Qui Nhon. This would have been a fine strategy except for the battery problem.

I climbed down from the roof and called the crew chief over. The grumbling from the passengers was becoming louder and more pointed: "What the hell does a pilot know about maintenance? Why don't you just fly the thing like you're paid to do?" By coincidence, the most outspoken member of the group was Specialist Marsh, who had flown as my door gunner the time I got shot down up by LZ English. He'd performed very poorly that day, his first and last trial by fire in scouts, and I'd replaced him with an experienced scout gunner. A crowd was beginning to gather, attracted by the heckling. My future passengers began pleading their case to the sympathetic onlookers. The situation was becoming embarrassing; there are certain elements of military courtesy regarding behavior toward officers that were not being heeded. Understanding their frustration, however, I exhibited patience and went about the business of determining if the aircraft was reasonably safe to fly.

"Ray," I said to the crew chief, "when was that blade grip reservoir last filled?"

Ray looked sheepish, avoiding eye contact. "Last night, sir. After dinner."

"About fourteen hours ago, would you say?"

"Yes, sir."

"Then why isn't it grounded?"

"The major said this mission was not to be canceled—morale of the troops and all that—and this was the best bird Mr. Watkins could make available."

"I'd hate to see what the others are like. Tell me about the battery."

"Like it says in the logbook, it won't hold a charge. We'll have to start it with external power and keep it running till we get to Qui Nhon. They'll put a new battery in when they fix the other stuff."

"So we've got an excessive leak on a blade grip reservoir, and we can't shut down at Cam Ranh to check it because the battery won't restart the engine. And getting external power there is next to impossible."

"You got it, sir."

"And Mr. Watkins really expects me to fly this thing."

"You got it again, sir."

"Well," I said, "it's not the first time he's been wrong." I took my red-leaded pencil and put an X in the logbook, writing up the excessive leak. The Huey was grounded. By regulations, only the commanding officer—in effect, via the maintenance officer—could return the bird to flying status. And neither would risk doing that until it had been repaired. The army treated red Xs with respect.

"I don't think the passengers are going to take too kindly to this," Ray commented, looking toward the disgruntled passengers and their growing band of supporters.

"You grounded it!" one of them exclaimed, proceeding with a profane dissertation on my limited knowledge of maintenance and maintenance procedures.

Turning to address the unhappy group, I responded, "Gentlemen, here's the situation: We've got an excessive leak on a blade grip reservoir. I might risk that if we could shut down at Cam Ranh and check the oil level. Unfortunately, we also have a bad battery, and we wouldn't be able to shut down and then restart the engine. In my judgment, the aircraft is not safe to fly. I know that—"

"Bullshit," Specialist Marsh interrupted, "how do you know the leak is excessive?"

Keeping my calm, I replied, "Because the maintenance manual tells me so. Specifically, if the reservoir drains completely during a twenty-four-hour period, the leak is excessive."

"Since when does a pilot read a maintenance manual?"

Ignoring the question, I gave him a hard look and said,

"Specialist, let's have a private conversation." I turned and moved a short distance away from the angry soldiers. He reluctantly followed, realizing that his sarcasm had crossed the threshold of acceptable military courtesy.

Turning to face him, I looked him steady in the eye and quietly said, "March 3, 1969. LZ English."

The abbreviated comment served its intended purpose, reminding him of his less-than-stellar performance as my door gunner on that date. Embarrassed, his face flushed, and he stared sheepishly at his boots. Napoleon once said that only the individual soldier and those immediately surrounding him during the battle knew the true value of any particular medal. Only Specialist Marsh and I knew the truth of what went on inside the cockpit that day . . . and I had maintained my silence, allowing him to boast of his own exploits during the encounter and wear his bronze star with "V" device proudly.

I waited a few seconds to ensure that my point had been adequately made. "Now, you know and I know that this aircraft is not safe to fly. We're going back over there, and I expect you either to keep your mouth shut or to change your tune. You got that?"

"Yes, sir," he responded demurely.

We returned to the mob of potential passengers and sympathetic onlookers. "Now, guys," I said, "I know you're disappointed—anyone would be—but its time to exercise a little patience. It's far better to be a day late getting home than not to get there at all. One of the lessons I've learned about aviation is that it's much better to be on the ground wishing you were in the air than to be in the air wishing you were on the ground."

Specialist Marsh maintained his silence, and the group's anger began losing steam, emotion slowly giving way to logic. "Now you guys go on over to Operations and get them to schedule you for another flight."

As they departed, still grumbling, Ray remarked, "Nice job of public relations. How'd you quieten down Marsh?"

"It's private. Let's go have a chat with Mr. Watkins."

I do not think the major was pleased that I had grounded the Huey. Two things led me to believe this. First, he told me so . . . for about ten uninterrupted minutes. Second, he assigned me an unscheduled stint as squadron C & C pilot, which was the worst duty a Delta Troop pilot could pull. By analogy, it ranked right down there with KP for an enlisted man. Normally Operations used the duty roster method to ensure that the distasteful job was fairly and equally distributed among the pilots in four-day shifts. The major had bypassed the duty roster and assigned the next shift directly to me.

This C & C duty had started about a week after we arrived in country. Since Delta Troop was an air cavalry troop in a ground cavalry squadron, we were the only organic aviation assets that belonged to the squadron commander. Rank having its privileges, he had ordained that we were to furnish him with a round-the-clock helicopter and crew. While he called it his C & C bird, in truth there was very little C & C and a whole lot of very bad, and frequently dangerous, ash-and-trash missions.

The most serious drawback to the duty was the lack of crew rest, which caused the flying to be somewhat hazardous. Being ground-oriented, squadron had no operational conception that helicopter crews were fundamentally different from tank crews. Thus we were treated as a tank crew. We typically logged ten to twelve hours a day of actual flight, at sporadic intervals. That translates into very little rest, and what rest occurred came in snatches. After four days of this the crew resembled walking zombies. Initially the duty was pulled in a Charley Model, and with its crew of four the workload could at least be somewhat distributed among crew members. Eventually, however, the major was able to convince the squadron commander that his requirements could be better handled with a Loach, thereby leaving more of the troop's resources available for our primary mission. This two-edged sword made the C & C duty even more demanding for the one-person Loach crew. By the fourth day it was not unusual for your right arm to become so fatigued that you were barely able to move the cyclic.

Squadron also had no concept about proper aviation tactics. They would use a Huey as a scout, or a slick Loach as a single-ship scout "team," or a single Huey for airmobile operations in a hot LZ or PZ.

The first time I'd pulled the C & C duty had been shortly after the troop arrived in country. I was an inexperienced aircraft commander with an inexperienced crew in an under-powered, slick Charley Model. By the fourth day of the duty we were also a very tired crew, and Squadron called on us to perform one of their single-ship airmobile operations. In short, we had all the necessary ingredients for disaster, particularly if you added buffalo grass to the list.

The C & C bird was scrambled at 1500 hours on a clear, sunny day in early September, the messenger from squadron TOC excitedly informing us that an LRRP team northeast of Blackhawk Firebase was in trouble. While I raced to the "heliport"—a dirt field with a PSP landing pad and some JP-4 drums with a hand pump—to get the aircraft cranked, my copilot rounded up the crew chief and door gunner. Within twenty minutes we were on a very steep final approach to the smallest and roughest PZ I ever hoped to encounter: surrounded by eighty-foot trees, covered with buffalo grass, and pockmarked with tree stumps ranging from one to eight feet in height. The PZ was barely large enough to accommodate the weak-powered Charley Model.

Avoiding the trees by maintaining precision control via the prayer method, I guided the bird to a smooth touch-down, the tail boom nicely centered between several stumps. Relatively speaking, landing was the easy part. The hard part would be trying to clear the trees on departure with the helicopter fully loaded. Four of the eight LRRPs—laden with full packs, weapons, and radios—scrambled aboard. No way in hell will we be able to do this, I thought. My copilot looked at me, passing a silent message of agreement. Lifting four passengers out of this particular PZ would have been iffy enough in the Charley Model, but with all the equipment they were carrying it represented an impossibility. I started to tell one of them to get off and wait for the next sortie but, looking at their frightened faces, didn't have the heart to do so. Whatever encounter they'd just experienced in that jungle under-growth had sapped their machismo.

What the hell, I thought, maybe I'm underestimating the

old bird. Bringing the aircraft to a hover, I checked the go/no-go indicator; we had a couple of percent to spare. However, I was about to learn that this power margin was incorrect, resulting from an abnormal ground effect provided by the tall buffalo grass. I slowly eased up the collective, the Charley Model rising in response. Things went smoothly for about fifty feet, then the bottom fell out. The RPM needle began dropping, and the low-RPM audio warning began blaring. To be expected, the helicopter followed suit, falling like a rock. The copilot, crew chief, and gunner were simultaneously screeching on the intercom about tree stumps and no place to land. I slightly lowered the collective, and the RPM built back up, the helicopter stabilizing at a thirty-foot hover. Everyone breathed a sigh of relief, including the passengers, who by this time had concluded that things were not progressing as expected. This was only a temporary respite, however. We couldn't hover out of ground effect indefinitely. Whatever random aerodynamic property had caused the helicopter to stabilize could be withdrawn as quickly as it had been issued.

We were between the proverbial rock and hard spot; we had to either take off or land. The point from which we had attempted our departure was the only place to sit the bird down without hitting tree stumps, and it was now several feet to our rear. There was no way the underpowered helicopter was going to back up. That left only one option: try again.

I cautiously eased the collective up, eyes glued to the tachometer. The helicopter began rising, then dramatically changed its mind and plummeted earthward. This time there would be no respite. Once more my headset was filled with shouting about tree stumps and don't land, coupled with the hideous blaring of the RPM audio warning. I wanted to shout back at my crew members that I really didn't have much to say about whether or not we were going to land, but I was concentrating on holding the helicopter level and cushioning our impact with the ground. A loud cracking noise occurred as the main rotor clipped a large branch during our quasi-controlled descent. Then the skids settled onto terra firma. I held my breath, expecting tree stumps to emerge through the bottom of the aircraft

*and the tail rotor to disintegrate from a blade strike. None
of these things happened. Miraculously, the tail boom was
nestled snugly between several tree stumps, and the tail
rotor was spinning freely. We had a few minor scratches
on the skin, but a little spot painting would make it as good
as new.*

*I motioned for two of the LRRPs to vacate the aircraft.
After some discussion among themselves regarding who
would go and who would stay, the losers of the decision
remained on board, and we departed, the lightened helicopter having no trouble clearing the trees.*

*Fifteen minutes later we landed at Blackhawk Firebase
and shut down to check the damage to the main rotor
blades. They finally spun to a halt, revealing gaping holes
about a foot inboard on each blade. Apparently the damage had been equally distributed, since there had been no
abnormal vibration in the controls. Bell sure makes good
helicopters, I thought. My copilot notified the squadron
TOC that we were down for maintenance and would be
unable to complete the LRRP extraction until we could get
a replacement aircraft from An Khe. They replied that
there was no rush, the remaining LRRPs having requested
permission to walk the twenty miles back to the firebase. I
radioed Joe Watkins to inform him that I'd damaged one
of his birds.*

Things hadn't changed much with the C & C duty since
that day so many months before, except we used Loaches
now. Squadron still treated us like tank crews, and they
still had no conception of proper aviation tactics. And the
duty was lonelier and harder, since you were a solo operation. I took my Loach and headed for Blackhawk Firebase,
the one bright spot being that my transfer orders were likely
to be waiting for me when I returned. The first three days
of the duty passed routinely with the typical intermittent
missions that kept you from getting any real rest. Then
the fourth day came around, and the squadron commander
decided to play aeroscout.

I was on my final day of the C & C shift, exhausted and
looking forward to getting back to Phan Thiet to check on

the status of my transfer request. It was mid-afternoon, no breeze, hot and humid. The only available shade in the vicinity of the squadron heliport was located beneath the helicopter, and I was attempting to make the most of it with a quick nap between missions. The flies, which came in multitudes, were doing their best to prevent this inactivity. I discovered, however, that by properly balancing my arm against my head I could create a pendulum-like effect, continuously shooing the flies with a minimum expenditure of energy. We had almost achieved a harmonious existence when the squadron commander's jeep came roaring to a stop next to the Loach, engulfing the aircraft in a cloud of dust.

As the colonel, his aide, and the Sergeant Major scrambled out of the jeep and into the helicopter I climbed into the cockpit and cranked the engine. The colonel plugged his headset into the intercom and provided instructions: "We've got a patrol in contact with the VC about ten miles northwest." Pointing to a spot on his map, he continued, "They're located in these mountains, moving along this ridge."

I acknowledged the colonel's information and headed the heavily loaded aircraft to the northwest. Reluctantly. I did not have a good feeling about using a single, overloaded Loach with four pistols for armament as a scout. The colonel didn't really understand the aeroscout concept. Where was my door gunner? Where was my wingman? Where were my Cobras? And the four hundred pounds of extra weight—two additional passengers—took away the scout's most important asset: maneuverability. Scouting was a sufficiently risky business even when proper tactics were employed.

Twenty minutes later we arrived in the AO, and the colonel had me doing a low-level zigzag search pattern across the peaks and valleys of the mountainous terrain while he carried on a running commentary with the ground troops, who claimed to be in hot pursuit of a group of heavily armed VC. The colonel's strategy was to use the Loach to "head the VC off at the pass." The weakness in this approach was what we would do with them if we did head them off. I wasn't convinced that the colonel had thought this all the way through. Consequently, I implemented a slightly modified strategy: Whenever the colonel told me to zig, I zagged. This continued for about half an hour, with the three passengers fiercely scanning the jungle for the enemy soldiers. Suddenly the colonel shouted, "There they go!" and he pulled out his pistol as he motioned me to swing the helicopter around in pursuit.

There had also been a weakness to my strategy: The probability of finding the VC by zigging was apparently equal to the probability of finding them by zagging. To my horror, the colonel was absolutely right: Three pajama-clad VC were scurrying down the mountain on an open trail. Each of them was carrying an AK-47. For heaven's sake, I thought, where'd these guys get their jungle training? Panicked by the pursuing ground troops, they had apparently thrown caution aside.

"Come on! Come on! Swing it around so I can get a shot," the colonel commanded. I suspected he had never tried to shoot a moving target on the ground with a .45-caliber pistol while airborne in a helicopter. The reason I suspected this was that it's virtually impossible to perform such a feat, contrary to what Hollywood would have you believe. On the other hand, shooting an overweight Loach from the ground with an automatic rifle from a distance of a few feet is not difficult at all. Aiming is not even required.

Enmeshed in his own enthusiasm, the colonel did not seem to be aware of the odds for a favorable outcome in this situation. I was accustomed to eyeball-to-eyeball confrontations with the enemy, but with a reasonable chance for survival. Living on the ragged edge of danger is one thing, committing suicide quite another.

While the colonel and his entourage attempted to bring their weapons to bear on the quarry, I reached behind the instrument panel and jerked a wire from the oil pressure gauge. I then swung the helicopter in the opposite direction from the VC, heading back toward Blackhawk Firebase.

"No, no. The other way," the colonel yelled, gesticulating wildly.

"Sorry, sir," I said, pointing to the oil pressure gauge, "we've lost our oil pressure. Those VC may have hit us in the engine. I'm going to try to make it back to Blackhawk Firebase."

"What rotten luck. Just when we had them where we wanted them."

"Some days they get lucky; some days we get lucky. I guess this was their day."

The rotation C & C ship was on station when we arrived back at the firebase. I dropped off the colonel and his companions, refueled the Loach, and headed for Phan Thiet. I was getting too short for this stuff. I hoped my transfer orders had arrived so I could head for greener pastures. If that were the case, I'd just flown my last mission in Vietnam, a distasteful finale to what had been a reasonably good performance. On the other hand, it suddenly occurred to me, I had just saved four American lives on my final mission, including my own. Perhaps I was viewing the episode from the wrong perspective. In fact, I probably deserved a medal. Unfortunately, the army's existing inventory of medals did not include a Congressional Medal of Common Sense.

When I got to Phan Thiet I discovered that my orders had arrived. I was scheduled to be transported by Huey to DIVARTY, Ninth Infantry Division on the following day, ultimate destination Hawaii. I spent a solitary night with my Wild Turkey and memories; half celebration, half mourning. My last night in Delta Troop.

I was awakened by pounding on the door of my hooch. I groggily checked my watch through the haze of early-morning hangover. It was almost noon. The exhaustion from the four days of C & C duty, coupled with last night's bourbon, had caught up with me.

"Who's there?" I grumbled.

"Specialist Connors, sir. I've got some mail for you, a package. Also, a message form Operations: The Huey to take you to the Ninth Division is leaving in fifteen minutes."

I unlatched the door, taking the package, and told Connors to let Operations know I'd be a few minutes late. Tossing the package on my bed, I went about the business of my morning toilet. With the exception of throwing in my shaving kit, my two duffel bags were already packed.

Twenty minutes later I was ready to embark on my journey, freshly showered and shaved and wearing a clean flight suit. I grabbed my bags to head for the flight line. As I took a final look around my quarters, remembering the good and bad times that had been housed there, my eyes fell on the forgotten package lying on the bed.

I picked it up, noting the return address: Mrs. Wilma Masterson, 1615 Cherry Lane, Joplin, Missouri. Eric's mother, I thought, a sinking feeling of foreboding striking the pit of my stomach. The package contained a letter and a smaller package, a jewelry box. I opened the one-page letter:

August 3, 1969

Dear Charles,

Eric has told us so much about you that we feel as if we know you. We certainly know of your friendship and we're very sorry to have to write this letter.

Eric was killed in an automobile accident last week. The doctor said he died instantly. For that, we're grateful.

He told us that if he had a single friend in this world it was you. We know you grieve as we grieve. The package is from him. He'd told us to send it to you if anything ever happened to him.

Sincerely,
Wilma Masterson

P.S.—*When some time has passed and we've adjusted to this, please come and see us. His father and I would like to know more about Eric's final year.*

Stunned, I vacantly stuffed the letter into a zippered pocket on my fight suit. I opened the jewelry box, knowing what it would contain: a gleaming tiger's tooth on a gold chain. *"The only way you'll get this tooth is* over *my dead body."* I sat for some time staring at the bejeweled tooth.

A messenger from Operations pounded on my door, reminding me that the Huey was impatiently waiting.

It was necessary, however, to perform the agreed-upon

ritual. I opened my duffel bag, extracting a half-empty bottle of Wild Turkey. I turned to face northward, toward home, held the bottle aloft, and toasted Eric: "I'll take care of Old Paint." I completed the toast by taking a long pull on the bourbon.

Replacing the Wild Turkey, I picked up my duffel bags and headed for my Freedom Bird. On the way out the door I hesitated, almost tossing the tiger tooth in the wastebasket, feeling that in some way this would remove the pain and erase the memories. Reconsidering, I put the chain around my neck and fastened the clasp. I didn't want to erase the memories.

Epilogue

When I got to Hawaii in the fall of 1969 the war in Vietnam had started on its downswing, at least with respect to U.S. troop strength. The withdrawal of the Ninth Infantry Division had begun a deescalation process that would continue for several years. The division moved on to Fort Lewis, Washington, but I stayed in Hawaii. Noteworthy historical events that lay in the immediate future included the Kent State massacre and the long-overdue invasion of Cambodia.

In Hawaii I had time to reflect on the events in which I had participated for the previous fourteen months. The most confusing aspect had been the various personalities I encountered. In general, we all behaved chaotically in a chaotic situation. What I could never understand were those individuals who could not adjust, either during or after their tours.

In postwar life Audie Murphy frequently complained that "nothing excited him anymore." This I could understand. I had experienced this phenomenon during my scout interlude. There is an aliveness about continuously facing immediate and compelling danger that cannot otherwise be experienced. Had Major Talbot not been so arbitrary in reassigning me to the scouts, I would have chosen to continue flying the Loaches. The danger was like a narcotic.

239

The type of adjustment that I could not understand was those soldiers who simply "fell apart." I have witnessed this behavior both in Vietnam and subsequently. I have concluded that these soldiers shared a common fallible belief: They took the war seriously. Perhaps they had not read Clauswitz, whose first principle of war is: All wars are political. Now, when you combine this premise with the implicit premise in Will Rogers's observation that he couldn't understand why he had to work so hard at being funny when Congress could do it with no effort whatsoever, the conclusion seems inescapable: War should not be taken seriously. The entire exercise is under the control of amateur comedians. I believe that the soldiers who had difficulty adjusting simply took the war too seriously. After all, it was only a matter of life and death.

In his recent book *Rolling Thunder*, Mark Berent states: "[During Vietnam] the army had developed a rotary-wing contingent that was successful beyond their wildest dreams. . . . Nearly one hundred percent of the pilots were nineteen- and twenty-year-old warrant officers who flew in the best scarf-in-the-breeze tradition." Except for the statistics, the complimentary quote is accurate. Warrant officers probably made up about eighty percent of the pilots who were assigned to flying slots. Until the army's creation of an aviation branch in the mid-eighties, commissioned officers were assigned to flying slots as a secondary duty, owing their allegiance to their own branch; consequently, there were probably as many commissioned aviators as warrant aviators, but only about twenty percent of the flying slots were designated for commissioned officers. Also, while there were a number of nineteen- and twenty-year-old warrant officers, most were in their early to mid-twenties. I was twenty-two when I arrived in Vietnam.

However, Mr. Berent is correct about "the best scarf-in-the-breeze tradition," although the statement should be expanded to include all army aviators. I hope I have communicated some of the spirit associated with that tradition. It is, of course, a tradition necessarily laden with a darker side: our fallen comrades.

During the Vietnam War 1,913 army aviators were killed in action (of these, eighty-six were classified as missing in action and have subsequently been declared dead by the Department of Defense). The first army aviator to be killed was WO1 Edgar Wilken Weitkamp (March 23, 1961); the last was 2LT Richard Vande Geer (May 15, 1975); and the youngest was WO1 Raymond Howard Chase, Jr. (November 10, 1967, 19.3 years of age). (Statistical source: Vietnam Helicopter Pilots Association.) More than nineteen hundred of America's finest are buried between these extremes. Their heritage lives on in the silver wings of every army aviator.

Finally, no book on Vietnam would be complete without a statement on the American public's inexcusable treatment of the Vietnam veteran. Perhaps the most eloquent commentary on this subject was provided by General Norman Schwarzkopf on his 1991 return from commanding Operation Desert Storm in the Middle East: "It's nice to be welcomed home in such a manner. Nobody noticed when I came home from Vietnam . . . twice."

Glossary

ADF. Automatic direction finder. A navigational instrument. It also provides audio reception for the radio frequency. Thus pilots can listen to radio stations as well as having navigational assistance.

AGL. Absolute ground level; altitude above the ground.

AH-1. See Cobra.

Air cavalry. An air cavalry troop emphasizes speed and mobility. It has a primary role of reconnaissance: finding the enemy. It has organic capability only for limited engagements with the enemy; consequently, it strives to avoid contacts that would lead to decisive engagements. Its task is to locate the enemy so that other types of units can decisively engage him. In Vietnam, an air cav troop was comprised of an aeroscout platoon (approximately ten Loaches), an aeroweapons platoon (approximately ten gunships), and an aerolift platoon (approximately ten Hueys). Additionally, an air cav troop had an organic infantry platoon (Blue Platoon), which was used for ground reconnaissance and security. See Cavalry.

AK-47. Rifle used by the Vietcong and NVA.

AO. Area of operations.

APC. Armored personnel carrier. A lightly armored,

243

tracked vehicle used for transporting combat soldiers, usually infantrymen.

AR-15. This rifle is a variation of the M-16. It is often equipped with a scope for precision firing. See M-16.

Ash-and-Trash. Slang, referring to noncombat missions.

Attack helicopter. See Gunship, Cobra, UH-1C.

Autorotate/autorotation. A procedure for landing a helicopter without engine power. Pitch is removed from the main rotor blades by lowering the collective (see Collective). The weight of the falling helicopter creates a "pinwheel" effect that turns the blades, thereby allowing the helicopter to "glide." There are sufficient frictional forces in the rotor system to allow the pilot one shot at a landing. However, the timing of the pilot is crucial to the success of the maneuver. Different models of helicopters have differing inherent autorational capabilities, ranging from very good to very poor.

Blue Platoon. The organic infantry platoon in an air cavalry troop. See Air cavalry.

C & C. Command and control. Usually referring to the person in charge of the mission, who provides command and control from an airborne helicopter via radio.

Cav. Abbreviation for cavalry. See Cavalry.

Cavalry. A military organization and concept with primary emphasis on speed and mobility. Technological evolution has replaced the cavalryman's horse with modern vehicles. At the unit level (troop or squadron) a principal role is reconnaissance: finding the enemy. Cavalry troops may be either air or ground, with the designation referring to their fighting vehicles (helicopters vis-à-vis tanks or APCs). Typically, an air cavalry squadron was comprised of three air cav troops and one ground cav troop, whereas a ground cav squadron was comprised of three ground cav troops and one air cav troop. See Air cavalry.

CEOI. Communications-electronics operating instructions.

Chalk. Referring to relative positions of helicopters in a formation flight, Chalk 1 being the lead aircraft, etc.

Chicken plate. Bullet-proof vest. It provides limited protection against small-caliber weapons.

Charlie. Synonym for Vietcong. See Victor Charlie.

Charley Model. UH-1C (Huey) normally configured as a

gunship, it was subsequently replaced by the Cobra. See Huey.

CO. Commanding officer. See Old Man.

Cobra. The first helicopter originally designed as a gunship. The Cobra was a transformed Huey, built by Bell Helicopter, and was introduced in Vietnam in 1967. Subsequent versions are currently active in the U.S. Army and U.S. Marine Corps as well as in armed forces of other nations. Military designation: AH-1 series, Cobra; slang: Snake.

Collective. A control lever that changes the pitch or angle of attack of the main rotor blades. It is manipulated by the pilot with his left hand. Raising (increasing) the collective causes the helicopter to climb or ascend; lowering (decreasing) the collective causes the helicopter to descend (with a turbine-powered helicopter, the throttle is coupled to the collective and automatically increases or decreases, as appropriate). The collective must also be adjusted to maintain current altitude if forward, rearward, or sideward movement of the helicopter is changed (see Cyclic, Pedals). The terms collective, pitch, and power are often used synonymously.

CYA. Cover your ass.

Cyclic. A control lever that changes the tilt of the main rotor system, thereby causing the helicopter to move in the direction of the tilt. The cyclic is manipulated by the pilot with his right hand. Changes in cyclic position are coordinated with changes in collective and pedal positions to produce the desired flight path. See Collective, Pedals.

Dead man's zone. A flight condition characterized by low airspeed and low altitude, from which an autorotative landing cannot be successfully performed.

Defense Contract Audit Agency (DCAA). Similar to the IRS, but more Gestapo-like.

Density altitude. An indicator of the "heaviness" of the air, which is measured through an interaction of such things as altitude and temperature. The higher the density altitude, the more power the helicopter requires, particularly to hover. In general, flying in Vietnam was in high density altitude conditions.

Deuce-and-a-half. Two-and-one-half-ton cargo truck.

DFC. Distinguished Flying Cross. A medal for valor that is specific to aviation.

Didi mau. Vietnamese expression for make haste or hurry.

DROS. Date rotated overseas. Normal return from Vietnam was twelve months later.

Dustoff. Synonym for medevac. See Medevac.

Duty officer. The commissioned or warrant officer who is placed in administrative charge of the unit during non-duty hours.

EGT. Exhaust gas temperature. Analogous to the engine temperature gauge on an automobile. See TOT.

ETA. Estimated time of arrival.

ETD. Estimated time of departure.

Flight idle. A throttle position that determines the engine idling speed.

Flight line. The parking area for aircraft.

40mm. See Grenade launcher.

Fox Mike. International alphabet pronunciation for F M, referring to an FM radio.

FM. Frequency modulation.

Free fire zone. A battlefield control measure that in effect allowed individual soldiers to freely engage the enemy without obtaining specific permission from higher headquarters.

Frag order. Fragmentary (abbreviated) version of an operations order. See Operations order.

G-2. The "2" refers to an army organizational element specializing in intelligence operations. The "G" indicates that the level of the organization is Division or higher.

G-5. The "5" refers to an army organizational element specializing in psychological operations. The "G" indicates that the level of the organization is Division or higher.

Go/no-go. A decision regarding whether the helicopter has sufficient power available to perform a takeoff.

Green personality. Slang for purchasing sexual favors for money (i.e., money is green).

Grenade launcher. A weapon resembling a single-shot shotgun. It fires a 40mm grenade that explodes when it strikes a solid object. Military designation: M-79. A gunship carries an automated version of the grenade launcher that also fires a 40mm projectile.

Ground pounder. Slang for non-aviation personnel, usually referring to infantry.

Grunt. Slang for infantry soldier.

Guard. Radio frequency reserved for emergency transmissions.

Gunship. An aircraft equipped with weapons whose mission was to provide aerial fire support. In Vietnam the primary helicopter gunship was the Cobra, although other types of helicopters were sometimes equipped with weapons and used as gunships. For example, early gunships were Hueys equipped with weapons. See Cobra, Huey, UH-1C.

Hooch. Synonym for personal quarters.

Hot start. Exceeding the engine temperature limits while starting the engine, an ever-present danger with turbine engines. As a minimum, the engine must be taken apart and inspected for damage after a hot start.

Huey. A colloquialism for the utility helicopter that became known as the workhorse of Vietnam. The Huey, in its various versions, was built by Bell Helicopter and was principally used for troop transport, including medical evacuation and resupply missions. Depending on the particular version, the Huey could carry from six to ten combat soldiers and their individual equipment. Several versions of the Huey have evolved; it is currently active in all branches of the U.S. armed forces, as well as in the armed forces of other nations. Early versions of helicopter gunships were armed Hueys, in particular the UH-1B and UH-1C. In the troop transport configuration a Huey was referred to as a slick. Military designation: UH-1 series, Iroquois. See UH-1C.

IP. Instructor pilot.

Jesus nut. A retaining nut located on top of the mast that holds the main rotor system together.

JP-4. Jet fuel; similar to kerosene.

Klick. Slang for kilometer.

Knots. Nautical miles per hour. There are 6076.115 feet in a nautical mile vis-à-vis 5280 feet in a statute mile.

Consequently, 100 knots is equivalent to about 115 statute miles per hour.

Leg. Slang for infantry.

Lift Platoon. See Air cavalry.

Lima Charlie. Slang for "loud and clear." Typically, used in responding to a radio check, indicating satisfactory communications.

Loach. A colloquialism derived from the acronym LOH (light observation helicopter). The army's LOH procurement program was initiated in the mid-sixties to modernize its inventory of Korean War–vintage small helicopters and to expand the role of the light helicopter. The principal role of the Loach in Vietnam was as an aeroscout in air cavalry troops. Specifically, the task of the aeroscout was to locate the enemy; this was frequently accomplished by hovering around the jungle until he was fired on by the enemy. The original Loach (OH-6) was produced by Hughes Helicopter Company (later McDonnell Douglas Helicopter Company) and was introduced in Vietnam in 1967. Due to contract and production problems, the original Loach was replaced with a version produced by Bell Helicopter (OH-8) that was introduced in Vietnam in the early seventies. The Loach colloquialism technically refers to the model built by Hughes. Military designation: OH-6 series, Cayuse (Hughes); OH-58 series, Kiowa (Bell).

LOH. Light observation helicopter. See Loach.

Low-RPM audio. An audio warning that alerts the pilot if engine or main rotor RPM has deteriorated below operating limits.

LRRP. Long-range reconnaissance patrol. LRRPs were small teams of U.S. infantrymen who prowled the jungles, particularly at night, searching for the enemy.

LT. Lieutenant. Each letter is articulated separately: L, T.

LZ. Landing Zone. The location where friendly troops are to be dropped off by helicopters. See PZ.

M-2. A 30-caliber carbine that was issued to helicopter pilots (in Vietnam) in lieu of the M-16 rifle.

M-16. The primary rifle issued to U.S. military personnel in Vietnam. This lightweight weapon is magazine-fed (twenty or thirty rounds), can be fired in automatic or semiautomatic mode, and uses a 5.56mm bullet.

M-60. A belt-fed machine gun that fires a 7.62mm bullet. (M-60 is also a military designation for a type of tank.)

M-79. See Grenade launcher.

Mattel Messerschmidt. Colloquialism for the TH-55A. A small two-place training helicopter built by Hughes Helicopter Company.

McGuire rig. A "basket" contraption that is lowered by "rope" from a helicopter, using a hoist, to insert or extract personnel in locations where the helicopter cannot land.

Medevac. Abbreviation for medical evacuation, usually referring to a helicopter that is specially equipped for medical evacuation. In Vietnam this was normally a specially configured Huey. Sometimes misspelled as medivac.

METT-T. Mission, enemy, terrain, time, and troops available. Factors used in mission planning.

MSL. Mean sea level. Altitude above sea level.

Minigun. A Gatling-like machine gun that can be mounted on a variety of aircraft. It was typically standard equipment on gunships but was sometimes used on scout aircraft in air cav troops; a Cobra could be equipped with as many as three miniguns. The electrically operated minigun can fire several thousand rounds per minute. It is belt-fed and uses a 7.62mm bullet (in Vietnam).

Newby. Slang for a person newly assigned to Vietnam or to the unit, usually the former.

NVA. North Vietnamese Army. NVA or NVA regulars refers to uniformed soldiers of North Vietnam (vis-à-vis Vietcong soldiers). See Vietcong.

Orderly room. The administrative headquarters of a troop or company.

OD. Olive drab. The omnipresent olive-green color used by the army.

OH-6. See Loach.

OH-58. See Loach.

Old Man. Slang for commanding officer.

Operations order (OPORD). A standardized (five-paragraph) document that details a mission. See Frag order.

Papa Tango. Slang for pilot technique.

Pedals. Control devices manipulated by the helicopter pilot with his feet to change the pitch angle of the tail rotor blades. Pedals are used to turn the aircraft while hovering or to trim the aircraft while in forward flight. Movement of the pedals is coordinated with changes in cyclic or collective positions. See Cyclic, Collective.

Peter pilot. Slang for copilot.

Pink elephant. An elephant used by the NVA and VC as a pack animal for transporting supplies into South Vietnam. The pink referred to the pinkish coloring that they acquired from the dust along the southbound trails, particularly the Ho Chi Minh Trail.

Pink slip. In flight school, instructor pilots used color-coded grading sheets for evaluating your flying during a training session. Pink sheets were used for giving an unsatisfactory evaluation.

Pitch. See Collective.

Power. See Collective.

PRC-25. FM radio carried in a backpack.

Preflight. The maintenance-oriented inspection that is performed by pilots prior to takeoff. Usually a detailed preflight is performed prior to the first flight of the day, with abbreviated versions thereafter. The term was also used to refer to the first four weeks of flight school for warrant officer candidates, since no flying was done during this period.

PSP. Pierced steel planking. Among other things, used to make "improved" runways and to line the bottoms of revetments.

Push-pull tubes. Mechanical linkages that connect the pilot's controls to the rotor system.

PZ. Pickup zone. The location where friendly troops are to be picked up by helicopters. See LZ.

R & R. Rest and recreation. Depending on allocations, during each soldier's tour of duty in Vietnam he was allowed to take at least one five-day, out-of-country leave to a specified location. Typical R & R sites included Australia, Hawaii, Hong Kong, and Taiwan.

Relief on station. Tactical procedure for rotating aircraft, particularly gunships, so that as one team ran low on fuel or ammunition another team arrived on station, thereby providing uninterrupted support.

Retrograde operations. The U.S. Army no longer retreats. It performs retrograde operations.

Revetment. A rectangular parking space for aircraft that is enclosed on three sides by approximately five-foot walls that are reinforced with sandbags. Also, see PSP.

RLO. Real live officer. Slang for a commissioned officer.

Romeo Foxtrot. Slang for Rat Fuck, referring to an extremely fouled-up situation.

RTO. Radio-telephone operator.

RVN. Republic of Vietnam (South).

Scout. See Loach, Air Cavalry.

Scout nosebleed. Slang reference to risking a nosebleed by climbing to an altitude that is higher than a scout normally flies, which is typically less than fifty feet.

SITREP. Situation report.

Skids. Non-wheeled landing gear on a helicopter; resemble skis.

Slick. Slang for a helicopter that is configured to carry troops, usually a Huey. See Huey.

Snake. A colloquialism for the Cobra gunship. See Cobra.

Staging field. An "improved" landing area for helicopters, usually with paved runways.

SOP. Standing Operating Procedure.

Straphanger. Slang (derogatory) for support personnel that do not perform combat missions.

Time-on-station. The amount of time that a helicopter can remain on station (i.e., in the actual target area), excluding the time required to get to and from the rearm/refuel point.

TOC. Tactical operations center. The location from which battlefield operations are conducted. TOCs are located at battalion/squadron level and above.

Top. Slang for first sergeant, the highest-ranking noncommissioned officer in a troop or company.

TOT. Turbine outlet temperature. See EGT.

UH-1. See Huey.

UH-1C. See Charley Model.

UHF. Ultra high frequency.

VC. Vietcong. See Vietcong.

GLOSSARY

VHF. Very high frequency.

Victor Charlie. Slang for Vietcong. See Vietcong.

Vietcong. Vietnamese guerrilla soldiers in South Vietnam who fought for (and were organized and supported by) North Vietnam. See NVA.

VOQ. Visiting officers quarters.

Wobbly One. Slang for warrant officer, grade 1. The warrant officer ranks range from warrant officer-1 through chief warrant officer-4.

WOC. Warrant Officer Candidate. Also, something thrown at wabbits.

Xinh loi. Vietnamese expression for "sorry about that" or "tough luck" or "too bad."

XO. Executive officer.

About the Author

Charles D. Holley received his Ph.D. in experimental psychology from Texas Christian University. After several years in academia, he returned to his true vocation, aviation, and is currently employed as a group engineer with Bell Helicopter-Textron. His military background ranges from combat duty in Vietnam as a scout pilot and gunship pilot to his current reserve assignment with the Army's Aviation Research and Technology Activity at NASA/Ames Research center.

America's Fighter Aces Tell Their Stories

TOP GUNS

Joe Foss and Matthew Brennan

They were high-flying heroes who fought our wars, inspired the country, and left a proud legacy. Now, America's greatest living fighter aces tell their personal stories—many for the first time—in this extraordinary record of aerial combat from World War I through Vietnam.

Legendary WWII Marine ace Joe Foss and highly decorated Vietnam veteran and distinguished author Matthew Brennan bring together twenty-seven fighter pilots to create this astonishing volume of oral history. You are there, in the major theaters of four wars—in the cockpit.

POCKET
BOOKS

Available in paperback from Pocket Books

419-02

STEPHEN COONTS

AN AERIAL ODYSSEY ACROSS AMERICA

THE CANNIBAL QUEEN

New York Times bestselling novelist Stephen Coonts
has been hailed as the best contemporary author
writing about flying. Now Coonts takes us on an
extraordinary adventure, following highways,
railroad lines, and rivers, and touching down in all
forty-eight of the continental United States,
from sea to shining sea.

POCKET BOOKS

**Available in hardcover
from Pocket Books
June 1992**